RELENTLESS PURSUIT

RELENTLESS PURSUIT

A True Story of Family, Murder, and
the Prosecutor Who Wouldn't Quit

KEVIN FLYNN

G. P. PUTNAM'S SONS
NEW YORK

⫼P

G. P. PUTNAM'S SONS
Publishers Since 1838
Published by the Penguin Group
Penguin Group (USA) Inc., 375 Hudson Street, New York, New York 10014, USA •
Penguin Group (Canada), 90 Eglinton Avenue East, Suite 700, Toronto, Ontario
M4P 2Y3, Canada (a division of Pearson Penguin Canada Inc.) • Penguin Books Ltd,
80 Strand, London WC2R 0RL, England • Penguin Ireland, 25 St Stephen's Green,
Dublin 2, Ireland (a division of Penguin Books Ltd) • Penguin Group (Australia),
250 Camberwell Road, Camberwell, Victoria 3124, Australia (a division of Pearson
Australia Group Pty Ltd) • Penguin Books India Pvt Ltd, 11 Community Centre,
Panchsheel Park, New Delhi–110 017, India • Penguin Group (NZ), 67 Apollo
Drive, Mairangi Bay, Auckland 1311, New Zealand (a division of Pearson New
Zealand Ltd) • Penguin Books (South Africa) (Pty) Ltd, 24 Sturdee Avenue,
Rosebank, Johannesburg 2196, South Africa

Penguin Books Ltd, Registered Offices: 80 Strand, London WC2R 0RL, England

Library of Congress Cataloging-in-Publication Data

Flynn, Kevin, date.
Relentless pursuit : a true story of family, murder, and
the prosecutor who wouldn't quit / Kevin Flynn.
p.   cm.
ISBN 978-0-399-15406-5
1. Flynn, Kevin, date.   2. Harris, Katrina, 1979–1993.   3. Hawkins, Diane,
d. 1993.   4. Harrell, Norman.   5. Murder—Washington (D.C.)—Case studies.
6. Trials (Murder)—Washington (D.C.)—Case studies.   I. Title.
HV6534.W18F59   2007
364.152'3092—dc22   2006037338

Printed in the United States of America
1   3   5   7   9   10   8   6   4   2

Book design by Lovedog Studio

Any views and opinions expressed herein are solely those of the author, and should not
necessarily be attributed to the U.S. Department of Justice or the Office of the United
States Attorney for the District of Columbia.

To my mother,
Kathryn Cunningham Flynn,
the natural writer in the family,
and in memory of my mother-in-law,
Annette Kopistansky

RELENTLESS PURSUIT

PROLOGUE

ONE SEPTEMBER DAY, I took a trip to a cemetery with my baby girl.

Megan had been born in the spring, and I'd spent less time with her than I should have. The day after my wife and I brought her home from the hospital, I was in court starting a grueling gang-murder trial. It had been the same way when my son, Connor, was born two years earlier: two murder trials the month before and another a month after, the ceremonies of birth sadly surrounded by those of death. But at the end of my daughter's first summer, I took a two-month break to be with her and my son while both were still fresh and new in the world. It was a time that would prove to be the most treasured of my life.

Still, for any man who's ever had it in him to want to be a homicide prosecutor, every day falls in a bittersweet autumn, and death is never that far away, nor is work. It was an afternoon in Indian summer 1995, with all the brightness and ominous portent of the season. My son was with my wife, Patrice; my daughter with me. It was time to go someplace.

As I write this, my daughter is eleven years old, still in childhood but leaning over the edge to see what's next. To drive her anywhere in a car is to be treated to a movie glimpsed on the letterbox screen of a rearview mirror, with the characters of school and softball and family and Girl Scouts and everything else in her life playing across the features of a young lady flush with the potential of creative observation. I have to force myself to remember her as she was on that day not all that long ago: sleeping in the backseat, strapped and mute in a baby seat turned away from me for safety's sake, when all I could see of her was a pink-blue hand that jerked occasionally with a bump or a turn. Right now, I couldn't get her in a car without a full accounting: Where are we going and when are we going there, and when are we coming back, and do I really have to go? Back then, she didn't ask, didn't care; the concept of *going* was still far beyond her. She was three years from knowing what her father did for a living ("Put bad men in jail"), another three years from knowing why he sometimes didn't come home at night ("He's in a court, and the judge is making him stay late"), a few more from sitting with her mom and her brother in a courtroom ringed by U.S. marshals, watching a jury convict three young men charged by her dad with many murders. And, God willing, many years from knowing from her own experience the feeling in the gut that would compel a person to get into a car and drive to a cemetery on a lovely day better suited to a long walk by a lake.

She didn't know, doesn't know, about Katrina Harris, a girl who'd crossed over that edge of childhood but never got the chance to go much farther. She didn't know, doesn't know, about Katrina's mother, Diane. And she didn't know, doesn't know, about how the special grace of these two lives was extinguished in a few minutes of unfathomable brutality.

Our destination that day was a graveyard in Maryland, farther away from us than it appeared on a map. I was born and raised in northern Virginia and knew that area well. I could navigate in and out of many of Washington's neighborhoods, particularly those that had spawned my violent crime cases; Maryland was a different story. To many lifelong Virginians it might as well be Mississippi, and the Potomac River dividing the two states looms wider in the mind than it does in real life. After forty-five minutes of meandering on roads I'd never seen before, I came to what I was looking for: a brick structure with a white sign that read HARMONY MEMORIAL PARK. It was the first time I'd been in a cemetery since I'd buried my father nine months before, on a mild December day in a park much like this one. That desolate scene rushed back to me as I surveyed this place: rolling hills of spotty sod, hundreds of bronze markers sunk into the soil, acres of empty expanse awaiting more arrivals.

I went to the cemetery office. Here worked the postmaster for this small, silent town, and she gave me the address I needed for the people I was visiting: Diane Hawkins and her daughter, Katrina Harris. No more "3461 Eads Street, NE, Washington, D.C.," of course; now their home was Section 16, Parcels A-39 and A-42.

I drove to where the graves were. Megan had roused herself earlier in the ride but now was asleep again. I didn't want to wake her and take her from the car. Not then, not there. There were no other cars on the winding road, no visitors walking about on the hills. I could hear landscapers toiling around the bend, but the whine of their machinery sounded distant. The weather was warm but not oppressive. If the graves were close to the road, I could lock Megan in the car and walk a short distance, as long as I was able to keep her in view. But I knew I wouldn't have much time.

I bounded a small bluff to find the plots. Suddenly a marker appeared beneath my feet: "Katrina Harris. In Loving Memory. July 15, 1979–May 26, 1993." Like my father's, it was mint-condition bronze, Olympic-medal bronze, marred only by grass shavings tossed from a mower. But where was Diane? In an unmarked plot, as it turned out. A rectangle of fresh turf outlined her place, catty-corner from her daughter's. The family, it seemed, couldn't afford to pay for both plaques at once. One of Diane's sisters would have made the arrangements, and I knew them, and I knew enough about Diane, to know that her voice had been in their ears. "Girl, do Trina's first," she would have said with a soft chuckle. "Not like I'm going anywhere."

I stood there for a moment, and a breeze kicked up. I placed myself between the two of them, as you might if you were standing in somebody's living room and wanted to be heard by everyone. I looked over my shoulder at my car; everything was still. A pause. Out of habit I lapsed into the Catholic prayer for the dead. "Eternal rest grant unto them, oh Lord," I murmured, "and let perpetual light shine upon them. May their souls and the souls of all the faithfully departed rest in peace, Amen." Another pause. "Diane, Trina." A glance at the car. "I'm going to be telling your story. I promise you I'm going to get it right. Just help me." I leaned down and patted the marker. I shot a wave to Diane's patch of sod. And I was gone.

I knew I'd be writing this book. I needed a blessing, a benediction. That's why I went there.

What I didn't know was that it would take me more than ten years to get the story right.

CHAPTER 1

IT'S WHAT WE DO.

That's a phrase I hear many times around my office, with different meanings depending on the context in which it's used and the intonation with which it's spoken, but its implication is always the same: Prosecutors are different from other people, and definitely different from other lawyers. Sometimes the phrase means that we're the good guys, so of course we have to meet a higher standard. Used in this way, the phrase gives expression to the arrogance of righteousness. Unlike private lawyers, we're beholden to no single client but only the public at large, and our own inchoate sense of right and wrong. If we can't prove a defendant's guilt, if we don't believe in a case, we drop it; if we come across evidence that a defendant can use at his trial to try to prove his innocence, we turn it over to his lawyer. *It's what we do.* Sometimes the phrase means that whatever success we achieve, it's never anything more than what was expected. *It's what we do.* Sometimes the phrase means that we're tough customers in a tough business; we ride everyone hard, especially each other. A friend of mine, an academic with a guileless spirit, sat around one night with a group of us and watched from the sidelines as we all traded sarcastic barbs for hours. Later he observed to me: "You guys are brutal." Well, *it's what we do*. And sometimes the phrase is simply a laconic summary of everything that's exhilarating about the job, about applying your talents on a public stage and bringing the worst of society's offenders to justice.

Recently I handled a gang-murder trial over an almost unendurable three months. I had three defendants charged with four homicides and numerous other violent crimes going back over five years, and my witnesses were primarily other gang members who were only slightly less compromised than the targets of their testimony. Many spoke only Spanish, and most were in some form of protective custody. Keeping the case together was a daily challenge; the days in court were long and the evenings that followed were longer. As if that weren't enough, the bureaucracy of my office—the dark side of government service—unexpectedly reared its head in a way that would be too tedious to read about, but that, trust me, made matters no easier. One night I called home from work and learned from my wife that my children were both in bed and she was fading fast. When I came home, I knew, I'd be moving about the house by myself. My back was hurting, and I was going to be taking a bath to soak it, so I stopped at a convenience store to pick up a magazine—something light that wouldn't remind me of work—to read in the tub. On the rack I glimpsed a magazine cover advertising an article inside: "The Ten Best Jobs in America." I was tired. I was frustrated. I was angry at my bosses. Still, without thinking, I picked up the magazine—on the off chance that my job was listed. Even with everything that was going on, I still couldn't help believing that any such roster should be led by "Homicide Prosecutor in the Nation's Capital."

IT WAS LATE SPRING 1993, and I was a thirty-six-year-old assistant U.S. attorney in Washington, D.C. Though I'd grown up in a small northern Virginia town named Annandale and now lived in another Virginia suburb, it had been my dream since law school to prosecute violent crimes in the capital. For the past year I'd been handling homicides and had had four murder trials in the last nine months. I'd lost the first and was still plagued by it, mentally reducing the experience to its most minute elements and pondering whether a question better phrased, a sentence better worded, might have kept a killer from getting back out on the street. And what about the next three trials, all of which I'd won? I barely gave them a second thought. My conscience rested easily where those cases were concerned, and the facts were already receding into a distant place in my mind reserved for nameless moments of satisfaction.

One day in late May 1993, a detective named Dean Combee appeared at my door. He was with D.C.'s Metropolitan Police Department (MPD) and he'd started working homicides a few years before, just as D.C.'s murder rate was accelerating. The cases were coming in so quickly that the details tended to blur together as if they were all just pieces of one long, epic tragedy. Most of Combee's cases were bad-guy-on-bad-guy murders, drug dealers exterminating one another in fevered battles over territory. On this day, though, he started talking about one case that stood out from the rest. Combee described the crime scene to me, for no other reason than that he knew me and he wanted to talk about it. A mother and daughter, innocent victims, had been left mutilated. The mother was named Diane Hawkins, the daughter Katrina Harris. The mother had been eviscerated; the daughter's heart had been cut from her body. They'd never had a chance. And their killer was still on the loose.

The average person hears this story and thinks: *Where did it happen? How far is that from here? Could I be next?*

The prosecutor hears this story and thinks: *God, just give me the chance to get that guy.*

Why? Part of the answer derives from the hubris of the committed public servant. We see ourselves as partners with the police in protecting the people, and we like to think of ourselves in action, springing to respond to metaphorical distress signals in the sky. Part of it, undeniably, has to do with the thrill of the chase, whatever it is that first seizes children when they play cops and robbers and that some of us never outgrow. It's the feeling that something is out there that you don't want to miss, something that will take you from the everyday commonplace—not to mention a fleeting opportunity to redirect the ceaseless flow of human events, if only by a fraction and only for a moment.

Much of it, though, is far more personal than any of us would easily admit. To a prosecutor—to me, at least—the private becomes public, the public private. The psychic paraphernalia of my family life and my work life are no longer kept in separate boxes but instead are jumbled together in the same large crate. My job is to plunge into cases that involve the most elemental human impulses—feelings of love and greed and hatred and resentment so extreme that they can move a person to want to render another nonexistent—and then to glean the essential truth from them and act on that truth in a setting where the stakes are very high. To do my job—to relate to the reality of a case and make it my own—I must draw on my own elemental impulses, the thoughts and feelings by which I am most driven. Hearing from Detective Combee about the mother and daughter murders, I didn't think first of all the children and all the mothers in the world; I thought of my baby boy, and of the woman with whom I'd chosen to share my life and who had joined me in conceiving him. That's the way I entered this case: *What if this madman had gutted someone I love?*

I knew in an instant that I wanted the chance to go after this killer. By sheer luck, the thought became reality for me. On Saturday, May 29, just three days after the murders, a man was arrested and charged with the murders. He would go before a judge on Memorial Day. In my office, holiday court duties were assigned at random. It just so happened that I'd drawn this particular day and by office policy would retain any case that came into court on my watch.

The clerk called the case and I walked to the front of the courtroom, case file in hand. The defendant strode forward. This was my first look at him. His attorney, a woman of average height, stood next to him. She had to crane her neck to look at his face, which was long and dominated by heavy-lidded eyes and a downturned mouth. He had a small mustache that I imagined he'd probably first grown when he was ten years old. On a good day, with proper posture, I top out at about five feet nine. He looked to be at least eight inches taller, maybe 100 pounds heavier. He didn't appear to be heavily muscled, but having enjoyed every other advantage of size, he'd probably never needed to be.

The hearing was over in minutes. The judge decided there was enough evidence to hold him in jail for now. It would now be up to me to lead the investigation of the case.

As I left court, an older man approached me. "Some of Diane's family is in the back," he said. "Can you come speak to them?" A few months before, I'd handled a murder case in which the victim was a drug dealer. None of his family or friends cared enough about him to come to the trial, or even to return my phone calls, and so every day for more than a week I put on the drama of his death in an empty courtroom. That was unusual but not unheard of. So this day I thought, if one or two people from this family care enough to come down to the first hearing in the case, it's a good sign for the future.

Behind the courtroom was an anteroom. I knocked lightly on the door and went in. Crammed into a space no bigger than a child's bedroom was a group of at least twenty-five people; more came in the back as we all talked, and I could see them strain their necks to hear everything. They were all African American. After spending every day of my working life in Washington, D.C., where most crime victims and many police officers are black, it was a regular occurrence for me to be the only white person in a room. What I wasn't used to was the experience of encountering a group so bereft, so unmoored as this. They varied in age from teenagers to senior citizens, and most seemed incapable of speech. Almost all of the men were standing, shifting back and forth; almost all of the women were sitting, wringing their hands.

I began by describing the schedule for the case and the procedures it would follow. I said that if anyone thought they'd like grief counseling, I could arrange for free services. I made one suggestion: Don't substitute the court process for the grieving process. I'd seen survivors of homicide invest all of their emotional energies in a prosecution only to suffer the ultimate letdown when the case was over: Whatever the outcome, it didn't bring their loved one back.

It was all pretty dry stuff. I looked around the room. No one was looking up, except one man. He appeared to be about fifty-five years old, and he had a round face and kind eyes behind wire-framed glasses. In a few seconds of silence I watched a tear follow a path down his cheek to his jawline; he didn't bother to stop it. I couldn't hold back. "Don't worry," I said. "We're going to get this son of a bitch."

Looking back, I realize this was a false moment, a cheap play to the emotions; I didn't know the case, the defendant, or this family well enough to utter an oath like that. I realize this now because of a voice that still moves about, gently but reprovingly, in my memory. It's the voice of maturity, the voice of reason. That day it came from an older woman standing to one side, but it could just as easily have come from anyone in the room. "Attorney Flynn," the voice said quietly. "All we want is justice." There was a brief silence.

"You're right, ma'am," I said. "That's what we want too."

I AM A PROSECUTOR.

I carry other titles that I cherish more: father, husband, son. But the specifics of my character, good and bad, are best defined by the job title that I've held for more than eighteen years: competitive, by turns idealistic and cynical, dramatic to a fault, with an occasional tendency to paint the world with a palette that lacks the color gray. Add, for good measure, world-weary. In 1993, I had thirteen fewer years on the job than I have now, but I'd already been stamped with the brand of my profession. I had an easy familiarity with humanity at its most base, and my career had consisted of an extended tour through a veritable museum of amorality and depravity. Cases in point: a young man whose MO was targeting females riding in vehicles at nighttime and shooting them in the head; two women who for no apparent reason beat and stabbed to death a defenseless seventy-year-old man and then sodomized him with his own broken cane; two youths who sprayed children at a school bus stop with gunfire four days before Christmas. The star witness in one case was a trigger-happy sixteen-year-old nicknamed Ant Man. He was the friend, surrogate, and moral equivalent of the victim. Ant Man paid me the ultimate compliment during one of our witness conferences when he interjected, "Mr. Flynn, you're all right. Have you ever killed anybody?" It seemed as if I'd left in another life the feeling of being surprised by any act of human cruelty. Encounters with the better angels of human nature were more rare.

Prosecutors tend to put themselves at a distance from others; I certainly did. Our job calls on us to pass judgment on other people's conduct every day of our lives. Defendants, suspects, victims, witnesses—all are fair game. Police officers don't receive favored treatment, nor do fellow prosecutors; on those rare occasions when one of our own is revealed to have compromised the system's integrity, it's our job to pursue them as vigorously as we would anyone else. The turnover rate in my job is high; many find it's not for them and drift away after a few years. Those who stay committed to it tend to be of a certain type: driven, focused loners. Those words, no doubt, applied to me in 1993. I was an only child. I had a small group of family and friends to whom I was very devoted, but I'd seen other friendships come and go with time. I had a tendency to expect too much from others—maybe more than I was willing to give to others myself—and so found myself disappointed with people more often than I had any right to. I worked by myself and I tried my cases by myself; in the courtroom, my table was my turf, and I needed no one else on it. It was said that the easiest job in my office was that of my secretary; I didn't delegate much. And I had the virtue—or vice—of training my sights on a case or a defendant and blocking out everything else.

The man who killed Diane Hawkins and Katrina Harris was in my sights. Hell, he still is. It's thirteen years later, and I'm still writing about him. I saw him again not long ago—later on I'll tell you why—and it was May 1993 all over again. It's tempting to say that this is his story, but it's not. It's a story of extremes: the worst and the best the world can offer, humanity at its most brutal and most noble. It's the story of two families—mine and another from a world that I thought I knew but didn't—two families full of ordinary people who did their best under awful circumstances. The story needs to be told and I, by default, am the best one to tell it. It isn't an easy story to tell, just as it wasn't an easy story to live. I'm still trying to get a grasp on it, all these years later: why it all came together as it did, why these lives folded themselves over each other so tightly.

And why any of it had to happen in the first place.

AFTER THE FIRST court hearing, I went to my office. It was Memorial Day, and there was nobody around to bother me, but I still closed my door; I didn't stray lightly from old habits.

I know many prosecutors whose offices are bereft of personal touches. Most days, convicted criminals move about in our halls: witnesses in our cases, they've been served with subpoenas, meaning that they know we can have them arrested if they don't show up. We need them, and they, in a way, need us. But our alliance is temporary and tenuous, and mistrust prevails on both sides. For many years a friend of mine has maintained a workspace as ascetic as the cell of a Trappist monk. "I don't want anybody who comes in here," he told me, "to know a damned thing about me." With more sentimentality than practicality, I long ago took the opposite tack. If my job was going to take me away from home, I reasoned, I could at least create a version of home in my office. And so my walls and desk space have offered up a hodgepodge of past and present, with the desk from my childhood room serving as a makeshift stand for a refrigerator and family pictures in cheap frames teetering precariously atop overstuffed file cabinets. If my office in 1993 was marginally less cluttered than it is now, it's only because I had less of a past to clutter it with. It was in this place—surrounded by the artifacts of family members long dead and still living, watched over by my son's ingenuous gaze as captured in a studio-posed eight-by-ten—that I contemplated Diane Hawkins and Katrina Harris and the man charged with taking their lives.

Before anything else, I knew I had to see something. I'd heard Detective Dean Combee describe the horror on Eads Street. I'd read the newspaper stories and watched the news broadcasts. Every account had been sensitively but vividly rendered. But in the end, words fail to capture a scene like this.

I had to see all the pictures, all of them.

I had to see the house, the rooms where the killings happened, everything the killer left behind.

I had to see the victims, their wounds, their faces.

I had to see the killer's handiwork.

I had to see what I was up against.

ON THE NIGHT of the murders, a police officer took a video to preserve all of the details of the crime scene. I needed to watch the tape, to pause it at places, to compare certain frames to the crime-scene stills.

The first scene on the Hawkins murder tape: a nondescript row house, captured from the outside.

Every murder case is just a story, and every story happens in a place. In fact, the concept of place is a key factor in *any* story. The place shapes the story. A man shooting from a car riding down a street, for example, has a freedom of movement that a man chasing a woman through a house doesn't. If a prosecutor has no sense of the place where a crime occurred—the neighborhood, the house, the room—he has no sense of the crime.

The camera is trained unflinchingly on the Hawkins place. Standing alone, dark, it gives no hint of what is inside. One detail catches the eye, a simple sign that, before her death, Diane Hawkins was having trouble making ends meet: The glass in both front windows is missing, with clear plastic covering the rectangular openings. Notably, the plastic hasn't been broken. A close-up of the front screen door and the wooden door behind also shows no signs of forced entry, though they do bear bloodstains.

Inside the front door is the living room. The focal point is a large television set topped by a VCR. Surrounding the television is the standard array of living room furniture and accessories. The sofa has been upended. Like its owner, whose feet can be seen in a wide shot of the room, the sofa is lying on its back and covered with blood. There is only one other sign of a struggle: Across from the sofa, a small table lies on its side, and on the floor next to it is a lamp and framed picture. Other items, magazines and the like, are scattered about the room, as if left there in the course of a family's hectic everyday life. A wide shot shows the sofa's position in the context of the entire room; a tighter shot focuses on bloodstains on parts of the sofa. A sizable stain, apparently still wet, covers one end at the place where one might rest one's head; long streams of blood, also still fresh, emanate from the stain toward the bottom of the sofa. Behind it a white curtain conceals the clear plastic in the living room window.

A wide shot of the living room shows a small brown table standing upright next to the sofa. The table holds two objects. One is a framed photograph of a young girl with a small gap-toothed smile and a large pair of women's earrings; I recognize her at once as Katrina. The other object is a Mother's Day card signed by Katrina— given just weeks before to the mother now lying dead on the floor just a few feet away.

A shot of the area between the living room and dining room shows no blood trail. None of the furniture in the dining room appears to be out of place: a dining room set, a china closet, and a microwave oven sitting on top of a small table in the corner. Resting precariously on top of the microwave is a napkin full of what looks like cheese chips. The glass in the china closet is unbroken. Behind the glass, on a shelf, a certificate is displayed: a prize won by Katrina at a school science fair.

Now the focus turns to the body of Diane Hawkins, and the camera advances closer and closer to it.

She lies near the doorway to her kitchen. The two walls closest to her body are covered with small bloodstains. A large smear, possibly caused by contact with a blood-covered object, and small smears mar the frame and adjacent walls. She is lying on her back with her right arm over her head and her left by her side, her legs slightly apart. The rug beneath her is saturated in blood. Her long, wavy hair is fanned out on the floor, her eyes are half-open. Her T-shirt has been drawn up close to her neck, exposing her belly. A massive hole has been carved into her chest; through it has been pulled a large amount of what appear to be intestines. A pile of bright yellow and red viscera, unattached from the rest, lies behind her head. Her heart is floating free in the chest cavity, cut from the tethers that had held it there.

The camera turns to Diane's face. It bears little resemblance to how a face would look in life. So much blood covers it that various tracks and patterns can be charted like troop movements on a Civil War battlefield. Her nose looks broken, the skin around her eyes is swollen, and her mouth is bruised and cut. Compared with the wounds that caused her death these are minor, but they tell me that a beating preceded the stabbing.

The focus turns lower, to a gaping wound around Diane's neck. It is several inches wide and exposes the neck's tendons and muscles in the same way that the chest wound reveals the viscera beneath. Its depth and length suggest that it isn't the product of a single impulsive slash but a vigorous sawing engaged in over a prolonged period of time. The camera moves to Diane's arms and legs. Her right arm is pressed against a child's plastic play chair. Her left hand is covered in a gauze bandage. The wrapping raises a question: Was the assault interrupted long enough for her to try to treat herself, or was the bandage the remnant of earlier treatment for an unrelated injury? Below, I see that Diane Hawkins's killer saw fit to unbutton and unzip her pants, for no particular reason; forensic tests have already shown that he didn't sexually assault her. Still lower, another oddity: a stab wound to the victim's inner thigh, far removed from her other wounds, which has bled heavily onto her blue jeans. Perhaps it was the opening salvo of the attack, perhaps a parting shot delivered while the victim was lying prone and defenseless.

The scene shifts from dining room to kitchen and blood drops on the worn linoleum floor. There are no large pools or smears between Diane's body and the kitchen; it appears unlikely that Diane Hawkins was killed in the kitchen and dragged to the dining room. On the sink and drainboard are dishes and silverware, washed but not yet put away. There is no blood around the sink, no sign that the killer washed off either himself or a weapon. There's a blood smear on the cabinet over the sink, a large round drop on the countertop, and a smear on the cabinet over the sink. There are similar smears on the inside door and outside screen door, which lead into a backyard.

The scene shifts again, to a narrow staircase, evidently going from first to second floor. There are blood streaks on the wall. There's a shot of a bathroom on the second floor: no signs of cleanup. This is puzzling; I assume the killer was drenched in blood. Wouldn't he have wanted to wash off before leaving? Next to the bathroom is a bedroom, as cramped as all the other rooms in the house. Two sets of bunk beds flank the room, and an ironing board is opened up in between, impeding easy passage. Sheets and a blanket are lying on the floor but nothing else appears to be out of place, and there are no signs of an altercation here.

Moving farther down the hall, the camera shows two bedrooms. The door to the bedroom to the left stays closed, apparently locked. The bedroom to the right holds Katrina Harris, captured in the frame at a distance. Throughout the room are children's clothes and women's shoes piled in various places, the headboard from a disassembled bed is propped up against two walls, and the floor can barely be seen beneath the mess. On a desk to the right is a television set playing at low volume. Unless police officers in the room turned it on—unlikely, given the solemnity of the scene—it was on when the murders occurred, and the only question is, who watched it last?

The camera scans the room: again, no signs of a struggle. A dresser sits in front of a window. It holds numerous perfume bottles and other fragile containers standing upright and untouched. Whatever else preceded Katrina Harris's death, she didn't flail about the room either in flight or self-defense.

There's a narrow strip of carpeting in front of where Katrina's body lies. No blood trail links the victim's body with the rest of the room or the hallway outside. Like her mother, Katrina Harris apparently died on the spot where she was left and wasn't dragged there from elsewhere. On the wall above the girl's head is a large blood pattern shaped like a fountain spray. On the wall above the bed next to her is the inscription "Reco" written in pencil. The wall is grimy and badly needs washing and painting.

Katrina is wedged in between her mother's bed and a large box of diapers: symbols of the conception and the nurturing of life. Her feet and legs are covered by two pillows; above the waist, she is still clothed and her shirt is pulled down, unlike her mother—who was left with arms outspread, gutted, and undraped for all the world to see. It appears dark red, but a closer look reveals that a small patch has retained its original green color; the rest is from blood, soaked through from the chest. Encircling the girl's neck is a wound, shown in close-up. It is at least as deep and as long as Diane's. Her chin is tilted oddly against her chest; her head, evidently, is unsupported by the muscles at the back of the neck. A small gold chain is twisted through the several-inch-wide gash in her throat. Her short, wavy hair is matted with already-congealing blood.

A still picture, apparently taken after the body was moved to be analyzed, adds detail. The girl's shirt has been lifted. A massive oval-shaped hole runs horizontally down the midline of her upper chest.

Here is where Katrina Harris's heart once beat.

I KNEW AN MPD homicide detective who kept a scrapbook of photos of dead bodies from cases he had worked. He wasn't the only police officer to pursue this macabre hobby: One such scrapbook, compiled by a Los Angeles homicide detective in the 1930s, found its way into print a few years ago. Even the grimmest photos were accompanied by laconic commentary and morbid humor offered by the detective. In the book's introduction, a writer noted:

The surgeon, the burn ward nurse, emergency room attendants, paramedics, firefighters and cops, all those who scrape the still-screaming remains out of car wrecks, must cultivate their off-switch. Those who can't learn to crack wise and discuss baseball over a corpse must find a gentler line of work.

Prosecutors are once removed from the worst of it. Only occasionally do we ride around with the police, so we rarely if ever have to see the corpses, let alone touch them or smell them. But we do have to see their pictures, meet their families, and carry their death visages around in our heads for weeks or months or even years. I'd put in enough time as a violent-crime prosecutor that my off-switch was fully operational. Around the office, gallows humor was my stock-in-trade, and nothing was sacred. My friends and I had only one rule: Let twenty-four hours pass before mocking a death. But after I saw the photos from Eads Street, something strange happened: I didn't joke about this case as I did the others. Not at all. And any time I tried to talk with anyone about Katrina, I had to stop in the middle of the conversation.

NOW THE MOST important task before me could be summarized in three words: Talk to people. For the simplest of reasons, I would never know everything about how this mother and daughter had died: I wasn't there. Every criminal trial brings together a prosecutor, a defense attorney, a judge, and a jury who share one limitation: We all have to rely on other people to tell us about what happened. I now had to bring before me everyone who *was* there—in the days, the hours, the minutes before and after those terrible moments.

After a few weeks' time, I could see these events in my mind as if they were actually happening. I could feel myself in the body of the man who'd walked in the house and found the bodies: bone-weary from a day's work, suddenly flailing about in a dark, death-filled house. I could feel myself in the body of the teenage boy who'd just looked down on his slaughtered mother and sister, blind with grief and anger and fear, trying to answer an officer's questions and only hearing words as if they were being spoken underwater. I could feel myself inside the body of the killer, sitting in a police station, thinking back to a truck left on a roadside, telling myself I'm just as smart as these cops are even though they think I'm not. And it would all be so real to me that when I went back through the story, it would all be in the present, and there would be no past or future.

CHAPTER 2

I T'S JUST AFTER 11:30 P.M. on May 25, 1993, and an aging
BMW is laboring through the city's deserted commercial district.
It's heading south toward familiar landmarks: the White House, the
Lincoln Memorial, and the Jefferson Memorial beyond. But its destination isn't the official Washington of postcards and tourist trams,
and within a few miles of the White House it turns east, then takes
a series of side streets around the lighted, alabaster Capitol building.
The dome shrinks to a dot of light in the rearview mirror as the
car leaves the official Washington of politics and enters the living
Washington of neighborhoods, mostly black and self-contained and
church-oriented and Southern-influenced, where people go about
their daily lives unnoticed by the national press.

Just after midnight, the BMW enters the Northeast Washington
neighborhood of River Terrace. Aptly named, it sits above a river, the
Potomac, just across a bridge from Robert F. Kennedy Memorial
Stadium, home of the Washington Redskins. On autumn Sunday
afternoons the air in River Terrace is charged with crowd noise from
the nearby stadium, but on this late spring evening the stadium is
dark and deserted. As the car rolls down the narrow streets, it passes

row houses handed down from generation to generation of black middle-class families for more than half a century. Like every other pocket of the city, River Terrace has in recent years been touched by a crime plague that shows no signs of letting up, and drug dealers move about sporadically in some of its parks and parking lots. But in a city pockmarked by decaying slums and projects, this community—with its tree-lined streets, tidy dwellings, and backbone of longtime inhabitants—is notable for its relative normalcy. For those of a certain age who live in this neighborhood, or even walk through its streets on a late spring day, River Terrace serves as a poignant reminder of the way things used to be. Even its name evokes its place in the city, if only by accident: on a plateau, above life's ebb and flow.

It's too quiet, thinks Mike Harwood, one of the BMW's passengers, as he and his friends drive through River Terrace. The car itself makes more noise than anything else nearby; needing a new muffler and probably more, it announces its arrival from at least a block away. The car slows to a stop in front of a row house in the center of River Terrace. It discharges Harwood and leaves, its engine rattle dwindling to a buzz and then to nothing. The house, 3461 Eads Street, is a regular way station for Harwood in his travels around town. He's twenty-eight years old, small and wiry, with large, wary brown eyes and a small mustache, and he has a coiled energy and a swagger fashioned over years of having to assert himself against larger people. Once adrift, caught up in petty crime, he is now a success story: a rehabilitated ex-offender, working two jobs. For this he credits his parents, Malcolm and Jean Harwood, both staid working people and contributors to the community, and the other members of his extended family—especially his aunt, Diane Hawkins, in whose house he is looking forward to laying down his head for the night.

His parents actually own the house. They bought it thirty years ago and now lease it to his mother's sister, forty-two-year-old Diane.

The house sits at the end of a block. To its left is an alley; to its right an adjoining house, vacant for some months, which in turn is attached to another vacant house. Across the street is a small, lushly foliated park said to be home to some dope peddlers but empty this night. Inside the tiny house at the end of Eads Street live, virtually on top of one another, Diane Hawkins and five of her six children: Reco, age twenty; Shante, age fifteen; Katrina, age thirteen; Rasheen (also known as Rock), age nine; and Kiki, age twenty-two months. A seventh person lived in the house until recently: Diane's boyfriend, Skeeter, evicted when their romantic relationship ruptured. Mike Harwood is a frequent visitor to the house, as are many members of his family; it's a center of activity for them as well as for Diane Hawkins's wide circle of friends.

So it's with some trepidation that Mike Harwood regards the house, which on other occasions has seemed to rock on its foundation with activity but which this night is dead still. He notes the time: 12:10 A.M. He'd wanted to arrive at his aunt's house before midnight, but now he's late. As he approaches Diane's house, he sees that while the outside and downstairs lights are off, the upstairs lights are on. This makes him even more anxious, maybe because he isn't used to seeing the lower level look so dark.

Of course, if the outside lights were on, he might see the trail of blood drops leading from the front door and down the walk, and if the downstairs lights were on, he might see the crimson smudges on the door frame, and he might run for help and never go inside the house.

Instead, not seeing these things, he walks up to the front door and finds it not only unlocked but ajar. It isn't Diane's way to leave her door open after midnight. Harwood pushes the door inward and enters the living room. The sofa is overturned. Perhaps his aunt upended it while cleaning or painting the room. He doesn't see that the sofa's beige brocade pattern is red-smeared. He takes tentative half steps toward the staircase immediately to his right. As he makes his way to the stairs, the merciful darkness spares him the sight of another bright red smudge on the white foyer wall, a series of circular red spots already sinking into the plain living room rug, and a piece of human flesh sitting on the living room floor. And he's also oblivious to the still form lying supine in the dining room less than ten feet away.

He continues up the stairs and into the house's lighted upper half, makes a hard right into a bathroom on the landing, and stops to relieve himself. Somewhere in the distance he hears a baby crying. He doesn't react to the sound until it becomes a scream, and he realizes it's coming from his two-year-old cousin, Kiki. He walks toward the sound, to a bedroom down the hall that he knows from his many past visits is his aunt Diane's. But she's nowhere in sight. He enters the bedroom and sees the baby poised unsteadily on the bed, looking over the side and wailing hysterically. He navigates his way around considerable clutter, including an ironing board and a basket overflowing with laundry, to a wall that's bare but for a framed, fading photograph of Diane and a small child. Beneath the photograph, lying on her back wedged between the bed and a jumbo box of Huggies brand diapers, is the same child now on the brink of adolescence: Mike's thirteen-year-old cousin, Katrina. Her hands are resting on her chest, her head propped up against the wall. Her eyes are closed and her expression serene. In fact, it's fair to say that Katrina Harris in the immediate aftermath of her violent death looks as if she's just fallen asleep on the floor, except for two things: Her head rests against her chest at a grotesque angle, and her clothing is soaked in blood so thick and fresh that it catches the light.

He comes close to Katrina, stares at her, but doesn't touch her. He thinks to himself that he needs to get out, that he needs to get help, even that the killer might still be in the house. He doesn't have any notion that he can save his cousin's life. He has seen the angle of her head and the blood on her clothes, and he knows.

The baby is still wailing, but Harwood, afflicted with his own form of hysteria, doesn't pick her up. He runs down the stairs, not seeing the long blood streaks on the wall and molding, and runs out the front door, not seeing the body in the dining room. He goes to the house two doors down from the Hawkins house and pounds on the door, shouting gibberish. But the house is vacant and his cries go unheard. He runs down the block until he finds a house with its lights still on, and here his pounding and yelling are answered. Harwood manages to tell the woman at the door that he has come upon something terrible in the Hawkins house.

At 12:21 A.M. on May 26, 1993, a police dispatcher receives a call from a female: "3461 Eads E-A-D-S. There's a whole lot of blood all over the house. There's blood everywhere and people laying down, and we need an ambulance."

The dispatcher fumbles for words, and the caller continues: "Yes, 3461 Eads Street E-A-D-S. It's in River Terrace. It's a private home on an alley. . . . It's the house the police have been watching for some time."

The dispatcher broadcasts a bulletin that is heard by officers on patrol in the vicinity. Two officers are close to Eads Street, and they drive straight to the house, arriving in minutes. Two other officers, Sergeant James Williams and Officer Elizabeth Sharp-Hamlet, are farther away from the scene when they hear the summons and drive into the area just a few minutes behind the others.

Meanwhile, Harwood is running back toward his aunt's house and sees his cousin Shante—sister of Katrina and daughter of Diane—as she rides up to the front of the house. Shante is fifteen years old and has recently begun spending more time outside the house than in, running with company that her mother has viewed with suspicion. Shante was with several friends early in the evening, staying near her home but being made ever aware that her mother was keeping watch over her comings and goings. Several times, Diane came out on her porch to make sure she was still nearby. She even asked Shante to stay in the house with her, and the look on her face was furtive and fearful. It was a look that will stay in Shante's mind for months to come. Following one of her brief visits to the house, and chafing under her mother's attention, she left to go for a drive. It was about 11:30 P.M. On her way out, she passed her brother Reco, driving away from the house in the opposite direction.

It's shortly after 12:20 A.M. when Shante returns alone and sees Mike Harwood at the curb. In an instant, Harwood shatters her world and then preserves a piece of it: He tells her what he has seen in the house, then he holds her back from going inside, saving her from a vision that will long cloud the memories of those not similarly spared.

After surrendering in her struggle with Harwood, Shante goes to find her brother Reco. She thinks to look first at the home of one of his best friends, Eric Fisher. Shante's hunch is sound; Reco is in the backyard of Fisher's house with him and two other friends. They're doing what they do many nights, which is not much of anything. All are in their late teens or early twenties, and none has a particular direction in life. (One will be dead a little more than a year later, a victim in a murder unrelated to the events of this May night; another will find himself a defendant in yet another unrelated murder.) They're like countless youths in every American city: living aimless lives on the fringes of illegality, losing their potential to poverty and listlessness. Reco is an especially frustrating case: a tall, handsome young man with a diffident manner that conceals a keen intellect and an abiding loyalty to those closest to him.

Shante runs up to Reco and tries to tell him what Mike Harwood has told her, but all she can say is "Blood is everywhere, blood is everywhere," over and over. Reco races to his house, with Shante and his two friends trailing behind, and sees Mike pacing in circles outside. The police and paramedics are on their way but haven't yet arrived. Reco runs through the front door, now open wide following Harwood's rushed exit. The downstairs lights are still off when he goes into the living room. Unlike Harwood, Reco sees the prone form lying in the semi-darkness as soon as he enters the room, and sees it's his mother.

He looks down at the woman who brought him into the world and whose buoyant spirit has filled the only home he's ever known. Even in the dim light he can see that she's dead; worse still, if that's possible, he can see that she's been mutilated.

Reco takes it all in. Questions of who or why haven't yet occurred to him. Reco knows that his mother is dead, but he still shakes her leg and says, "Mom, Mom," as if trying to wake her. Then he rises from the body, stumbles upstairs, and finds Trina lying in the bedroom.

Reco runs from the house, then returns with several of his friends. Rumors are already spreading outside about the murders at 3461. Reco's friends huddle first around Diane and then go upstairs to Katrina. Moments later, paramedics arrive on the scene, followed by the police and members of the Hawkins family who live nearby and have received word that something is very wrong in the house on Eads Street. No one touches either body. Paramedics hang back in a cluster. A police officer walks in, sees Diane Hawkins's body, pivots, leaves the house, and vomits. Tomorrow, before reporting for work, he'll request psychological counseling.

In the midst of all the confusion, one person has been forgotten: twenty-two-month-old Kiki, moving around the house and crying softly for her mother. A police officer picks her up and searches for someone in the family to take care of her. The girl becomes quiet, then falls asleep.

Meanwhile, Reco and his companions have left the house and are running down Dix Street, one block away from his home. They're seen by Sergeant Williams and Officer Sharp-Hamlet, who are driving in a marked car toward Eads Street. To a police officer, no one appears as suspicious as a group of people running from the scene of a murder. Sergeant Williams decides to stop the group.

The young men are wild, out of control. One, the tall youth who will later become known to them as Reco Hawkins, is in worse shape than the others. He's weeping incomprehensibly for several seconds as the officers try to calm him down. Sergeant Williams is a veteran officer with considerable experience in handling situations such as this; Officer Sharp-Hamlet, while junior to her partner, is also trained in crisis control. But they have their hands full with the Hawkins boy. He continues to wander back and forth in the street, saying over and over: "I know he did it. I know he did it. He killed them. He killed them. He killed them both." And then, about Katrina: "He didn't have to kill her. He didn't have to kill her. He didn't have to kill her. She was just a baby." And then he cries some more and circles around the officers, rebuffing all their entreaties. Sergeant Williams says several times, with increasing impatience, "What are you talking about? Who did what?" Williams and Sharp-Hamlet figure that the boy is referring to the murders on Eads Street and know they need to detain him long enough in one place so they can get his story from him. But every time the officers get close to him, he either moves back or swats away their proffered hands. Finally they handcuff him, simply to sit him still and get a logical account from him.

The tactic seems to work. Reco struggles to think of the name of the person he's talking about but draws a blank—this man he has known for most of his life—and he waves his cuffed hands around in front of him as if trying to conjure the name from the air. His friends are still around him and try to help. Reco appears to the officers as if he might be about to hyperventilate. He finally makes some reference to his "mother's boyfriend." One of his friends chimes in, "You mean Skeeter?" referring to Diane Hawkins's ex-boyfriend, the one who recently moved out of the house. "No, no," he says, finally remembering. "Norman. Norman! He'd just left."

At this moment, the police have their first leads. They now need to find out more about Norman, and Skeeter as well.

———

AT ABOUT 12:45 A.M., the second wave of police personnel arrives at the Hawkins house: plainclothes detectives. Some go inside the house; others go door-to-door to try to locate anyone who might have seen or heard anything suspicious in the last several hours. Without exception, all those interviewed claim to have been oblivious to the commotion, the yelling and screaming, which had to have accompanied the murders.

Inside the house, homicide detectives Herman Johnson, Dean Combee, and James Johnson tiptoe through the premises, jotting down detached observations in dog-eared notebooks. These notes, memorialized in formal police reports, will capture the scene with dry objectivity. But they won't capture the emotions of the men and women who are here this night. Detective Herman Johnson, for one, has been a detective for twenty-three years, a homicide detective for eight. He has been on thousands of crime scenes and hundreds of murder scenes, and has long since concluded that his job can offer him no more surprises—until tonight, when he walks through the Hawkins house and says to himself and anyone nearby, over and over: "This is the worst."

Two other homicide detectives drive up to the Hawkins house but don't linger there for long. Detectives Dan Whalen and Eric Gainey are told at the front door about the state of the bodies inside, and can see that there's no shortage of law enforcement personnel handling the scene. They decide that their time might be put to better use elsewhere and drive over to Dix Street, where they've heard by police radio that uniformed officers have a potential witness detained.

Indeed, Reco Hawkins has calmed down enough that Sergeant Williams and Officer Sharp-Hamlet have removed the handcuffs from his wrists. The young man is still acting as if he's in a daze, walking aimlessly in the street, and Sergeant Williams is relieved to see the homicide detectives arrive so that he can turn this witness over to them. Whalen and Gainey approach Reco to ask if he can get into the backseat of their car to take a drive with them, and he agrees. All the detectives know at that point, from their conversation with Sergeant Williams, is that someone named Norman was with the victims before they died, that Reco can take them to his house, and that he seems to believe very strongly that Norman had something to do with what happened. Why, the sergeant doesn't know. Well, they have to start somewhere.

AT ABOUT 1:00 A.M., three crime scene search officers—evidence collectors—arrive at the crime scene. All are on a permanent midnight assignment, meaning that their tour of duty coincides with the peak hours of violent crime throughout the town. Their job: sifting through the wreckage of lives lost to brutality, night after night.

Responsibilities for various duties are divided at the start. Officer Lamont Allen will draft a diagram of the floors of the house where the bodies were located; Officer Curtis Lancaster will photograph the scene and gather evidence for later use; Officer A. P. Holmes will take a video of the house's interior. The video has been requested by the homicide detectives, who decided upon entering the house that this was such a vivid scene that mere still photographs, while helpful, wouldn't suffice to capture the many details that might prove significant.

Outside, a crowd gathers.

Among Diane Hawkins's living relatives are seven sisters, three brothers, six aunts, two uncles, fifty-nine nieces and nephews, and many, many friends who are just like family to her. Many keep in regular contact with her and with each other, at least by telephone and often in person. Now they're linked in tragedy. Some are still awake when they hear the news; others are roused from a sound sleep, the last moments of peace they would enjoy for some time to come.

Understandably, given the circumstances, these initial reports sometimes garble the facts. Carlene Hawkins, one of Diane's many nieces,
is among the first to arrive at the house, bursting onto the scene as
Reco is fleeing down Eads Street. Carlene has received a telephone
call from a cousin, telling her to hurry over to River Terrace because
"somebody's sprayed Diane's with gunfire and they're all gone." The
same erroneous report, passed on by a different source, summons Barbara Harwood, Diane's sister and landlord. But unlike Carlene and
many others, Barbara and her husband, Ty, don't rush to Diane's house.
They tarry in getting ready and then take such a leisurely and cir-
cuitous drive to River Terrace that they get there well after the rest
of the family, even though they were among the first to hear the news
and didn't have far to travel. In months to come, they will have only
a hazy memory of the trip, recalling it as one might a sleepwalking
episode. But they will know the cause of their lethargic meandering:
It was a psychological contrivance to delay the inevitable, even for a
little while.

Barbara and Ty join the crowd milling about outside the Hawkins
house. Those who have risen from bed to answer the call in the night
are readily distinguished by the nightgowns and pajamas peeking out
from their coats and trousers. Rumors are already spreading through
the crowd about who the killer might be, and some in the anguished
group angrily vow retaliation. The truth is that no one in the group
has anything but a private hunch to rely on at the moment, and
cooler heads among them—the older family members, primarily—
prevail on the others not to rush to judgment. Many are crying
loudly. None of the group is being permitted past a certain point by
the police, who are concerned about tainting the crime scene. But
the fact that family and friends aren't able to see the remains of their
loved ones, combined with the rumors that are circulating about the
state in which the bodies were found and the sense of powerlessness
that they all feel, makes the experience all the more excruciating for
those on the outside.

Someday, some will ask investigators if they can see the police photographs of Diane and Katrina, so they can achieve some sort of emotional closure. Incredibly, as gruesome as the photographs are, those family members who view them will invariably say that they imagined the slaughter to have been even worse.

ONE MEMBER of the Hawkins family is riding through the streets of D.C. in the back of a police cruiser.

Homicide detectives Whalen and Gainey have decided that the only way that they can hope to get anything from Reco Hawkins is to take him away from the neighborhood. As the detectives drive farther away from River Terrace, with no destination in mind, Reco becomes calmer, the hysteria now dulled into numbness. His thoughts are beginning to come together as well, and as the wave of shock that hit him earlier recedes, his memory of the events of a few hours before—it already seems as if years have passed—becomes clearer. While Detective Gainey drives, Detective Whalen asks questions—gently, without persistence, letting Reco answer as he can. Gainey and Whalen are physical opposites—Gainey is a tall, light-skinned black male, Whalen a shorter, fair-skinned white male with Irish features—but they share a low-key approach to situations such as this. Within minutes, the detectives have the full name of the person whom Reco referred to earlier on the street: Norman Harold, a former boyfriend of Diane. They learn other identifying information as well: that he's a black male, thirty to forty years old, about six feet four to six feet six, stocky, brown skinned; that his nickname is Danky or Dank; that he generally drives a brown and tan Ford pickup truck with a camper shell on the back; and that he was last seen earlier that night wearing a blue jacket with a hole in the back, blue work uniform pants, a white T-shirt, and black boots. They also learn something else: that if Norman isn't the actual killer, he may have been the last adult except for the killer who was with them. Reco tells the detectives that when he left his house a short time before the bodies were discovered, he left behind his mother, Katrina, two-year-old Kiki—and Norman. There is, of course, another possibility: that this Norman is a victim himself, that he was taken from the scene, alive or dead. Detective Whalen presses Reco on whether he knows where Norman lives. Reco does not know the exact address, but he can take them there. Finally, the detectives have a destination, after some minutes of aimless driving. It is now 1:15 A.M.

They travel down Central Avenue, which runs directly east-west from the U.S. Capitol into Maryland. Gainey is driving away from River Terrace, toward the state line. Five minutes from the Hawkins house, Reco tells them to take a right onto A Street, then to the 4600 block. He points to a freestanding brick house at 4615 A Street and says, "That's where he lives." The detectives go to the door and knock. No one's home, and the brown and tan truck isn't in the driveway. Two other vehicles are on the side of the house: an abandoned automobile and a blue Dodge van that Reco says Norman regularly drives. Whalen writes down the tag number on the Dodge van for future reference. The detectives decide that Reco should be taken to the MPD homicide office to give a formal written statement.

First, though, they need more information on the pickup truck, which is at that moment missing, along with its owner. Gainey drops Whalen off at a police station not far from the A Street address and continues riding with Reco on the slim chance that they can locate Norman in the area around his residence. At the station, Whalen signs on at a computer terminal and punches in the identifying information on the Dodge van parked at 4615 A Street. On the screen pops up the name of the registered owner of the vehicle: a Norman Harrell, not Harold; black male; date of birth January 1, 1949; living at 4615 A Street, SE. Now that Whalen has Norman Harrell's full name and other identifying information, he can find out if any other vehicles are registered in that name—including, he hopes, the brown and tan pickup truck. In less than a second, the following flashes on the screen:

HARRELL, NORMAN RODERICK

VEHICLE REGISTRATION RECORD

TAG: 935181   TYPE: PASSENGER   EXPIRES: 11/28/93

VIN: FI5HNDC3679   VEH: 79 FORD PK

OWNER: HARRELL, NORMAN RODERICK   DOB: 01/01/49

ADDRESS: 4615 A ST. SE   WASH DC 20019

This is the vehicle they need to find. Whalen immediately radios the MPD dispatcher and gives a description of Harrell and the truck, which is then broadcast across police channels throughout the city and in neighboring jurisdictions. It is 1:30 A.M.

The chase is on.

RECO HAWKINS is with Whalen and Gainey at police headquarters. He is no longer the hysterical young man who required forcible restraint just an hour ago. In fact, he's so quiet, so still, that Whalen wonders if he's in shock. But Reco has his wits sufficiently about him for Whalen to begin a formal interview at about 2:00 A.M. Reco sits in a chair next to Whalen's slate-gray metal desk.

"Mr. Hawkins," begins Whalen, "the homicide squad is investigating the murder of your mother and sister Katrina. Could you please tell me about your family history?"

"My mother's name is Diane Hawkins. Her birthday is October 16. I think she would have been forty-one this year. I have an older brother, Tyrone Jackson Junior, who'll be twenty-four this year. His birthday is September 20. He's currently incarcerated at Lorton. His father is Tyrone Jackson Senior, who's deceased. I'm the next in line. My father is also Tyrone Jackson Senior. I took my mother's last name, Hawkins. The next oldest is a sister, Shante Jackson. She'll be sixteen on July 20. Her father is also Tyrone Jackson Senior. The next is my sister Katrina Harris. She would have been fourteen this year; I don't recall her birthday. Her father is Willie Harris. The next in line is my brother Rasheen Hawkins. I think he's nine; I don't know his birthday. He's currently in Florida on a school trip. His father is Norman Harrell. The youngest is my sister Keymari Huggins. She'll be two on June 20. Her father is Lamar Wilkinson."

"Can you tell me what happened tonight?"

"This evening, Norman Harrell came over to our house on Eads Street in Northeast D.C. He said that he walked to our house. I found this kind of odd, because of the time of night. He stopped by to see if we'd heard from my brother Rasheen. Norman stopped by because the phone was out of order, and he couldn't have called. Norman stayed downstairs in the living room and watched some TV. I went up to my room with my friend Toi Cohen. My mother was in her bedroom lying down. Katrina was in her room in bed. Keymari was in the room with my mother. Toi and I went to the store to get some sodas. Toi drove me in her mother's car. We came back, and I gave the sodas to Norman—he was still in the living room—and my mother—she was still in her bedroom. Toi and myself left the house. Toi went home. I went down the alley to my friend's house. His name is Eric Fisher. About half an hour later, my sister Shante showed up at Eric's house and told me that blood was everywhere in the house. I ran up the alley to my house. I went in and saw blood everywhere. I found my mother dead in the dining room. I ran upstairs and found my sister Katrina stabbed to death too. I went out of the house, and a short time later the fire department and the police showed up."

"Where was Norman when you ran home and found your mother and sister dead?"

"He was gone."

"Were there any problems in your house tonight that you know of?"

"No."

"Is there any reason anybody would want to kill your family members?"

"The only thing I can think of was that my mother was taking Norman to court over child support for Rasheen. I didn't know if this caused any friction, because we hadn't talked about it. Norman was acting kind of odd tonight—he was perspiring a lot, and he said he'd walked over to our house—but I didn't pay it much attention." Reco pauses for a long moment. "There'd be no other reason for anybody to do this."

"How often did Norman come by your house?"

"He came by roughly about twice a week. He didn't have a key to the house. He didn't keep anything in the house. He had no private area in the house to store things."

For the record, Detective Whalen asks Reco to state again the identifying information about Harrell that he provided to the detectives during their ride together, then asks a series of concluding questions:

"Had Norman made any threats to your family in the past?"

"No."

"Did Norman ever carry a knife?"

"No. Not that I know of."

"Is there anything else you can think of?"

"No, sir."

It's almost 3:00 A.M. when Dan Whalen rises from his desk. He isn't sure what he has here. He may have happened upon a possible motive—animosity between Harrell and Diane Hawkins concerning a child support action—but the question remains: Who would do this to two human beings because of resentment over a court filing? Reco Hawkins has also told him that Harrell acted strangely before the murders. This could be a sign of a guilty mind, but then again it could just as easily amount to nothing.

Whalen is certain of only one thing: He has a lot of questions for Mr. Harrell.

As for Reco, he and his cousin Mike Harwood, who has also made a statement to the police, are given a ride by an officer to the house on Eads Street. There Mike rejoins his parents, and the Harwoods offer Reco a place to stay for as long as he wants. Reco lost his father, Tyrone, to AIDS just a few months ago, he's now lost his mother and sister to violence, and the Harwoods are worried about him. With good reason: At the sight of his mother's house Reco collapses, and an ambulance is called to take him to a nearby hospital. But once in the emergency room, he flees, and the Harwoods and others tackle him outside and return him to the hospital. Again, as before, Reco is able to compose himself. A short time later he's discharged in the conventional manner and agrees to stay with one of his aunts and her family. For him the rest of the night is uneventful but restless, marked by frequent trips to the bathroom to wash his hands, over and over again.

For a long time to come, Mike Harwood will remember what Reco says as they leave the MPD homicide office together. "Are you all right?" Mike asks, seeing Reco walking toward him with his head down. In his usual monotone, flatter now and without tears, Reco replies: "My father's gone; now my mother and sister's gone. Ain't nothing gonna ever be all right again."

INSIDE THE HOUSE, morgue personnel have placed the bodies of Diane and Katrina on stretchers and wrapped them in sheets. Mother and daughter now leave their house for the last time, shrouded like mummies and carried by strangers. As the stretchers appear, one then the other, the crowd outside convulses. In the morgue wagon, the driver sits behind the wheel. Like Detective Johnson, like many of the others there, he has been on hundreds of crime scenes, seen hundreds of corpses. But months from now, he will still be haunted by the memory of this night: "No human being on earth ever deserves to die like that. I want someone to talk to me about that. I want someone to explain why something like that could happen. You can't." And he will wipe tears from his eyes as it all comes back to him.

As despair mounts among the family members posted outside the Hawkins house, a figure arrives, and the crowd parts for him. He's dressed in a crisp dark suit, which he threw on when he heard news of the murders. His name is Richard Wooten, a nephew of Diane Hawkins who is also a clergyman and counselor to many there. "Just imagine they're on a long trip, a long peaceful trip," he says to a woman who has collapsed into his arms. His presence has a calming effect on the group, which, as if by instinct, begins to form a large circle on the lawn, each person tentatively extending hands to others on both sides. Not everyone there falls in. Some stand to the side and hold on to their private grief with clenched fists. But enough join in that the circle envelops the front yard of the house. Led by Reverend Wooten, the family and friends of Diane Hawkins and Katrina Harris join hands in prayer for the repose of the souls of their loved ones. "We are spiritual beings," the reverend intones, "and the spirit never dies. Our lives really begin when we're six feet under the ground."

And then the group prays for the strength to refrain from seeking vengeance against the killer.

WASHINGTON, D.C., shares its eastern borders with Prince George's County, Maryland, which, to D.C. residents, is "P.G. County" or just "the county." Once a largely Caucasian enclave, the county's 1993 population is more than 50 percent black, and many of its African-American residents have moved there from D.C. in the last decade. Their migration to P.G. County had changed the racial composition and attitudes of the county's police force, long criticized by blacks for overzealousness. The force's cowboy image became the stuff of urban folklore in the late 1970s with the case of one Terrence

Johnson, an African-American teenager who killed two white P.G. officers while in custody in a police station. Johnson claimed he was being brutalized by racist cops and acted in self-defense. A jury disagreed, but Johnson became a legend in the black community. Through the years, though, the legend receded and the force reformed. It has even been successful in forging a cordial and cooperative relationship with its counterpart in D.C. This is largely by necessity; no body of water separates D.C. from the county, as the Potomac River divides D.C. and Virginia, hence the crime problems of one often spill into the other and require joint action.

It's a short drive from River Terrace to the P.G. County border, especially if it's late, traffic is light, and you're a man in a hurry.

Just minutes after the MPD dispatcher's broadcast of Detective Whalen's description of Norman Harrell and his vehicle, a P.G. County dispatcher is putting it out to units in the county. The time is 1:55 A.M.: "Lookout for suspect for a homicide that occurred in MPD—in D.C.—3400 Eads Street, D.C. Lookout is going to be for a suspect vehicle: a brown 1979 Ford pickup truck with a license tag of 935–181, with a camper on the rear, unknown direction of travel. The driver is believed to be a Norman Harrell, H-A-R-R-E-L-L, a black male that resides in Southeast D.C. He's described as being about six-five, last seen wearing a long full-length work uniform with no markings on it. It's going to be authority of MPD homicide."

Corporal Michael Hunt, a six-year police veteran, is working routine patrol on the midnight shift when the broadcast goes over the air. He's driving south on a two-lane street called Richie Road, a two-lane thoroughfare with long undeveloped intervals, lined on both sides by dense foliage. But it's still close enough to the city, and to the location of the murders referred to in the lookout, that Hunt's ears perk up when he hears the broadcast.

Coming to the intersection of Richie Road and another street called Walker Mill Road, he sees a vehicle coming fast toward him: It's the same truck that's wanted in D.C. He radios the county dispatcher: "I've got a vehicle on Walker Mill Road. I'm turning to see what direction he went."

He puts on his flashing lights and makes a U-turn. When he comes out of the turn, he sees the truck ahead and radios again to his dispatcher: "He's on Walker Mill, from Richie Road."

"Ten-four. Units go to the area of Walker Mill and Richie Road. That homicide suspect vehicle was just seen. Look out for a brown and tan 1979 Ford pickup truck, D.C. tag 935–181."

With this last transmission, the dispatcher summons other officers to assist. Corporal Mike Barnhardt is a short distance away on Walker Mill Road, by himself in a marked police car, driving toward Corporal Hunt. He hears the broadcast and accelerates, radioing to the dispatcher: "Is that Walker Mill towards Richie?" The dispatcher directs the question to Hunt, who responds: "He's headed towards Walker Mill at Richie Road." And then: "I think he just cut his lights off."

Indeed, as soon as Corporal Hunt begins his pursuit of the vehicle after coming out of his U-turn, he sees that the rear lights of the brown and tan truck have been turned off. Corporal Hunt tries to catch up to the vehicle, but he loses sight of it when the road curves. Hunt takes a left turn off of Walker Mill Road, thinking that the vehicle will be heading back toward the city, but it continues on straight and Hunt is off the trail. But Barnhardt is on it now, doing a quick U-turn when he sees the truck pass him going the other way. When Barnhardt comes out of his turn, he sees that the vehicle's rear lights are back on. Barnhardt follows it down Walker Mill Road and radios Hunt, who gets back on track on Walker Mill. A third officer, Sergeant Mike Butler, joins the pursuit after hearing the communications among Hunt, the dispatcher, and Barnhardt. As the truck turns off Walker Mill Road onto a less heavily traveled street called Karen Boulevard, it's in the vanguard of a police convoy.

Barnhardt put on his flashing lights before the truck turned onto Karen Boulevard. Now, finally, several miles from the point where

Corporal Hunt first saw it, the truck comes to a slow stop at curbside in front of newly constructed town houses. Neither Barnhardt nor any of the other P.G. County officers on the scene knows any details about the murders on Eads Street. They don't know that the role of the driver of this vehicle has yet to be ascertained by MPD homicide. All they know is what they have heard from their dispatcher: that this vehicle is connected with a homicide, that its driver is a "suspect," and that they need to proceed with caution. Barnhardt, the first in the line of officers arriving, switches on a loudspeaker in his car and tells the defendant to leave his vehicle, keep his hands visible, and lay down on the ground.

The truck has stopped on a downward curve. The driver's-side door swings open and stays open. For several seconds, no one comes out. Then a man dressed in blue emerges from the driver's side. He is every inch the height described, a hefty man with sloping shoulders. He slowly moves away from the truck and lies down on his stomach. Barnhardt pats him down for weapons and places handcuffs on him, for his own safety and that of his fellow officers. Barnhardt then tells him, "You need to stay here. Some detectives need to talk with you." The man says nothing. Barnhardt finds it strange that the man never asks why he was stopped, or why on earth some detectives want to talk with him about anything.

Barnhardt eyes him up and down and notices two things. The man is sweating profusely even though it's a cool evening, and he's wearing an odd outfit: coveralls, dress shoes, and no socks.

The officers on the scene radio their dispatcher and tell her that the "suspect vehicle" has been stopped; she passes the word to MPD. Detective Whalen is still interviewing Reco Hawkins when he learns of the stop. He and Detective Gainey agree that Gainey will go to the county and Whalen will join him after finishing with Reco.

Back on Karen Boulevard, Sergeant Butler and Corporal Hunt approach the truck and size it up. The driver's-side door has remained open. The officers look inside, being careful not to touch anything, and see nothing suspicious. Outside, water is dripping from the bottom and the tires appear to be very clean. But none of the officers asks the driver about the water; this is a D.C. murder case, and the P.G. County police are involved in it purely because the man chose to come into the county instead of heading another way.

As the P.G. County officers and the man from the truck silently await the arrival of the MPD detectives, a television news van pulls into the area and a cameraman carrying video equipment jumps out. He's a freelancer who monitors the police band radio every night. He's heard about the double homicide on Eads Street, assessed this as a newsworthy story, and then overheard a police communication concerning the stop of the pickup truck. Watching the cameraman turn bright klieg lights on the area and begin filming, Officer Barnhardt draws close to the man on the ground. He leans over to him, lightly touches his arm, and escorts him to a place on the curb where he'll be shielded from the camera. He might be a murderer, Barnhardt thinks, but then again, he might not, and it could ruin an innocent man if he gets his face on TV like this. (A while from now, despite Barnhardt's efforts, the cameraman will be able to capture footage of the man entering a P.G. County police vehicle.)

More P.G. County officers have arrived on Karen Boulevard, and they all begin to discuss among themselves the disposition of the Ford truck, which can't remain indefinitely on this residential street. Someone has a suggestion: Why not call one of the man's family members and ask them to come and claim it?

Lieutenant Grady Baker drives up after all the others. He's a troubleshooter on the midnight shift, riding around the county all night long and seeking out situations such as this. He's working on his third decade in uniform, and in the course of his nightly rounds is usually the senior officer on any crime scene he covers. He can tell immediately that matters are under control on this one, so he hangs back at first. But his curiosity about the truck draws him closer to it. He advances to the open driver's-side door, still open, and passes his flashlight over the armrest on the door. Then he steps back and calls to the assembled officers: "Fellas, this truck isn't going anywhere right now. Take a look at this."

THE BODIES of the victims have been taken from the house on Eads Street, but the work of the officers there is far from done; the scene still has to be fingerprinted and any tangible evidence processed. Numerous prints are lifted from various surfaces but none in blood; unless the killer was a stranger to the house, the fingerprints won't help close the case. All in all, the officers' search for evidence is less notable for what it yields than for what it doesn't: no bloody weapon, though numerous kitchen knives, one broken-tipped, are seized for further inspection; no metaphorical smoking gun, though a real firearm is found wedged between the mattress and box spring of the bed near Katrina's body.

Curtis Lancaster, one of the evidence technicians on the scene, begins using cotton swabs to collect blood samples from various surfaces of the house. He starts at the front of the house on the first floor and works his way back, and then upstairs. He swabs a blood smear from the outer front doorknob, then moves to the kitchen and swabs one from the kitchen cabinet doors. Directly beneath the cabinet is a large blood drop, different in appearance from the smudges and smears in the other areas, which looks as if it might have fallen from an object. Lancaster swabs the drop, then moves to the back door and swabs a smear on the inside. He works his way up to the bedroom where Katrina was found and swabs the door and a light switch, and finally a bloody area on the railing in the hall near the steps. Lancaster uses a separate swab for each sample and saves it in a ziplock bag, then marks each location on a diagram of the house floor plan.

It's a standard technique of crime scene processing, and it will help investigators reconstruct the murders. In the end, though, none of the blood evidence recovered on the scene will tie any particular suspect to the crime.

A different story is developing in P.G. County.

MPD DETECTIVE TONY DUVALL pulls his car to a screeching stop on Karen Boulevard, followed within minutes by Detective Gainey. Both are briefed by Officers Barnhardt and Hunt, then directed to Lieutenant Baker.

Baker walks Gainey and Duvall over to the Ford truck and shines his flashlight on the driver's-side armrest. There on the beige armrest, almost imperceptible to the naked eye in the semidarkness but illuminated by Baker's light, is a series of dark red smudges. "And look at this here," Baker says, waving his light around the passenger compartment. Gainey leans in and sees what looks like small dark drops on the tan seat. In a flash he decides the fate of the truck—it's going over to D.C.—and radios for a police tow truck to take it to an MPD impounding lot.

Gainey goes over to the man sitting on the curb and gives him the once-over, seeing no sign of injury. He also notices the man's dress shoes, worn with no socks.

"Hey, how you doin', sir?" Gainey asks.

"Fine," says the man.

Gainey says, "What's your name?"

"Norman Harrell," says the man.

Gainey now has to decide what to do with him. He broaches the subject gingerly. "We'd like to talk to you about an incident which occurred in D.C."

At first, Harrell says nothing. Then he asks, "What incident?"

Gainey pauses for a moment and considers each word. "There's been some trouble at the Hawkins residence on Eads Street."

Harrell doesn't say "What trouble?" He doesn't say "Whose residence?" He says nothing at all.

Gainey now thinks to himself: *Maybe this is the guy; maybe we're going to have to charge him. I can't keep talking with him here, I've got to give him rights so I can talk to him somewhere else.* He says to Harrell, "I'd like to have some further conversation with you about this matter at the police station." Harrell doesn't blink. Gainey goes through the Miranda rights, pauses, and says, "Would you mind accompanying us to the Prince George's County police facility?"

Harrell hesitates a moment, maybe two, then says yes, he'll go to the station.

Within minutes, a police car arrives to take Harrell to the county police facility. In accordance with P.G. County police procedures, Harrell has to remain handcuffed during the short trip in the transport car. Harrell says nothing during the ride.

At the station, Harrell is taken out of the vehicle. Gainey parks his car and walks to where Harrell is standing. Gainey is more than six feet one inch, but he feels like a small boy next to Harrell. He thinks: *This is the biggest motherfucker I've stood next to in my life.* They walk into the station and down to the county's homicide squad office, where Gainey solicits officers to assist him in setting up the interview.

Sergeant Butler, one of the officers who chased Harrell down Walker Mill Road, has come back to the station and now begins to remove Harrell's handcuffs. In the half-apologetic tone of voice that police officers use when explaining to a civilian that they were just following procedures, Butler tells Harrell that he had to handcuff him for the officers' own safety. Harrell says, "Okay," nothing more.

Gainey finds a locker where he can check his police firearm—a standard routine when about to encounter a suspect in confined quarters—while Butler escorts Harrell to an interview room. Small, windowless, and unadorned, it's about the size of Diane Hawkins's kitchen.

Gainey walks into the fluorescent-lit room and regards the man he last saw in shadows under streetlights. Even sitting back in his wooden chair, massive arms folded, Harrell seems to fill the room. He's brown-skinned and has a large head and hands. He's taken off the black peaked hat that he had on when the police stopped him. He's wearing a short-sleeved blue work shirt under blue jean overalls. There's no sign of blood on him.

Harrell sits still, staring at the detective with eyes that could be impassive or menacing or sad, depending on your point of view, and waits for Gainey to speak first.

Gainey repeats Harrell's Miranda rights, adding that he isn't under arrest and can leave at any time. Harrell says he understands his rights and agrees to talk. Gainey begins: "We're investigating a stabbing incident at 3461 Eads Street, the Hawkins residence. Diane Hawkins has been stabbed to death. Did you know her?"

Harrell shows no reaction. "Yeah, she's my son's mother, my son Rasheen."

"Were you at the home earlier last evening?"

"Yeah, I arrived at about nine thirty."

"Who was there?"

"I saw Diane, Reco, Reco's girlfriend, and Diane's baby, Kiki."

"Why did you go there?"

"I was trying to find out if they'd heard anything from Rasheen. He lives there with Diane, but he left to go to Disney World on Sunday. I'd gone by his cousin Tracy's home to find out if he'd heard anything from Rock, but he wasn't home."

"Why did you leave?"

"Some guys knocked on the door. I thought they were looking for Reco. So I left."

As he answers each question, Harrell remains in the same position: leaning back in his chair, arms folded across his chest. He looks ill at ease, but his eyes meet Gainey's with every word. It doesn't escape Gainey's attention that Harrell is only answering what's asked and volunteering nothing.

"Where did you go after you left?"

"I went home and got my truck, then I drove out Central Avenue to 202 and then to White House Road. I then cut through Richie Road to Walker Mill Road. That was when the police pulled me over."

Gainey traces the route in his mind. To get from Diane Hawkins's house to Harrell's own house, he would have gotten on East Capitol Street no more than a mile away from the Hawkins residence, then driven less than five minutes to A Street, which was right off East Capitol. To go from his home to the place where he was stopped by P.G. County police, Harrell would have gotten back on East Capitol, which becomes Central Avenue as one travels east toward Maryland. Which leaves a question: Why did he take the other streets between Central and Walker Mill? And how did he fill the time between his visit to the Hawkins house and his stop by the police? Harrell isn't saying.

There's a knock on the door, and Detective Dan Whalen appears at the threshold. It's about 3:30 A.M. Whalen has finished the interview with Reco Hawkins and driven to the county station. Gainey excuses himself from the room and steps outside to speak with Whalen. In five words, he summarizes the interview so far: "He's not giving it up." Gainey tells Whalen that he's advised Harrell of his Miranda rights, which Harrell has waived, and that he's broached the subject with him of Diane Hawkins's murder but not Katrina's. Gainey also mentions Harrell's nonreaction to the news of Diane Hawkins's death. Whalen, fresh from taking Reco Hawkins's statement and learning by police radio of the discovery of red stains in Harrell's vehicle, now has more questions.

Eric Gainey and Dan Whalen are an ill-suited tandem to play "good cop/bad cop." Both are "good cops," preferring to ingratiate themselves with their subject rather than intimidate him. Easygoing Eric Gainey, a cheerful man of simple pleasures—playing the horses, bowling in a weekly league, knocking back a few at the police union bar—would have little credibility posing as an intimidator in any interview. As for Whalen, his approach is dictated by his personal makeup as well as by more complicated concerns. He's a white male, the son of a former congressman and a resident of a fashionable Georgetown neighborhood, working in a city whose inhabitants are predominantly black and maintain a healthy skepticism toward the police. Whalen has learned that the best way to gain the trust of his sources and suspects alike is to invoke his authority with deft subtlety. It's his style to try to convey to even the most hardened criminal that he should consider himself allied with the police in solving a common problem.

All of which explains Detective Whalen's first words to Harrell when he enters the interview room with Gainey: "Hello, sir, my name is Dan Whalen, and I'm with the Metropolitan Police Department. We're just trying to find out what went on at the Hawkins house. You've said that you were there earlier. Do you think you might be able to help us figure out what happened?"

But the brief delay in the interview seems to have stiffened Harrell's resolve. He repeats, as if by rote, his earlier answers to Gainey and adds, "When I left, there were no unusual problems." Whalen asks him where he went after leaving the Hawkins house, and he says only, "For a drive. I went for a drive."

Harrell rises slightly in his chair and looks at Whalen. "I need to use the bathroom. Can I use the bathroom?"

"Absolutely. You're not under arrest. Using the bathroom is one of your freedoms."

Whalen finds a county officer and tells him that Harrell wants to use the bathroom, and since he isn't under arrest it isn't necessary that he be guarded. Whalen turns to Harrell before he leaves: "Mr. Harrell, you're free to leave, but we'd like to have your assistance in working this out." Harrell nods and heads toward the public men's room.

About two minutes later, Harrell, unguarded and unrestrained, returns to the room, and Whalen starts again: "Now, I understand that Detective Gainey has already told you that Diane Hawkins is dead."

Harrell nods yes.

Whalen continues: "I'm not sure if you know this, but her thirteen-year-old daughter Katrina was found dead also."

Harrell's expression doesn't change. A second passes, perhaps two. He turns to Gainey: "Why didn't you tell me about that?"

Gainey shrugs and looks back to Whalen, who is mentally marking the seconds going by before Harrell asks how it happened.

Harrell never asks.

Whalen: "You don't seem very upset about that."

Harrell: "I can't do anything about it, can I?"

Whalen changes the subject. "You were driving a Ford truck when you were stopped by the police, right?"

"Yeah, I was."

"Is there any reason for blood to be inside your truck?"

"No."

"Has Diane Hawkins ever been inside your truck?"

"No."

"Has Katrina Harris ever been inside your truck?"

Harrell thinks a moment and says, "Almost a week ago, I took her to McDonald's."

"Has she been in there since?"

"No."

"Did you wash your truck tonight?"

"No."

Whalen takes one final shot: "Sir, I'm not saying I don't believe you or anything, but we do need to clear this up, and I was wondering if you would agree to take a polygraph test—a lie detector test— for us, so we could eliminate you as a suspect."

"Yeah, I'd be interested in that . . . Well . . . well no, I don't think so."

Harrell looks hard at Whalen. "You know," he says, "people put themselves in jail. And I'm not going to do that."

With that, Whalen rises to leave. He has interviewed hundreds of suspects in his career. He knows when further discussion is futile. He has a last question for Harrell, and he tries to put it to him as nonchalantly as possible under the circumstances: "Sir, before I go, would you mind if I inspect your person from head to toe?" Harrell agrees, and Whalen goes one step further: "Can you take down the coverall straps, too?" Harrell complies. Whalen circles around him and eyes Harrell's body and clothing. He sees no sign of blood and no scratches or cuts. Harrell buckles his coveralls and reclaims his seat in the interview room.

Before leaving, Whalen sticks his head into the room: "Mr. Harrell, I'm going back to Washington. Do you want me to drive you home?"

"No, that's all right, I'm going to walk."

Whalen is taken aback. "Are you sure? You know, that's quite a ways from here." The P.G. County police station is at least ten miles from Harrell's house.

"No, that's all right."

Whalen walks out shaking his head. Gainey returns to ask Harrell if he can wait around for a little while longer, since the detectives are checking on some things and might have a couple of more questions for him. Harrell says he will.

It's now 4:40 A.M. Just five hours ago, Diane Hawkins and Katrina Harris were still alive.

BACK AT THE HAWKINS HOUSE, evidence technician Lancaster is collecting his kit, camera, and other equipment. Like a hotel guest doing a final check around his room before leaving, he sweeps through the premises to make sure he hasn't missed anything significant. It's now time for Lancaster to leave this crime scene for another. A call has gone out for a shooting in another part of town that demands his attention: another case with another victim with a story all his own.

"IS HE STILL out there?"

Detective Herman Johnson is calling Detective Gainey on the telephone in the detective cruiser being driven by his partner, Detective Dwayne Stanton. It's close to 6:00 A.M., and Johnson and Stanton are just leaving the Hawkins house.

All of the MPD detectives involved in the case are members of the same squad, working it together. Fanned out throughout the city, they've been in radio contact with each other for the last five hours, so Johnson and Stanton know about everything that's been going on. Most recently, they've learned that Diane's ex-boyfriend Lamar "Skeeter" Wilkinson—recently evicted from Diane's home and possibly still bearing a grudge against her—had an airtight alibi for the time of the murders and several hours on either side. This reduces by one the dwindling field of potential suspects.

Johnson and Stanton now want to face Harrell directly, and they're hoping he hasn't left the P.G. County facility. They were among the last officers to leave the murder scene and have more ammunition to use against him. They're taking this case very personally. They were inside the house longer than most of the others, and when Diane and Katrina were carried down the steps to the waiting morgue wagon, Herman Johnson and Dwayne Stanton were steadying them on either side. Now they need to get out to the P.G. County station before Harrell leaves. Gainey confirms to Johnson over the telephone that Harrell is still there but becoming impatient and might wish to leave at any time. Stanton steps on the gas.

As they pull up in front of the station just after 6:15 A.M., they see a towering man ambling out the front door with Eric Gainey a few paces behind. Figuring the man to be Norman Harrell, they jump from their car to head him off. Stanton identifies himself and Johnson and says that they have a few more questions for him, then asks if he minds coming down to the D.C. homicide office. Harrell says no, he won't come to D.C. "Well, then," says Stanton, "can we talk with you here? Is that cool?" Harrell agrees. The three go to the same room where the earlier interview was conducted. Here yet another discussion with Norman Harrell begins, and Stanton thinks: Either he's entirely innocent or he's entirely convinced he can talk his way out of anything.

Stanton is younger than Johnson, and he has a baby face and a bounce in his stride. He takes the first run at Harrell. "You're not under arrest," he begins. "You don't have to talk to us if you don't want to. We just want to ask some additional questions that Detective Whalen and Detective Gainey didn't know to ask. Is that all right with you?" Harrell says it is and settles back in his chair.

"How well did you know Diane Hawkins?"

"We were friends. We got along very well. At one point we were boyfriend-girlfriend. We have a ten-year-old son together."

"Is it true there's some child support battle or paternity hearing or something like that going on between you?"

"Well, she filed papers to take me to court, but I'm not worried about that. I make good money."

"Are you supposed to go to court on that anytime soon?"

"I don't know when the court date for the hearing is, you know, but I think it's a couple of months down the road."

The detectives already know that Reco Hawkins has told Whalen that the court hearing in the case was scheduled for later that very morning. Stanton doesn't let on what he knows and moves on: "Can you tell us what happened last evening?"

"I walked from my house to the Eads Street address. . . . "

"Where do you live again?"

"4615 A Street, Southeast."

"Why did you go to the Hawkins house?"

"I was looking to meet her nephew Tracy."

"That's a long walk, isn't it? Why didn't you drive?"

"I'm trying to lose weight, and I like to walk."

"Do you own any motor vehicle?"

Stanton and Johnson know the answer. They're testing Harrell, seeing if he'll tell them the truth.

"I own a truck, the one I was driving when I was stopped. I also have a van—that was parked at my house—but I have another car. It doesn't have an engine so it's parked at my house."

"Did you change clothes after leaving Diane's house?"

This is a pointed question. Stanton knows that Reco has described Harrell as wearing different clothes earlier, including black boots, from those he's wearing now. Harrell doesn't blink.

"No. I walked back to my house, but I didn't go in because I wasn't sleepy."

"What did you do then?"

"I got in my truck and started driving around because I had things on my mind."

"What things?"

"Just things."

"Where did you go?"

"Well, I ended up around Addison and Walker Mill Road, and then I got lost along one of the side roads. I think it's White House Road. That's when I got stopped by the police."

With each exchange, Stanton sees Harrell growing tenser. Perhaps he feels cornered. Stanton tries to give him a way out: "You know, if this was an accident, it can be handled that way, but you have to be the one to inform us of that."

Harrell stiffens.

Stanton continues: "We all have pressure points or boiling points or what have you, and people sometimes, especially women in relationships, well they have a tendency not to leave an issue alone but to continually press you until you react, and sometimes you react in a negative fashion."

Harrell folds his arms and tears well up in his eyes. Stanton waits a moment. Now he has him. He leans in and presses on: "We all have been in situations like that when women . . ."

Harrell raises up. "People put themselves in jail," he says evenly, his eyes suddenly dry. "I'm not going to do that."

"What's that again?"

"People put themselves in jail, and I'm not going to do that."

The window has closed as quickly as it opened. Stanton responds: "Well, that's not really true. It's people's actions that land them in jail, not doing the right thing. Telling the truth and clearing your conscience is the first step in righting a wrong."

"I didn't do this. I didn't kill those people. Why would I do something like that?"

Stanton surrenders. It's Herman Johnson's turn. He's a broad-shouldered man of impressive bearing with enough gray in his hair to make him look distinguished without looking old: the prototype for the seasoned detective. As Johnson leans forward to start, Stanton leaves the room. He's hoping that if Harrell is left alone, man to man, with a detective closer to his age, the interview can get back on track.

It doesn't. Johnson tells Harrell that all that the police want to do is to eliminate him as a suspect. Will he give them his consent to search his home and automobile? No. Well, then, would he take a polygraph? No. Why not? "I just don't want to," replies Harrell and goes on: "You know, I've been locked up before, but I always got out because the police always found out it was someone else that did the crime."

Johnson now sits back in his chair and folds his hands on his chest. Harrell looks at him: "If you're going to lock me up, just go ahead and lock me up." This isn't said in resignation; it's more of a taunt. Harrell seems to sense that the police don't have enough to hold him. Johnson can't detain Harrell further without arresting him, and Johnson doesn't believe that his proof is strong enough to do that. It's an exasperating situation: If this man didn't commit these murders, he surely knows more about them than he's told the detectives, and he can't credibly account for his whereabouts at the time they occurred—driving around by oneself not generally considered a solid alibi. To Johnson, this man had the motive and opportunity to commit the murders; he's linked to the crime by suspected bloodstains; and his denials are weak. But without something more—at least a scientific determination that the stains are in fact blood—the case against Harrell could be found wanting the first time it goes to court. Based on what the police have developed thus far, a judge might well decide that Norman Harrell is purely a victim of a convergence of coincidences.

"Let's leave it like this," says Johnson, going into his suit jacket for a business card holder. "Here's my card. You give me a call if you remember anything else." Harrell takes the card and says he will. Johnson asks if he can photograph him standing outside the interview room. Harrell agrees, and the picture is taken. The session is now over.

The sun is rising on a new morning as Norman Harrell walks unescorted through the doors of the police station, free and clear, at least for now.

IT'S NOT EVEN 6:00 A.M. when the telephone rings at the house of Aaron Barfield, Yellow Freight truck driver. The caller is Harrell, his coworker and fellow union member, asking for a ride from the police station to his job site. Harrell doesn't say much to Barfield on the phone—only that he was locked up for something he didn't do—but it sounds like he's in a fix, and Barfield is happy to help a fellow Teamster. Barfield is a shop steward at work, one of several officers elected by the employees to represent their interests before company management, and he takes his responsibilities seriously. He knows about the various complaints that Yellow Freight has lodged against Harrell over the years, and he's helped Harrell challenge a number of them. He thinks that Yellow Freight hasn't treated Harrell fairly and that the company has singled him out for two reasons: He's a loner, and he doesn't volunteer to do more work than the labor contract requires. Barfield, a man who also tends to keep to himself, is as close to him as anyone else in the company is, but even he feels he doesn't know him very well.

Conversation on the ride between the police station and the Yellow Freight offices is brief and awkward. Harrell says nothing about why the police stopped and questioned him. He does offer that he's not coming to work that day, and Barfield leaves it at that. He doesn't ask Harrell why he wants a ride to Yellow Freight if he isn't actually going to work. Norman isn't a person who invites inquiry.

ON THE D.C. SIDE, Minnesota Avenue runs hard by aging railroad tracks until it hits the Maryland line. At that point its name changes to Addison Road, and it gradually shifts direction and seeks higher ground. Passing schools and homes, it widens as it twists its way southeast, nearing but never again touching the D.C. border. It forms an intersection at a major subway station, meanders like a river through a residential neighborhood, then stops abruptly at Walker Mill Road. It begins again about a half mile to the north but at this point is more of a creek: a small, winding two-lane road flanked on both sides by a series of modest brick apartment buildings.

On May 26, 1993, a woman named Verdeen Wells is living in one of these buildings, which bears the address "2070" in unadorned script. She's a heavy-jowled woman of fifty-five, carrying too much weight for her own good. She's also Norman Harrell's mother-in-law. On this morning, Gale Tolson Harrell, Harrell's wife, is staying there as well, as she has been for the last several weeks. The apartment building sits on a bluff a mere mile away from where Norman Harrell was stopped by the police on Karen Boulevard—lost in strange territory, according to the story he gave the police.

Gale is asleep when her mother's alarm clock goes off at 7:00 A.M. Verdeen leans across the bed in her room and turns off the alarm before it awakens her daughter down the hall. Verdeen is half-watching a morning show on television when a local news segment comes on. She hears the words "slaughter" and "mother and daughter" and looks up to see news film of a group of people gathered in a circle. A man's voice comes from the set:

"At about the same time the Hawkins and Harwood families were praying in Northeast, Prince George's County police, acting on a tip, spotted the pickup truck of Ms. Hawkins's former boyfriend. He was detained for questioning but has not been charged."

Verdeen stares at the screen, watching Norman Harrell being led in handcuffs by a police officer to a waiting car. Her first thought springs from maternal instinct: She hopes her daughter didn't hear the broadcast. She knows she won't be able to keep the news from Gale for very long, but she sees no reason for her to know about it right now.

Long after the news show has ended, Verdeen sits in an easy chair, thinking. She's known Norman Harrell since he began a romantic relationship with her daughter some nine years ago. She's dimly aware of problems in the relationship, although she's never been particularly curious about other people's affairs. For the last several weeks, Gale and her six-year-old son, Torey, have been staying here with her, and Harrell visits them daily. Gale explained that she'd just undergone surgery, which limited her mobility, and it would be easier to move about in her mother's one-floor apartment than in the two-level house she shares with her husband. It doesn't occur to Verdeen that this might have been a pretext offered by her daughter to conceal marital difficulties. All she knows is that Harrell is her son-in-law, since last September 29, and the father of her grandson; as family, he's entitled to receive the benefit of the doubt. She's never spent more than a few hours in Norman's company, but sees no reason to believe that he's capable of committing the kind of crime she just heard described on television.

Verdeen recalls that he came to the apartment last night, sometime after 8:00 P.M., and he didn't act oddly in any way. The only thing that puzzles her now is that when she saw him then, he was wearing a long-sleeved blue work shirt and blue pants, yet when she saw him on television, he was wearing a short-sleeved blue shirt and blue coveralls. She isn't sure why this is sticking in her mind.

RON BRANCH is waiting for a telephone call. He is operations manager at Yellow Freight, Inc., a Maryland trucking company whose offices are within less than a five-minute drive from Karen Boulevard and Verdeen Wells's apartment. Branch is watching the clock with mounting impatience. One of his truck drivers is now fifteen minutes late for work. It's 8:15 A.M. and Branch's frustration is compounded by the fact that the late driver, a company employee since 1984, has long been a disciplinary problem and might have been fired if his union, the Teamsters, hadn't taken up his cause many times in the past.

The telephone rings, and Branch answers it. He immediately recognizes the voice of his missing employee, Norman Harrell: "I won't be coming in to work today."

"Don't you think you're late calling in?"

"I was in jail all night. The police picked me up."

"Why'd they do that?"

"The mother of my son was killed last night. I'd gone over to her house; she's taking me to court for child support today. Somebody killed them about an hour after I left. Somebody saw me in there, and the police picked me up."

Branch is struck by how matter-of-fact Harrell is being about the whole thing. He can't resist a shot: "You have to be pretty dumb to go by there last night if she's taking you to court today."

"Well, just like I told the police, if I did it, why don't I have blood on my clothes?"

As Harrell's supervisor, Branch has had to confront him about a number of work-related complaints, and Harrell has invariably been hostile and defensive. Branch thinks to himself, *If I can't get a straight answer out of him when I'm accusing him of loafing on the job, what's the point in talking with him about a murder?* He tells Harrell he'll see him tomorrow and makes a note to dock him one day's leave. *Isn't it just like Norman,* he muses, *to get out of a day's work by getting locked up for murder.*

VERDEEN WELLS has gone into the kitchen to get something to eat. An hour has passed since she saw Norman on the news. She walks back to her daughter's room and looks in. There sits Gale, watching television. She's crying.

KIKI HAWKINS is sleeping in a strange bed for the first time since her mother brought her home from the hospital twenty-two months ago. Soon after the MPD lieutenant found her in the midst of the confusion in her house earlier that morning, she landed, deep in unshakable slumber, in the arms of her cousin Carlene Hawkins. Carlene and her boyfriend, Donald Saunders, have three children of their own and live in a small, semidetached house in a neighborhood that has its share of crime problems. Still, they didn't hesitate when it was suggested, in a hurried family conference outside the Eads Street house, that Kiki go home with them that night. Carlene had a special relationship with Diane Hawkins. Because of Diane's place in the family's order—second youngest of eleven children—she got along as well with some of her nieces and nephews as she did with her older brothers and sisters. To Carlene, Diane was like a sister. Carlene has known Kiki from the first moments of the girl's life and treats her as if she were her own child.

And so it falls to her to deal with Kiki's first questions when the girl awakens Wednesday morning and bolts upright in the bed. But the look on Kiki's face tells Carlene that the little girl already knows where her mother and her sister are, so Carlene changes the subject.

IT'S JUST AFTER 9:30 A.M. on Wednesday, and child support cases are being heard in D.C. Superior Court. A courtroom clerk with a languid voice calls out a case name: "Hawkins, D. versus Harrell, N." No one responds, and she says the name again, more emphatically. No one in the courtroom knows that at that very moment, the petitioner in *Hawkins, D. v. Harrell, N.* is lying on a table at the morgue, being prepared for autopsy.

The judge decides to let the case live on—it isn't unusual for one party or the other to be a no-show for the first hearing in a case like this—and a new date is set. A notice for the next court date, September 27, 1993, will be sent to Norman Harrell, as well as to Diane Hawkins of 3461 Eads Street, NE.

IT'S EXACTLY 10:00 A.M.—Verdeen Wells looks at the clock— when her daughter Gale walks into the apartment with Norman. He telephoned for Gale a little while ago, and Verdeen heard her daughter's side of the conversation. Gale told her on her way out the door that she was going to the trucking company to pick up her husband. Verdeen knows that Gale knows that Norman was stopped by the police last night. Verdeen now waits for Gale to raise the subject. Gale never does.

Let's hope it's all over, Verdeen thinks. She looks down as Norman passes. He's wearing brown loafers and no socks. He was wearing something different on his feet last night, but she can't remember what.

AT 1:00 P.M., two unmarked police cars pull up outside Norman Harrell's house on A Street. Inside are Dean Combee, Dwayne Stanton, Herman Johnson, and two others. They have with them a warrant, signed by a judge, authorizing them to search Norman Harrell's house, whether he wants them to or not.

In daylight the property looks shabby from curbside. In the driveway sits the same Dodge van that Gainey and Whalen saw not twelve hours earlier. Two-by-fours and concrete blocks are strewn about the grassless front yard. In the backyard is more wood and concrete, straddled by a rusting metal construction: a swing set upended and as shapeless as a storm-twisted umbrella. The entrance to the house is overseen by a rickety white portico with chipping paint. Inside, the window is covered by venetian blinds, shuttered tight, so the detectives get no glimpse of the inside or who might be moving about there.

At the front door they knock and yell loudly, "Police. Open up. We have a search warrant." They listen for voices, footfall, anything— and hear nothing. Again they knock and yell; again there's no answer. They force their way in, look around furtively. No one is home.

In their first walk-through, the detectives see nothing unusual: no blood trail leading from entranceway to kitchen, no knife handle peeking from the rubbish in a trash pail. What they do find is a tidy and clean living space in stark contrast to the ramshackle exterior. The living room is small but welcoming. In one corner is a television with a VCR; in the opposite corner, a home entertainment center holding a turntable, cassette player, miniature stereo speakers, and three delicate Oriental figurines. One of the kimono-clad statuettes looks down demurely at a trinket sign that reads HOME SWEET HOME and sits uneasily on a rickety plastic stand. Saloon doors separate the living room from the kitchen, which is larger and neater than Diane's. On the Sears refrigerator is affixed a crayoned drawing of an apple titled "Red" and signed "Torey Tolson." The master bedroom is cluttered but well appointed. Dominated by a walnut bedroom set, it also features another television set and two VCRs, set up and ready for use.

All in all, it's an American middle-class house like countless others: rough on the outside with graceful touches concealed within. But further probing yields secrets and oddities. The first revelation: secreted in its corners and cubbyholes is a remarkable array of knives of all shapes and sizes, new and old, gleaming and rust-colored alike. Some are common kitchen instruments: a seven-piece cutlery set, for example, sitting in a box on top of the refrigerator. Others are so long and menacing in appearance as to inspire respect even when found resting in a kitchen drawer (a twenty-inch knife with a fourteen-and-one-half-inch blade) or propped against a wall (a three-foot-long sword). One knife catches the eye; it has a broken tip. At Katrina Harris's autopsy that morning, a blade tip was recovered from her skull.

Every pointed object in the house ends up in an evidence bag. Whether or not any can be linked to the murders, they all add to the developing picture of Norman Harrell: a man comfortable with bladed weapons.

In Norman Harrell's kitchen, Combee finds a ziplock bag of opaque rubber gloves. The bag is unmarked; there's no way to tell whether a set is missing. There are certain objects that carry the weight of ominous significance in a circumstantial murder case, and rubber gloves are among them.

Meanwhile, three detectives rummage through the master bedroom. A double bed divides the room into halves. On one side is a closet containing both men's and women's clothing. It's a typical marital bedroom but for two discordant notes. In the corner, next to the closet, stands the sword. And on top of the VCR on the dresser, in plain view, is a set of photographs of 1970s vintage, all featuring an unidentifiable female with various other people. In every photograph, the female's head has been cut off with a pair of scissors.

The detectives pick up other photographs from around the room for future reference, including one of two young boys holding what looks like a dead squirrel, the bounty from a hunting trip. No deductive gymnastics are needed to conclude that a hunter lives in this house. And so when Stanton comes across a book in a pile of magazines on an elevated shelf in the closet, he doesn't consider it a particularly momentous find. The book, *Maryland Hunter Safety Student Handbook*, is a ninety-two-page, government-printed publication devoted to the promotion of safe hunting techniques, with a written quiz that had been earnestly executed in number-two pencil. Stanton flips through the book's pages, and nothing jumps out at him, but he still decides to hold on to it. It certainly won't hurt to have it.

As it turns out, the detectives have no need to worry that their efforts will be interrupted by Norman Harrell himself. While the house he shares with Gale is being scoured for evidence, he sits with her in a darkened room at Verdeen's house, watching television all afternoon.

Among the programs available for viewing is the afternoon news on local Channel 9, which leads with an expanded version of its earlier story on the murders, including interviews with family members outside the Hawkins house: "On Eads Street early this morning the Hawkins and the Harwood families formed a circle and prayed. A short while earlier the aunt they all loved and her young daughter were found stabbed to death. The victims: forty-two-year-old Diane

Hawkins and her thirteen-year-old daughter, Trina Harris. They were found slaughtered inside by one of Diane Hawkins's nephews."

The face of Malcolm Tyrone Harwood Junior, brother of Mike and also a nephew of Diane, appears on the screen: "Mike came, and the door was open. And he thought someone had opened the door for him, seen him coming, and he went inside to the bathroom, came downstairs, cut on the lights, and that's when he heard the baby crying. He heard the baby crying, and he went upstairs and that's when he found Trina laying up in the bed there. And he just panicked and ran out of the house."

The footage of Norman Harrell in Prince George's County is now repeated: Harrell being escorted to the police car, his shirt unbuttoned. The reporter continues: "Family members said that Diane Hawkins's ex-boyfriend was known to be at the house last night. . . . It is unclear why he was there."

Daryl Hawkins, a twenty-nine-year-old nephew of Diane, now comes on the screen: "She worked hard at raising her kids, to give them a better life than what she had. You always try to give your children a better life than what you had, you know. I don't know what went wrong. She did the best she could with what she had, and somebody took that from her. And we want to know what happened."

The reporter again: "Diane Hawkins had been involved in a dispute with her ex-boyfriend over child support payments. Katrina Harris, an eighth-grader, was an A student at Woodson Junior High. They came from a large, close-knit family. Today many of their loved ones gathered, reminisced, and helped preoccupy Diane Hawkins's youngest daughter, two-year-old Kiki, who was found crying in the house last night."

Now thirty-year-old Eric Harwood, nephew of Diane and brother of Mike, appears: "That's what families are for. They get together at times like this and hug each other and grab each other and let everybody know how they feel."

Malcolm Harwood Junior, again: "Diane has been there for me through thick and thin. She came around to talk to me at times when I was down and out. She was always there for me, laughing, with that pretty smile, always brushing me off, giving me that smile. And that's how I'm going to remember her."

Daryl Hawkins again: "Every time you saw Diane she had that smile on her face. She was just a fun person. When you were down, she'd lift you up." These final words are accompanied by video of MPD officers lifting one of the stretchers onto a morgue wagon.

Later, Verdeen Wells will tell the police that she had no idea what her daughter and Norman Harrell watched that day or what they might have talked about. It was none of her business.

JUST EIGHT MILES AWAY, Norman Harrell is being betrayed by his pride and joy: his 1979 Ford truck. It's sitting in an MPD holding lot, its doors open wide as if resigned to the inevitable, while a mobile crime officer named Maureen Walsh systematically strips it of evidence.

In the light of day, the reddish smears on the driver's-side armrest are quite conspicuous, and similar blemishes can now be seen on the door panel. Officer Walsh considers simply taking swabs of the smears, as Lancaster did at the Hawkins house, to preserve the suspected bloodstains there. But unlike a wall or a kitchen countertop, the armrest can be removed from the vehicle and transported intact to a crime laboratory, and Walsh does just that.

The armrest and door panel aren't the only objects in the Ford truck dotted with what appears to be blood. Walsh moves gingerly into the front seat area. At her feet is a small cooler, turned upside down on the passenger-side floorboard. Walsh clutches it in a gloved hand and rights it. It's the kind of cooler that a man who spends a lot of time on the road would want near him on a long trip. White with red trim, it opens in the middle with the push of a button. It's empty, but on all four sides and the bottom it's speckled with as many as ten crimson spots. Walsh closes the lid and puts the cooler into a plastic bag, encased in a separate plastic container.

A white paper bag containing loose change is sitting among the refuse in the truck's front compartment. The bag is red-blotched and Walsh takes it. The overhead light catches an imperfection on the tan dashboard: another potential bloodstain. Since the entire dashboard is too cumbersome to remove, she cuts the suspicious section, puts her initials and the date on the back of it, and puts it in a bag. For good measure, she also removes the driver's-side visor, which bears a discoloration meriting further study.

In the back of the truck, tucked in a corner that was out of Harrell's reach as he drove through P.G. County, is a loaded pistol. Walsh retains it, even though it probably had as little to do with these murders as the gun found by Curtis Lancaster under Diane Hawkins's bed. Also in the back is apparel of varying styles, including camouflage and waterproofed jackets, all in size extra large. Notably missing: the blue work uniform and black boots that Reco Hawkins saw Harrell wearing at the Hawkins house last night.

Walsh separates the red-stained items from the rest; their next destination will be a forensic laboratory.

In a matter of hours, the police have secured a difficult crime scene, calmed a hysterical witness and gotten from him crucial information leading to a possible suspect, located and interviewed the suspect, searched his house and his truck, and seized evidence against him. Now everything will stop until science speaks.

RON BRANCH, Norman Harrell's supervisor at Yellow Freight, makes no secret of his disdain for Norman Harrell's work habits. Over the past few years Branch has repeatedly had to take disciplinary action against him. Harrell's personnel file is brimming with

complaints filed by Branch and other management officials, charging Harrell with offenses ranging from refusal to follow a supervisor's
direct instructions to failure to maintain a clean company truck. In
each case, Harrell has invoked grievance procedures and submitted
a formal rebuttal to the company's complaint. The rebuttals are usually ungrammatical, though sometimes Harrell files a typewritten,
smoothly phrased product that Branch assumes was written for him
by someone else. A constant theme runs through the rebuttals: that
he's being discriminated against because of—of all things—his size.
His disciplinary record, substantial as it is, is dwarfed by his medical
history: He's renowned for claiming leave for purported job-related
injuries, none of which ever seems disabling.

All of this goes through Branch's mind as he watches Norman
Harrell go about his work on Thursday and Friday. After taking
Wednesday off, Harrell returned to the job without even mentioning
his telephone conversation with Branch on Wednesday morning,
acting as if nothing had happened. In the past, even on the rare
occasions when Harrell was in a congenial mood, he struck Branch
as a man carrying considerable latent hostility. On Thursday and
Friday, however, Harrell is relaxed and even gregarious. What Branch
finds even more amazing is that he delivers all of his loads as instructed without delay or complaint. *My job would be a lot easier,*
Branch thinks, *if the police stopped Harrell for a murder every day.*

FRIDAY AFTERNOON finds MPD Detective Dean Combee at his
desk at headquarters, working his usual three-to-eleven shift. The
phone rings; it's the FBI serologist reporting test results. He confirmed the presence of human blood on four objects: an automobile
armrest, a cutting from an automobile dashboard, a white paper bag,
and a cooler. Then he compared the blood types with two samples
marked "Hawkins, Diane" and "Harris, Katrina." The results:

- Armrest: match to Hawkins and/or Harris
- Dashboard cutting: inconclusive
- White paper bag: match to Hawkins and/or Harris
- Cooler: match to Hawkins and/or Harris.

Combee is a bulky man with a mustache and thinning, reddish hair swept back from his forehead. He has a twang that betrays his roots in the American heartland, but just a few years as a D.C. police officer have broadened his vernacular, and his casual speech is a blend of country and city. His impassive personality conceals the mind of a natural criminologist whose interest in his cases is all-consuming. Usually his focus is analytical and detached. This case, though, touches him on another level, and he can't help feeling exultant after getting the news from the FBI. He knows he now has enough evidence to arrest Norman Harrell for the murders of Diane Hawkins and Katrina Harris, and he begins typing his warrant application. Born on the plains, at home in the woods, Combee can appreciate the irony of the situation. Norman Harrell—a hunter, a tracker of wounded prey—has been cornered at the end of a blood trail.

By sundown Friday, May 28, 1993, the warrant has been signed by a judge. It's a sealed warrant; it won't be made public until Harrell is arrested. Combee is well aware that the news media monitor the filing of arrest warrants, and he's concerned that Harrell will flee once he learns the police are looking for him. Not even the family of the victims will be told about the recent developments in the case until Harrell is safely in the hands of the police. Returning to the homicide office, Combee alerts his supervisors and fellow squad members that the warrant has been issued and then arranges for a special teletype to be transmitted to all police forces in the Washington area. The teletype gives basic details about the crime and the defendant and ends with a warning: "EXTREME CAUTION SHOULD BE USED. NORMAN RODERICK HARRELL, AKA 'DANK,' IS CONSIDERED ARMED AND DANGEROUS. NO WEAPON HAS BEEN RECOVERED."

Police units are dispatched to find Harrell. There's only one problem: Norman Harrell isn't staying at his house, won't be returning to work until Monday, and the police know nothing about his mother-in-law.

MORE THAN TWO days have passed since she first heard about the murders, and Verdeen Wells still hasn't spoken with her son-in-law Norman about them. She's watched him come and go over the past two days and has noticed no change in his demeanor. This gives her some feeling of optimism. Certainly, a man who murdered two people would be acting a bit strangely now, wouldn't he? She wants to talk with him about the whole thing but never does.

She does summon up enough courage to ask her daughter Gale one question that continues to trouble her. What was Norman doing over at that house, anyway? The only thing her daughter says is that her husband has told her he went over to Diane Hawkins's house to get his son Rock's telephone number. Gale says nothing further, and Verdeen never asks why Norman wouldn't already have his own son's phone number.

THE SUN HASN'T set on Friday evening when a bus pulls into a school parking lot in southeast Washington. Onboard is a contingent of children and adults returning from a five-day, school-sponsored trip to Disney World in Florida. Forty-two-year-old Deborah Courtney chaperoned a group that included her daughter, Gloria; ten-year-old Rasheen, the son of her best friend, Diane Hawkins; and Rasheen's cousins, the children of Diane's niece Carlene Hawkins. The drive was long, the youngsters predictably boisterous, and the adults are now exhausted, especially Deborah, who has a heart condition that needs to be watched closely. She's now looking forward to nothing more than being able to put her feet up in her own house.

She knows nothing about what happened three nights ago at Diane Hawkins's house.

Deborah has known Diane for thirty-five years. As little girls, they lived in the same neighborhood in Southeast D.C., where they first forged a friendship so close that Deborah's family became intertwined with Diane's. Each is called "aunt" by the other's children, and Deborah had once had a romantic relationship with Diane's brother James. The friendship is an attraction of opposites, Diane's open ebullience counterbalancing Deborah's natural reserve, and for as long as Deborah can remember, she's been energized by the sight of Diane's beaming face and the sound of her voice.

Through Diane, Deborah met Norman Harrell eleven or twelve years ago. When Diane began secretly seeing him while still involved with a man named Willie Harris, father of Katrina, Deborah voiced her disapproval, but to no avail. Still, as time has passed, she's gotten to know Danky well and socializes with him often, though always with other people. Deborah is a frequent visitor to Diane's house, especially in the summer months. Even now that Diane is no longer romantically involved with Danky, he still comes by weekly to see his son.

Over the years, Deborah and Danky have developed a contentious relationship. Though Deborah considers him a friend, they often argue with each other over trivial matters, and she feels he resents her stubborn independence. Their altercations have never become physical, but they've often raised their voices at each other. Memorably, one argument ended with Deborah drawing herself to her full height—a full foot shorter than Danky—and telling him that if he stepped up to her she would cut him "too short to shit." All he could do was shake his head and say "You're why I never mess with a black woman," a reference to his liking for light-skinned black females such as Diane. She laughed, and the tension passed, but she saw in those interludes signs of a dangerous temper barely suppressed.

One of the points of dispute between Deborah Courtney and Norman Harrell concerns the care of Rock, his son by Diane. Deborah feels that he doesn't do enough to help Diane care for the boy. Rock was able to go on the Disney World trip only because Deborah took the initiative. Rock isn't enrolled at the school sponsoring the trip, but his three cousins and Deborah's daughter are students there. Deborah learned about the trip from her daughter and thought that Rock would enjoy the experience if given the chance to go. She pressed Harrell to pay the $200 trip fee, knowing Diane couldn't afford it. After much prodding by Deborah, Harrell agreed to pay, but their conversations on the subject were so rancorous and disturbing that she told Diane about them, and they still trouble Deborah now.

As the group disembarks from the bus, Deborah sees a welcoming party awaiting them in the parking lot. Deborah thinks it unusual when Carlene Hawkins quietly whisks Rock away with her three children. Strained conversation follows; Deborah knows that something has happened but can't get anyone to tell her what it was. When they arrive at Deborah's house in Southeast D.C., several miles from Diane's, they're greeted by a larger group that includes members of both her family and Diane's, including Reco. She's well aware that in the past, when the people closest to her had bad news to tell her, they backed into it gently out of concern for her heart. She knows that she's receiving the same treatment now. For some reason she thinks that she's about to be told that her sister has died.

Deborah sits down in her living room, her head is swirling, and she hears someone say that Diane's been killed, then she hears someone else say that she wasn't the only one, that Katrina was killed too. As soon as she hears about Katrina, she sees Reco run downstairs crying, and all she can think is that she has to be strong for everybody else. She follows Reco down to the basement and puts her arms around him, wondering if she can hold up. She remembers that Rock went to Carlene's house, and she says to Reco, "Come on, Reco, we got to get it together, baby. Let's go around to Carlene's."

When they arrive at Carlene's to get Rock, the first thing she hears when she enters the house is the boy yelling into a telephone, "Danky, you killed my mother! You're a bastard. You cut my mother up!" And she turns to someone in the group and says, "What's he talking about?" and it's only then that she's told how Diane and Katrina were killed. What she doesn't know, what no one in the family knows, is that Norman Harrell is at that moment wanted by the police for the murders.

Deborah walks over to Rock, who is still holding the telephone and crying. "Get yourself together, baby," she says, and she takes the phone from his hand with the softest touch, not bothering to check whether anyone is on the other end of the line. She hands Rock off to someone else in the house and calmly dials the number of a friend who knew Diane Hawkins and Norman Harrell. Deborah tells her, "You know, he did this," and then she tells her how she knows.

For Deborah has carried with her for a month a secret she's shared with Diane and no one else, like all the secrets she's held since childhood. Now the other keeper of the secret is gone.

SATURDAY DAWNS CLOUDLESS and blindingly sunny and stays that way all day. Confined inside is MPD Detective Rod Wheeler, the only detective working in the Homicide office, and several other officials. All of the detectives in the squad assigned to what is now called the Harrell case are off duty, having worked the midnight shift all week.

At about 1:30 P.M., the main telephone line rings, and Wheeler answers it. A woman is calling to find out how she can arrange to have a vehicle released. She says it belongs to a Norman Harrell, and she's Mr. Harrell's lawyer.

Wheeler is familiar with the case and knows that Harrell is wanted on a warrant. "Ma'am, Mr. Harrell's car has been approved for release, but I can only release it to him personally. I'm the only detective working right now, and I leave work at two o'clock. I suggest that Mr. Harrell come and get it immediately."

"Can you hold on a minute?"

Wheeler has baited the trap. He now waits for a long minute before the woman comes back to the telephone.

"Mr. Harrell will come to your office to get his auto."

"Okay, fine. Like I said, I'll be leaving the office soon. But I'll be more than happy to get him his auto and all the release papers."

"That'll be fine."

Wheeler looks at his watch. He needs time to get help.

"I tell you what," Wheeler says. "Have him meet me in front of D.C. Superior Court in about ten minutes. You can come with him if you wish."

Wheeler goes straight to his supervisor, who then calls in the detectives on the case. Wheeler picks up a pair of handcuffs and his police radio and recruits a uniformed officer for assistance. Together they start walking toward Superior Court, one block away.

As they near the courthouse, they can see a man fitting Harrell's description standing with a much smaller white female. The man is looking around and shifting from foot to foot. Wheeler surreptitiously radioes the police dispatcher and asks him to send more officers to the area at once. Wheeler now approaches the man.

"Are you Norman Harrell?"

"Yes, I am."

"I'm Detective Rod Wheeler, MPD homicide. I have to inform you that I have a warrant for your arrest for murder."

The female looks flabbergasted; Harrell doesn't. Wheeler puts Harrell's hands behind his back and cuffs them.

Just that quickly it's over. Norman Harrell has been caught trying to reclaim the truck that held the most critical evidence against him.

DEAN COMBEE didn't have the chance to interview Harrell in P.G. County Wednesday morning. Sitting across the desk from him now, doing the paperwork on the arrest, Combee is struck by how unruffled he is in the face of his arrest. Then again, Combee has dealt with subjects being arrested for murders committed just hours before, who actually fell asleep during processing.

The rituals attending an arrest are largely ministerial, except for one: reading the defendant Miranda rights and asking if he'll waive those rights and answer questions about the charges. From Combee's point of view, his case against Harrell can't be hurt by getting him to give over more information. At worst, Harrell will simply repeat the account he gave Wednesday morning. At best, he'll give a conflicting account, which will be all the more incriminating because it varies from the first.

Reading from a small preprinted card, Combee recites the Miranda warnings. Harrell says he understands his rights and doesn't want to talk; in fact, he won't even sign the card. Combee says, "In that case, this interview is terminated."

Combee turns to his typewriter, and Harrell sits silently before him. Then Harrell speaks: "What kind of evidence do you have on me? Or is it just circumstantial?"

It's now Combee's turn to remain silent.

At 4:15 P.M., Combee and Sergeant Sharkey flank Harrell and lead him from the homicide office down a wide corridor, past reporters who have learned of the arrest, to an elevator that will carry him to a basement cell block. As the elevator moves between floors, Harrell speaks: "I think you only got me on circumstantial evidence." A few seconds pass, and he speaks again: "I was there, I'll admit that. I was at the house." Sharkey and Combee don't respond. The elevator stops at the basement level, and the three walk to the cell block. On arrival, Harrell speaks a third time: "I was just in the wrong place at the wrong time, that's all." Again, he receives no response.

As Sergeant Sharkey stands beside Harrell in the cell block, waiting for a guard to take custody of him, she watches him. Earlier, when Harrell saw her at the homicide office, he stared at her intently, and though he said nothing to her, his eyes rarely left her. Only much later would she realize what might have caused his preoccupation. Sharkey is a Caucasian female in her early thirties, with a round face, brown eyes, a dimpled smile, and long, wavy brown hair. According to Diane Hawkins's family and friends, she bears an uncanny resemblance to the light-skinned Diane of a decade before.

SATURDAY IS SHOPPING DAY for the Hawkins family: a day devoted to buying clothes to wear at the wake and funeral. Diane's sisters have decided to wear white, not black, to the ceremonies. For as long as they can remember, they've been taught that a person's passing isn't a tragic event but a "homegoing," a reunion with God and a return to something more transcendent than earth can offer. Now, in the midst of grieving, the lessons of childhood guide their choices. The only problem is that they don't all own white dresses, and Saturday is spent at a shopping mall in distant Charles County, Maryland, seeking appropriate clothes at bargain prices. Diane's children are worse off than anyone; all of their belongings are still locked inside the sealed murder scene on Eads Street. So Reco, Shante, and Rock are chaperoned through stores by older family members who help them buy the outfits they need. Diane's older sister Celestine takes on the task of going to a children's store to buy something for Kiki. To her mother's and sister's funeral, the little girl will wear a floral dress and tasseled socks.

It's only after the members of the group return to their homes late Saturday evening that they hear the news that an old friend has been arrested and charged with the murder of Diane and Katrina.

CHAPTER 3

E ARLY IN MY CAREER, someone advised me to prepare every case backward. Imagine yourself in trial, with the defendant sitting nearby. Imagine the arguments his lawyer will be making and how you'll respond. Imagine the defendant on the witness stand and what you'll ask him and how he'll answer. To know where you are, you first have to know where you're going.

The witnesses I interviewed in early June 1993, in the first weeks of my investigation, brought to life for me the places where this story happened—River Terrace, Eads Street, Richie Road, the curb where Harrell sat, the room where he was interviewed—but the people who were at the core of the story were still a mystery to me.

Who was Norman Harrell? The police documents in my file, duly and dispassionately spelling out the evidence implicating the man in a slaughter, left no room for equivocation: These were monstrous acts committed by a monster. But other documents in my file, prepared by a court agency that had done a background check on Harrell, introduced a paradox. They showed a man almost forty-five years old, with no pending criminal cases and a couple of minor criminal convictions from twenty years before. He had a steady job, a work history, family and friends in the D.C. area. Norman Harrell, apparent double murderer, seemed to have lived a life as normal as anyone's. Sitting here today, with twelve more years of exposure to the tangled mess that is the sociopathic mind, I've become more familiar with this phenomenon. I've since encountered the likes of Sydney Smith (respected engineer and wife killer), Oscar Chávez (decorated Marine and gang killer), and a host of other young men who've called me "sir" and shown me respect and lulled me into forgetting that if they ever saw me on the street and it suited their purpose they would gun me down and then go home and lustily eat a full meal. At that moment in my career, though, my defendants had been more stereotypically malevolent, and I had to remind myself that a hard-working man with devoted family and friends could have an unplumbed side sinister enough to compel him to great cruelty.

So what was the state of the evidence against Harrell? The case against him was circumstantial, to be sure, meaning that I had no eyewitnesses and would have to rely on the circumstances of the murder—a conglomeration of details—to prove he was guilty. If you've watched too many crime dramas on the high-numbered cable channels, you've no doubt seen the stock prosecutor character turn to the stock detective character at a pivotal scene break, shake his head, and say something like "We'll never win this. *It's just a circumstantial case.*" In reality, the law makes no distinction between eyewitness and circumstantial evidence, and having spent a number of years dealing with the imperfections of eyewitness observation—not to mention the interesting characters that tend to be outside when a cocaine dealer is killed in an open-air drug market at 4:00 A.M.—my response to any circumstantial case was *Come to Papa.*

This circumstantial case was stronger than most are this early in the investigation. There are only three words that matter in such a case: *motive, access,* and *opportunity.* Here, I already had evidence showing that Harrell had a motive: Diane Hawkins had taken him to court over child support for his son, and he'd voiced anger about it to several people. He had access to the kind of heavy knife that was used in the murders, and he had the opportunity to commit them, in the time that elapsed after he was left alone with the victims and the baby. The last point was crucial. The accounts of Diane's son Reco and his girlfriend, assuming they were reliable, established a narrow window of time in which the murders could have been committed. Even more significant was the damning evidence found in Harrell's truck: the blood of the dead on the property of the accused. Despite this, a part of me was saying, *He had nothing to do with it. I have the wrong man.*

You see, everything I learned in law school can be summarized in two phrases: "on the one hand" and "on the other hand." Most lawyers are specialists, and they go through their whole careers without ever applying any of what they learned in most of their law school subjects. But what survives is a way of thinking: surrounding an issue, breaking it down into small parts, and eyeing the parts from different angles. Around any law office you hear the saying "playing devil's advocate" so often that you'd think we're all on Satan's private retainer—something most nonlawyers believe anyway, come to think of it. By reflex, I could argue Norman Harrell's cause for him as vigorously as his defense attorney would—and I did, to myself, because it was the only way I knew to expand my view of the case to encompass its deficiencies.

And so, on the issue of motive: At first glance, it appeared that our case against Harrell was solid. Everything happens for a reason. There was only one person I knew of who had an ongoing issue with Diane Hawkins, and that was Norman Harrell. It wasn't just by coincidence that the murder happened the day before she was taking him to court. On the other hand: *Are you kidding? Thousands of people sue each other every day without anyone getting killed. You're trying to blame a petty court dispute for these horrific deaths? And what about Katrina? She wasn't involved in any court fight, was she? And by the way—what about the murder weapon?*

The police weren't able to find it. But Harrell had enough time to ditch it—after all, the police stopped him that night not far from a landfill. In fact, the haste with which he rid himself of the evidence suggested preplanning and premeditation; he thought about the cover-up before he ever even committed the crime. On the other hand: *Who cares that he was stopped near a landfill? The police searched it that night and didn't find any weapon, didn't find any evidence of the murders at all. The only fact that counts is that Norman Harrell didn't have the murder weapon when he was stopped by the police. Everything else is just speculation.*

But Harrell had the opportunity to commit the murders—that's what Reco Hawkins and his girlfriend said to the police. So the very person who had the best reason for wanting Diane Hawkins dead just *happened* to be in her home right before she was killed? What was this, the night of a thousand coincidences? *There you go again with the motive, which is flimsy in the first place. And who knows who came in and out of that house? The Hawkinses weren't exactly a small family. And why should you take Reco's word, anyway? The bottom line is, you only have one eyewitness to what actually happened and she's two years old.*

All right, maybe I'd never be able to get anything from Kiki. But what about the blood evidence? Lab tests showed that several of the stains from Harrell's truck were of the same type as the blood of the victims, and that Harrell was definitely not a source. What was he doing riding around with their blood in his truck? *Not so fast. That blood type is shared by 18 percent of the African-American population of the U.S.—millions of people. Other possible sources of the blood, including other family members of Harrell or of the victims, haven't been eliminated. And what about this—after the police stopped Harrell, they took him back to the station and looked him over under bright lighting. No scratches or cuts on his body, no blood on his clothes.*

Well, he could have changed his clothes after the murders; a couple of witnesses described him wearing a different outfit earlier that evening. *But could he have killed two people in this manner without a mark being left on him? And who are the people who gave the police information about Norman Harrell, anyway? Family members of Diane and Katrina, who knew him for years. What if they had some secret grudge against him that made them shade the truth a bit, cut a corner here or there to fit him more firmly into the picture?*

That's where more one-on-one meetings would come in—seeing all the witnesses, outside the setting of the grieving family gathering, and looking each of them in the eye. For all of the involvement of modern technology in the legal system—DNA and lie detectors and crime scene wizardry and the like—when it comes to getting the truth of another human being, there remains no substitute for sheer gut instinct.

I really only knew one thing for sure: I'd been blessed with an exemplary team of police detectives and officers on this case. Duvall, Combee, Whalen, Gainey, Lancaster, Walsh, all the rest—I'd worked with them before and they were as dedicated and resourceful and brave and honest as anyone who'd ever worn the badge. About that, at least, there was no internal debate, no "other hand."

There was a long list of things to do: ordering documents on Harrell's employment history, his custody disputes with Diane, and any prior court cases he'd been involved in; ordering another crime scene visit and additional fingerprint work; ordering further DNA analysis of the blood evidence, since only a conventional serological test had been used.

But before all that, we had to go back to the small child who'd sat in the center of it all as it happened. For all intents and purposes, two-year-old Kiki Hawkins had been orphaned by her mother's death, since her father had debilitating personal problems and couldn't take care of her. She'd ended up with one of Diane's sisters, a benevolent middle-aged woman named Ellen Neblett. What did Kiki know? Would she ever be able to tell anyone what she'd seen?

Would she ever be able to say it to strangers, or even say it in a courtroom? And would a judge even let her?

I'd heard that Kiki was a precocious little girl, reciting her ABCs and some of her numbers at an age when many children are only babbling. I'd also heard that she'd made comments suggesting that she'd not only seen the murders but still had the picture fixed in her head. One story, passed to me by an aunt, had Kiki coming upon a photograph of Harrell and saying, "He's the one who hurt Mommy."

If she could say this in the courtroom, it was possible that a judge would let her testify. All a witness has to do to be considered "competent" is to know the difference between the truth and a lie and tell a story in a coherent narrative—a pretty low standard, when you get right down to it. I even knew of one case in which a judge had ruled that a three-year-old was capable of testifying. *This girl is two,* I thought; *what difference would a year make?*

Ellen Neblett brought Kiki to my office on a bright day in June 1993. In the room with me were Sergeant Corey Sharkey, who'd interviewed hundreds of child victims as a sex offense investigator, and Detective Combee. Kiki was wearing a flowered dress for the occasion and had her hair in pigtails. She sat in a chair and began chewing her finger. Her large brown eyes, lovely and wary, never met ours.

We began by talking about other things: telling her how pretty her dress was, asking who'd done her hair. She looked beatific but distant and answered monosyllabically, if at all. She took no notice of any of us, even her aunt, but gazed at a point beyond my left shoulder.

I knew that there was a playroom in my building set up for the children of visitors. *Maybe,* I thought, *we can get something from the room that will distract Kiki enough that she'll forget herself and begin talking to us.* I turned to Sergeant Sharkey, who'd been standing in a corner behind Kiki, and asked her to get some coloring books and crayons for the girl.

Kiki's eyes followed mine and lighted on Corey. Without a word, she left her chair and went over to her. "Mommy," she said.

I looked over at Sharkey, then at Combee. We were all perplexed. Only Ellen knew: "You look just like Diane, dear," she said to Sharkey.

At that moment, we all welcomed the short break to get the crayons and coloring books.

After Sharkey returned, the little girl occupied herself by stretching out on the floor, coloring and doodling. We asked her about her family: no answer. We asked whether she'd seen anyone do anything bad to Trina or her mommy: no answer. There was only one time during the session when she was engaged and focused: when Corey Sharkey knelt on all fours and traced Kiki's hands with a crayon on a piece of paper. Kiki stood up and held the paper to her chest, looked at Corey, and smiled.

Ellen decided to try one last time. "Come here, honey," she said and lifted her gently to her lap. We all drew in closer. "Do you remember seeing anything bad happen to Mommy and Trina?" Kiki said nothing, and as Ellen went through her litany of questions, each simply phrased but heavy with meaning, I watched the girl's eyes close. Within seconds, she fell into a deep sleep. "That's the same thing she did the night this happened," Ellen said. She shook Kiki gingerly a couple of times and said her name into her ears, but Kiki didn't move, just continued snoring lightly.

By this time, I'd set aside any idea of ever trying to use Kiki Hawkins as a witness in the case.

It wasn't lost on me that I was giving up on what could be our most important evidence. I had no doubt that she'd locked away in her mind—behind the barricades of a child's defenses—the secret of the murders. I believed her family when they said she was smart and knew how to tell the truth. Under the law, a witness's competence is assessed at the time that she testifies; this case might drag on a year or two before going to trial, and by that time Kiki would be older and more mature. She knew Norman Harrell well and could be trusted to identify him just as any small child could identify, say, the next-door neighbor. It was conceivable that sensitive yet persistent investigative questioning, conducted over many months with the help of trained professionals, could draw from Kiki the story that would seal this case.

But the prosecution's strategic gain—a long shot at best—would be achieved to the lasting detriment of this little girl. Fresh in my mind was the famous McMartin preschool case, where charges of child abuse against the school proprietors were dismissed because the accounts of the children were found to have been improperly influenced by the doctors who interviewed them. Kiki Hawkins would be useless to me as a witness if her testimony could be effectively attacked as the molded handiwork of adults. So I would have to discourage her family from speaking with her about the murders—and possibly even from getting psychological counseling for her—until the trial was over. In the process, I would be depriving her of the very influences she would most need in facing life without her mother and sister.

Ellen Neblett still had Kiki on her lap when I sat down with her and said that I didn't want to put the child through any more questions. "Go get her some help," I said, and Ellen seemed relieved to hear those words.

I later heard that Kiki began seeing a psychologist soon after our interview. And not a moment too soon; she'd begun acting out the murders with her friends, passing a finger across her throat and falling to the ground.

I never regretted not trying to use Kiki Hawkins as a witness. But I was given a moment's pause by something told to me not long afterward, which made me wonder again if she might have had such rare qualities that she could have been qualified as a competent witness even as a two-year-old. One of her aunts, I heard, was driving around with her one day, talking with her about simple things, when the little girl fell into a long silence. Finally she spoke. "You know," she said, "he would have killed me too. But I laid down on the bed and pretended I was asleep so that he wouldn't hurt me."

ONE NAME CAME UP again and again in the early days of the investigation. Talk to Deborah Courtney, we kept hearing, she has something she needs to tell you, and she won't tell anyone else what it is.

Before I got around to following up, she called me herself. When she revealed what she wanted to discuss, I cleared the next day's calendar to talk with her. She agreed, with only one condition: She wanted to bring Kiki Hawkins with her, since she'd promised to take the girl for an outing and didn't want to disappoint her.

The next day, Kiki was entrusted to a babysitter: Corey Sharkey, the only person she would stay with as long as she was in our building. One product of their time together was another tracing of the child's hands. At the end of the day Kiki ceremoniously presented the drawing to me, and after she left I taped it to my office wall—right next to the color arrest photo of Norman Harrell.

Deborah walked into my office and settled heavily into a government-standard chair too narrow for her comfort. On the telephone, she'd sounded congenial and laconic, even easygoing. In person, she was a formidable presence, with leveling eyes and a bracing, direct manner. I could see why Norman Harrell had his hands full when they squabbled.

Before our meeting, I checked into her bona fides: She was who she said she was and worked where she said she worked, as a social worker for the D.C. government. I was still wary and began hesitantly. We need some personal information for our records, I told her, because we might have to get back in touch with you later. I didn't mention the other reason we needed the information: to run a criminal records check. She gave me her home and work addresses and telephone numbers, her social security number, and her birth date: July 6, 1951.

"That's my birthday," I said. "I'm six years younger, though you wouldn't know it to look at us."

She smiled for the first time.

I asked about Diane and Katrina: simple questions, background questions, but not innocuous, innocent questions. There's never anything innocent about any question a prosecutor asks a potential witness in a murder case.

I moved on to Harrell.

"Toward the end he and Diane didn't get along well, but she still let him come over to see his son. He'd come over whenever he wanted, and he always caused problems with Kiki's father—you know, Skeeter. Diane didn't need that, you know."

"When did things start to go bad between Diane and Danky?" I asked her.

"About three years ago. They'd been together for some years. She'd started seeing him when Trina was two or three years old, so they'd been with each other for what, eight years or so."

"Did you ever see them have any arguments?"

"Diane wouldn't argue. She just wouldn't. That wasn't her style."

"Was there ever any violence in the relationship?"

"Not that I ever saw, no. But I know she was scared of him, especially after they stopped seeing each other. Like he had some things that belonged to her, and he wouldn't give them back and she wouldn't confront him about it, because she was afraid of how he might react."

"What did you think of Danky? From what you knew about him, was he capable of doing these murders?"

"Oh, yes. Oh, yes." She rolled her eyes and shifted in her chair. "He's definitely capable of doing something like this. He has a violent temper. He could go into a rage over nothing."

"You saw this personally?"

"I did. One time, I had an argument with him over Rock. I thought he wasn't giving Diane enough for him. He got real mad, and he hopped up and rushed over to me. I said I wasn't scared of him, and he backed off." For an instant she was lost in the pleasant memory of a small triumph.

I broached the next subject carefully. "On the phone, you mentioned that he used to talk about Jamaicans . . ."

"Yes. Constantly." She took a deep breath. "He would brag all the time about these Jamaican friends he had and how Jamaicans kill people." The words came haltingly. "He said they would gut people—they'd cut their hearts out—as proof of what they did and then they'd pull out the intestines and splatter them up against the wall. He said if he ever wanted anything to get done he would get them to help him."

"Did you ever meet these Jamaican friends?"

"No. I never even knew if they really existed or if he just made them up, but he would talk about Jamaican killings all the time."

"When was it that you first heard him talk like this?"

She thought for a moment. "It was three or four years ago. We were outside his brother's apartment on Benning Road. A group of us were just talking, and it came up. A guy there was having some problems with a lady friend, and Danky said, 'You know them Jamaicans, you can pay them a couple of dollars and get anybody bumped off,' and then he went on from there."

"How many other times did he bring the subject up?"

"Oh, my. Six or seven, at least. Probably more."

"When was the last time?"

"Earlier this year." She hesitated. "It was just him and me. He brings up Rock. He says that he wants custody of Rock, but Diane won't give him up. So I say to him, 'You know, Diane's real sick; she doesn't need you to put this pressure on her. Work with her to help Rock; don't be trying to take Rock away from her.' And I say to him,

'Look, she's dying of cancer. You know, she had it before, had a breast removed, and the doctor told her it came back. And he seems shocked."

I hadn't heard this before. Maybe no one else in the family knew about it either. I started to interrupt her to probe further but stopped; I didn't want to get her sidetracked.

". . . So, anyway, he keeps talking, and he says he's gotten married and he wants Rock. He says he'll take the weight off her. And this is the first time I'm hearing that he'd gotten married, so I say to him, 'You never got over Diane; you still love her—'"

"Had he ever asked her to marry him?"

"Oh, yes. She refused. Maybe about four years ago. So anyway he answers, 'No, that has nothing to do with it.' And then he shows me his ring. So at this point I bring up the child support issue. Because I'm curious—I'm thinking then about going after my own ex-husband, and I'm curious about how a man feels about going to court on something like this. The thing is, I'm feeling as if I shouldn't have to go through the system, and so I'm curious. I want to ask his opinion. And so he says, 'A woman's no good to do that.' And I say, 'Why?' And he says, 'Shit, if Reds ever did anything like that to me, I'd hurt her.'"

"And Reds was—"

"Reds was Diane. That was what we all called her, because of her light skin. So then Danky starts saying about Jamaicans. He says, 'I'd go Jamaican style. You know them Jamaicans.' He talked about them gutting you and them cutting you right around the neck and then cutting straight down and taking everything out, just like they would a deer. And so now I try to cut him off. I say to him, 'Don't talk to me about Bambi. My husband brought a deer home one time, and I couldn't eat it, with his brown eyes and all.'"

The momentum of Deborah's narrative had carried her past her emotions. Now they were gaining on her, and she had to stop. On my desk was a napkin left over from a past lunch: a poor substitute for a tissue, but the closest thing available. I handed it to her and she went on, wiping her eyes.

"So I say to him, excuse me, Attorney Flynn, but I say to him, 'Why the fuck would you do that? You didn't do that to your other baby's mother.' Because I'd heard that another girlfriend had taken him to court for support too. And he says back, 'I didn't pay her either. I whipped her ass, and I did time in jail for it.' And he was laughing."

"I take it you knew as you were listening to him that Diane had already filed her case against him?"

"Yes, I did. But I didn't want to let on so I didn't say anything about it."

"Why would he make like he didn't know about Diane's case if he really did?"

"Maybe because he knew I'd tell her what he said, and it would scare her off."

"And did you?"

"Yes, I did, the next time I talked with her, but she went ahead anyway."

"Did you see Danky again before you and Rock left for Florida?"

"I saw him the Sunday we left—a few days, I guess it was, before the . . . the incident. We were all in front of the school—it's where Rock's cousins go, where the trip was leaving from. We were all boarding the buses and Danky was there."

"Was Diane?"

"No, she wasn't—I heard she wasn't feeling well, but Danky seemed mad she wasn't there."

"How was he acting?"

"Kind of strange. Like, somebody there asked him for his telephone number, in case Rock had an emergency while we were gone. And he wouldn't give it to them. They kept pressing, and he said, 'Y'all might be the police or something. I ain't giving it to you.' Then the lady said, 'What if Rock gets hurt? What if he's unconscious or something?' And Danky goes, 'Then wait till he comes around; he'll give it to you.' "

"And when did you find out about . . . about Diane and Trina dying?"

"The night we got back from Florida. The family told me what had happened, and they told me how it had happened, and . . . well, I just knew."

WE SAID GOOD-BYE in muted tones. I watched Deborah Courtney walk from my office and down the corridor toward the exit, holding Kiki's hand.

Deborah's contribution to the case appeared incalculable. She'd given us our best evidence of premeditation: the explicit, detailed threats. She'd given us not only one but two motives: a retaliatory strike for the child support challenge, fueled by romantic rejection. She'd given us leads to pursue and a blueprint to follow. In short, she seemed to be a dream witness.

To my jaded eye, this was reason enough to remain skeptical. Prosecutors tend to move about most comfortably in the shadows of the human soul. When someone asks what I do for a living, I sometimes respond: "I sit in an office where people come in and lie to me all day long."

But the more I learned about Deborah Courtney, the more my skepticism waned. She was described by all who knew her as a stable person, not prone to exaggeration or embellishment. She'd been deeply affected by the murders, but they hadn't disrupted her hold on reality; psychologically, she was rock solid. Her friendship with Diane Hawkins had been as staunch as she described, and she'd also been close enough to Norman Harrell to know his ways, but not so close as to have a hidden agenda. As best as we could tell, they'd never been involved romantically in any way. Sure, they'd argued in the past; she'd told us that herself. But ironically, it was Harrell himself who was her best character witness: he'd just entrusted her with his own son on a thousand-mile trip.

MY FRIENDS around the office refer to the usual drug-related murder as "JoJo shoots Stink over a fifty rock," nonchalantly using common street nicknames and narcotics lingo. If the hypothetical JoJo and Stink case is mine, then what I have to do has little to do with the past lives of shooter and victim. Leave those things to the urban sociologists; I don't have the time to obsess over why JoJo started hustling drugs, what twisted family pathos drove him out of the house too young, whether it was a lack of self-esteem or an unresolved Oedipal conflict that first compelled him to want to wrap his fingers around a cold metal firearm and point it at another man's head. Street relationships are transient: JoJo fronts Stink some crack to sell today; Stink sells it and tries to short JoJo tomorrow; JoJo kills Stink the next day. JoJo and Stink don't leave a paper trail charting their recriminations, and the fact that they may have tussled over a girl in junior high homeroom five years ago has nothing to do with my case. If I can find one or two people who are willing to say they saw JoJo kill Stink—and if they're telling me the truth, a big if—then I have a case. If not, I don't.

The Harrell case, like any domestic murder case, was different. Set aside Harrell for a moment and assume he was, as he told the police, in the wrong place at the wrong time. Look at the way the victims were killed, and you know that whoever was responsible, it was someone who knew one or both of them very, very well and hated one or both of them very, very much. Shootings are impersonal. I've had young men tell me about shooting somebody and describe it as if it were a video game: picture a man wielding a gun as if it's a joystick and the target is a blip on a black screen. But stabbings are personal. Getting so close to someone that her blood is all over you, feeling her last heaving breath and watching her eyes go sightless—that's personal. And personal killings are frequently planned—not just planned but brooded over, obsessed about, for hours and days and weeks before—which is why they're often carried out behind closed doors, where no one else is around, so the personal grudge can come to a private, final resolution.

I needed to know more about Diane Hawkins, more about Katrina Harris, than I'd known about any other victims in any other case I'd ever investigated. I needed to get a sense of how they moved about during the day and what they thought about at night. I needed to know about how they were raised, the friends they made and the friends they lost, and, most of all, the family that spawned them and the culture that nurtured them. I needed to know enough about them to be able to interweave their life story with my own—to absorb the similarities and reconcile the differences—so I could one day tell it from the heart to people I didn't know: a jury.

One of Diane's sisters called me one day in June. "I don't know if you'd find this interesting at all," she said, "but you know, there's a videotape of Diane's and Trina's viewing and funeral." A public interest group that was focused on domestic violence was sending camera crews up and down the East Coast, memorializing particular cases. They'd heard about this one, did some checking, and sent a crew to the service.

I got the tape and brought it back to my office. As I set up the VCR, I thought: *What's so special about a wake?* I'd been to a few in my day; my family's demographics were dominated by the elderly. I'd also been an altar boy at church for four years and had assisted at a number of funerals and weddings. Catholic rituals follow a predictable pattern, and as such they all run together in my mind, except for one thing. At the end of a wedding, somebody from the family usually slipped the altar boys an envelope with a ten or maybe even a twenty. But after a funeral everybody was distracted and they always forgot.

I PUT THE TAPE into a VCR in my office.

The screen flashes, turns white, and then a man in a black suit—a mortician?—is seen standing next to an open coffin. The face of the body isn't visible. The man looks into the camera self-consciously. The scene shifts to what appears to be a funeral chapel. Two caskets are lying end to end, separated by an arrangement of flowers standing on a pedestal. The camera closes in; I recognize Diane and Katrina from the photographs. A floral tribute stands nearby: carnations configured into the form of two hearts, a large red one superimposed upon and partly obscuring a smaller white one. The caskets are bathed in soft light cast by ivory-colored pole lamps posted like sentinels on either side.

A cluster of Diane's sisters enters the room. They huddle first around Diane, then Katrina, then Diane again, speaking to them between sobs and wails, their voices overlapping and merging together:

"I love you, Diane, I love you, Diane, don't worry about it, all right? You know I love you, Diane, I love y'all; I love both of y'all!"

"Oh Jesus, oh Jesus, Holy God—Thy kingdom come, Thy will be done, in heaven as it is on earth!"

"Oh, Jesus, oh no, Diane, oh, Diane, oh, Diane, oh, Diane, oh God!"

"We're all going to be in heaven tomorrow, Trina, we're all going to be there tomorrow, praise the Lord, praise Him."

One sister is shown walking away, then turning toward Diane's casket once again, edging her way up to it, then turning away again and biting her lip. Another—I recognize her as Ellen Neblett, who had brought Kiki down to see me—collapses. "I took care of her, I took care of her, that's my baby, I took care of her, oh Lord." She falls backward and is helped to her feet by men on either side. "Oh God," she says, "I took care of her, I changed her diapers, I carried her around with me, oh Lord Jesus!"

Others approach, one by one or in groups that crest at one casket or the other and turn back on themselves in waves of grief. One woman says, again and again, "That don't look like you. That's not you there. That's not her, that's not Diane, that's not Diane!"

An outside shot: A crowd is gathering. A steady rain falls, and the mourners seek shelter beneath the building's protruding roof line. Back inside: The chapel is filling up. Organ music plays unobtrusively in the background, broken by sporadic outbursts of fresh emotion from new arrivals. As the crowd swells, some of the older women begin fanning themselves with cards from the pews. Scattered throughout the congregation is a startling number of teenagers and children. The camera lingers on one, a boy no more than twelve years old, slouching against a wall and wearing sunglasses, completely still.

Someone begins to clap rhythmically. Within a few seconds more clapping resounds through the room, and then everyone is joining in. A choral group has begun singing:

Praise the name of Jesus, praise the name of Jesus,
Praise the name of Jesus, praise the name of Jesus.
He's my rock, He's my Lord,
He's my deliverer, in him is my reward,
Praise the name of Jesus!

The song sounds out in a stepped-up tempo. Some in the crowd sing along; others mouth the familiar words silently. Some vigorously clap, and some discreetly tap a toe. A middle-aged woman embraces the man next to her and unconsciously pats his back in time with the rhythm of the music. The verses ring out, over and over, ten, fifteen, twenty times.

Finally, as if on cue, the music stops abruptly, and a man in a dark suit, evidently a minister, stands at a microphone. "Quiet, please. Quiet! Glory be to God!" he implores the audience. The hubbub abates. "Glory be to God, Alleluia!" he cries out, and the crowd responds, "Alleluia! Alleluia! Alleluia!"

"Glory be to God," he begins again. "We're *excited* about being here tonight!"

"Yeah! Alleluia!"

"We're *excited* to be here tonight for one reason!"

"Yes!"

"We're *excited* to be here tonight because Jesus Christ is still Lord!"

"Yes!"

"Listen to me! You may not believe this, but who you see in the casket is *not there*!"

"No!"

"They are with *Jesus*!"

"Yes!"

The reaction begins slowly but rises to a crescendo of voices shouting "Alleluia" and applauding for half a minute.

"If the Lord is your Shepherd, you shall not want. And if you have come through the valley you already have *victory*. And so I say to you tonight, with all the things you are going through, you can *still* have joy, because victory is on the other side of the valley."

"Amen! Amen! Amen!"

A female vocalist sings a lilting solo, and the man in the suit reclaims the microphone: "In the name of the Lord, we want to thank all of you for coming tonight, and if you would just give us your attention and bow your heads and pray.

"Father, in the name of Jesus, we *thank* you for this time of sharing together. We *thank* you for the love that you have just brought out. Father, we *thank* you for the spirit of comfort that has come to every last one of us. Father, we *thank* you for this family because their joy in the Lord is *their* strength, and I know you have given them the spirit to continue on, and Father, as they continue on, their fullest joy will be before them and the glory of God will go behind them, surely sickness and mercy shall follow theirs, all the—"

"—days of our lives!"

The scene changes again to another day. A line of people, all African American, is entering the Maple Springs Baptist Church, an unembellished, one-story structure with white trim, whose name is posted on its face in matter-of-fact block letters. I see Diane's sisters in their white dresses; most of the other women are wearing white as well, though flashes of peach, turquoise, and other pastels can be seen. Most of the men wear blue or gray; here and there I see a beige or a seersucker suit. No one I see is wearing black. Still, the mood is somber, oppressive.

Then, inside, a choral group takes the stage above and behind the two caskets and the multitiered floral arrangements surrounding them, and the rhythmic clapping begins, followed by singing in double time:

This is the day that the Lord has made,
I will rejoice and be glad!
This is the day that the Lord has made,
I will rejoice and be glad!

Underneath these verses is a separate harmony rendered in deep bass by the choir leader:

He has made me glad,
Oh, he has made me glad,
I will rejoice for he has made me glad!

Over and over comes the refrain, and the service starts in a burst of exultation. The audience is standing and moving as one and hundreds of arms are waving. The insistent cadences of the church ensemble are supplemented by the private offerings of some in the congregation who have brought their own tambourines. The chorus moves seamlessly into a second selection and the walls seem to pulsate in rhythm:

> *What a mighty God we serve,*
> *What a mighty God we serve,*
> *Angels bow before him,*
> *Heaven and earth adore him,*
> *What a mighty God we serve!*

Now the pulpit is claimed by a young man with a high forehead and a small mustache. He is introduced as Calvin Hawkins Junior, one of Diane's many nephews. "All of us," he begins, "had a special connection to my aunt. I'm standing up here numbered among the ownership of pain; all of us are owners of that pain we are experiencing because of Diane's and Katrina's deaths.

"But I just want to say before I say anything, to my aunts and uncles and especially to you, Aunt Celestine, thanks for permitting me to come over to your house this past week. Because I don't think I could have said 'Joy, joy, joy!' I was one of those who said 'An eye for an eye.' But because I came around and saw how my aunts dealt with their pain"—at this a swell of sound begins to rise from the crowd—"and how they kept praising Jesus"—the swell becomes a full ovation—"I had to sing a new song inside of me." At this, cries of "All right!" and "Alleluia!" resound through the hall.

"I would like to take the liberty to say a few more things. If Diane was here, she would probably say to Reco, Shante, Rock, Kiki, and Tyrone that she would wish for you to find serenity and tranquility in a world you may not always understand. May the pain you have known in the last week and the conflict you have experienced give you the strength to walk through life facing each situation with courage."

"Yes!"

"Your mother knew that she was leaving some aunts and uncles behind, some cousins and friends, who will take care of you. She knew that their love and understanding would always be there for you, even when you feel alone—"

"Yes!"

"—and may you ever remember that the storm is passing over, remember the sunshine when the storm seems unending, and teach love to your friends, who right now may be feeling a little hate. Remember, Reco, Tyrone, Shante, little Rock, and Kiki, that life goes on—"

A deep, resigned voice responds from somewhere in the church, "No doubt about it."

"—and may you always be loved, and may you remember"—his voice rises, bringing the crowd with it—"that life is not an empty dream, for the soul is dead that slumbers, and things are not what they seem, and that though the causes of evil prosper yet"—he was now presiding over a convocation of waving arms, shouting into a wall of noise—"there stands Jesus in the shadows keeping watch."

And with that Calvin leaves the stage and is engulfed by the standing crowd.

IT WAS LIKE nothing I'd ever seen before.

The burial ceremonies of my Catholic past had a standard mode of behavior, with everyone trying to take their lead from the invariably stoic widow, following the Jackie Kennedy model of bereavement. They also had a standard, fixed liturgy, unchanging and restrained, with little tolerance for improvisation. In the more conservative churches personal touches were forbidden; in others, when permitted, they were often awkwardly rendered. Two neighbors of my parents, husband and wife, were killed when their car was hit head-on by a tractor trailer. At their funeral, the priest began his eulogy with a prayer of Thanksgiving: ". . . for the truck driver, who was found this week to have not been negligent, so we can all be glad he doesn't have that on his conscience." The theme of the traditional Catholic prayer at the grave site was "Thou are dust and unto dust now shalt return," a bracing, realistic message but not exactly an exuberant one. As much as I valued my religious upbringing, the Catholic view of death seemed to be: When it comes, act as if it's not there. And if it keeps hanging around, act as if you were expecting it the whole time.

Here, though, was a different way of dealing with death: naked, unabashed agony merging into defiant, resilient exultation. The message was: Death may have won this battle, and we're not going to pretend it didn't. But we're going to win the war.

CHAPTER 4

WATCHING HER FUNERAL as if I were there, listening to her family talk about her as if she were about to bound into the room, I knew one thing about Diane Hawkins: Until her last days, her life had been larger than everything else around it.

She was a big woman, not tall but ample, with a broad smile and a booming laugh. She came from generations of large families and was raising another, a mother of six children who herself was one of eleven, as her paternal great-grandfather had been one of twelve and her father had been one of nineteen. Her appetites and energies were equally outsized. She had long romantic relationships with four men but always resisted marriage, and so it was the Hawkins name—a name that first took root in the soil of an eighteenth-century slave plantation—that she would take to her grave. And it was the Hawkins family history that would foreshadow the story of her struggles in life and her persistence in the face of adversity.

It all began down in North Carolina, just a few miles south of the Virginia border, in a county called Halifax, in a place now known as Roanoke Rapids.

To the modern visitor from the urban north, Roanoke Rapids is a town shy about revealing its age. From the autobahn of Interstate 95 the visitor takes a feeder route toward the town's core. It's a route no different from thousands of others in an America dominated by chain stores: Winn-Dixies and Exxons and Builder's Squares and 7-Elevens, thrown together in uneven rows like tornado carnage, accidental neighbors with nothing in common. Traffic signals, timed out of sequence, act as checkpoints; they're small tests of will to deter anyone who doesn't really want to come here. But then the visitor arrives at a perpendicular, a main street, vintage 1950s, with home-grown merchants sharing space in brick and stone along a two-lane cruising strip, and the mind's eye conjures tail-finned Buicks idling under wide-arcing streetlights to the distant strains of doo-wop. Go further and the years recede. Take the winding road through the middle of town, a road laid before the bulldozers began imposing straight lines on the region's rolling contours. Pass the low-slung frame houses sitting gently by oblong tobacco patches. Find a world of greens and browns and towering pines topped by tufts of lush growth. Do these things and you might get some sense for the land as it was when it was worked by the ancestors of Diane Hawkins and Katrina Harris more than two and a half centuries ago.

A slave named Sary was born in 1740 and lived her entire life on a 10,000-acre spread on land that is now part of Roanoke Rapids. Her slaveholder was a white male named Ambrose Hawkins, who used his female slaves to breed a new generation of field hands. Sary gave birth to eight children over twenty-one years, all of whom assumed the slaveholder's last name by the custom of the time. There are no records to tell us who fathered any of the eight— probably one or more slaves from the Hawkins plantation or another in the area, though it's also possible that Ambrose Hawkins himself sired one or more, particularly since several of the children were referred to as "mulattos" in the census records of the day.

Far more significant than the paternity of Sary's children was the adoption of the Hawkins name on their behalf. The Hawkins family tree—white as a birch for hundreds of years—had now sprouted a sturdy branch of a richer hue.

Until slavery was abolished a half-century later, these children, and their children as well, knew only two things in life: backbreaking work and the boundaries of Ambrose Hawkins's plantation. Sary's daughter, born in 1809, married a fellow slave on the Ambrose Hawkins plantation in 1826; they had thirteen children, all raised in slavery. Their tenth child, Robert, was born in 1848. Robert's four children would be among the first members of the black Hawkins family born in freedom, during Reconstruction. Robert's youngest child, named Captain for reasons unknown, was born in 1871. He would eventually be the most prolific of Robert's children, fathering nineteen offspring by two women. Of these, Sallie Diggs, his first wife, bore eleven before dying in 1914 at age forty; his second wife, Vaggielean Flemming, bore eight.

A black-and-white posed photograph of Captain Hawkins has survived the years. It shows a solemn young man with coarse dark hair side-parted above a round face and widely spaced light eyes looking slightly off camera. In his face one sees the features of the granddaughter he would never know, Diane Hawkins.

With the end of the Civil War came the end of slavery. Many of the first generation of free African Americans chose not to stray far from what they knew, and Captain Hawkins was no exception, living in Halifax County for his whole life. He was an ordained Baptist minister who started Sunday school classes for those neighbors who were unable to travel to community churches. The school grew to become a church, first named simply The Hawkins Church, and later renamed The Walnut Grove Baptist Church. Still thriving today, it includes in its membership many of the hundreds of Sary's descendants still living in the area. Appropriately, it looks down on land once sown with the sweat of Ambrose Hawkins's slaves.

The tenth child of Captain Hawkins and Sallie Diggs was a boy named Wallace, born in 1909. At age five Wallace would lose his mother, and at age six he would see his father remarry. Just about every year of his childhood, a stepbrother or stepsister would come into his home. Wallace would remain in North Carolina until adulthood, nurtured by the family and the church built around him by his father. But he wouldn't live out his days there. Just as historical forces had once conspired to keep Wallace's ancestors on this land, historical forces would now act to draw him and many like him away from it.

In the 1930s and 1940s, millions of African Americans left the South for northern cities. The reason for this movement can be summarized simply: The South had Jim Crow laws and no jobs for blacks. Northern cities weren't models of racial tolerance, but at least they offered more opportunities than the South did. So thousands of black North Carolinians traveled north, to the point where entire high school classes vanished from the eastern part of the state. No city attracted more African Americans from North Carolina than Washington, D.C., partly because it was close by but also because of three other things: The federal government was by law an equal opportunity employer; the city had open housing; and World War II had started, so the government was mobilized and hiring.

Among those who made the journey, giving up what they knew for what might be better in the capital of the nation, were Wallace Hawkins and his wife, the former Magdeline Brown. Magdeline was also a native of Halifax County, born in Roanoke Rapids and educated in its public schools, and she and Wallace had married in 1933. Like Wallace, she had never traveled more than a few miles outside the county boundary before making the trek to Washington.

The migration of Wallace and Magdeline may not have been as arduous as the cramped, disease-ridden transatlantic voyages of the European immigrants in the early 1900s. But it also lacked the giddy optimism that made those trips more bearable. They were seeking a richer future but had no delusions that they would find more fairness where they were going. Washington, D.C., was still segregated in fact, if not by law, and many natives looked with dismay on the arrival of blacks in great numbers. Any misconceptions that Wallace and Magdeline might have had in this regard were dispelled as they were being deprived of the use of all public facilities along the route north.

They settled on L Street in Southeast D.C., near the Anacostia River and the Washington Navy Yard, a robust shipbuilding facility. It was there that they were living when Diane Magdeline Hawkins was born on October 16, 1950. Preceding Diane had been six girls and three boys, and one more girl would follow Diane in 1952. As in many households where older children serve as a buffer between parents and a newborn, basic duties in Diane's early care were taken on by some of her siblings, particularly some of her sisters, who were old enough to be so inclined without having to be coerced.

Diane was a light-skinned little girl with wavy hair the color of burnished copper, which led inevitably to her being nicknamed Reds. She was especially close to her mother, somewhat less so with her father. Wallace was already drifting into the alcoholism that would ultimately cause his early death at age fifty-seven, when Diane was just seventeen years old, and Diane's dealings with him were distant. But with her mother, things were different; it had been in Magdeline's honor that Diane had been given her middle name, and Diane's devotion to her would last until the day she died and broke her mother's heart.

Soon after coming to Washington, Wallace Hawkins had been able to get a job in Washington's sanitation department, which was growing to meet the needs of the city's population. He would work there every day for the next thirty years, retiring shortly before his death with months of unused annual and sick leave; if he was an alcoholic, he was certainly a functional one. Magdeline wasn't able to work, preoccupied as she was with a growing population in her own home, and so the family got by on one income. Money didn't flow freely into the house on L Street. Weeknight dinners for the whole family often consisted of just green beans and biscuits, and a weekend treat was fried chicken. But Wallace and Magdeline saved as much as possible, and before long they could afford a larger house one block away, and then another twenty blocks away, at 1713 C Street, Southeast. It was on C Street that Diane met the girl who would become her closest friend, Deborah Courtney. Diane attended the neighborhood elementary school, junior high school, and high school. She'd dreamed of becoming a nurse when she was a small child and went so far as to take courses in the field at a vocational school. Ultimately, though, her love of cooking became a career choice, and she took a job in the bakery department of a local grocery store. This would be the first of several jobs she would hold, all in bakeries.

She grew into a woman of uncommon exuberance, possessed of all of the virtues that accompany that trait. It was fitting that she spent much of her working life in the only department of a food store that could always bring a smile to a child's face. She was a toucher and a hugger, and so often did she punctuate an exclamation ("Go on, girl!") with a playful punch to the listener's arm that friends said if you stood too close to her, you bore bruises the next day. Her Sunday dinners were legendary: sprawling affairs attended by family, friends, and anyone she might have met the week before and taken a liking to, with heaping portions of kale, collards, candied yams, macaroni and cheese, glazed chicken, and pot roast. Mondays often found her hauling leftovers to a group of drifters who drank in a park across from her home. When she became a mother in her early twenties, she took to parenting as easily as to cooking and entertaining. Surprisingly, considering her easygoing nature, she was a true disciplinarian with her children, strict and demanding. She cherished them, lived and died for them, but wasn't the type of parent who believed they could do no wrong. When her oldest son got into trouble with the law as a young man, Diane called his probation officer more than once to report violations.

She was never on time for anything, ever. She was renowned in the Hawkins family for making a grand, grinning entrance to a niece's wedding reception in her bridesmaid's dress after missing the entire church ceremony. But no party really started until she arrived, nor did one last long after she left. She could be spontaneous to the point of being shortsighted, especially when rising to the defense of family and friends in situations where discretion was better advised. Her niece Carlene would long recall the night she joined Diane, Deborah Courtney, Carlene's cousin Kirk, and a few other friends for an outing that ended with a late-night visit to a pancake restaurant. A group of girls at the next table began disparaging Kirk's girlfriend; Diane took offense. Words were exchanged, with Diane's voice rising in anger with each rejoinder until one of the girls rose from her table and said she was getting a gun from her car outside. At that point, Diane and the others left quickly. Carlene would later wonder whether Diane would have stayed even longer if she hadn't felt that she had to leave with everyone else.

As the years passed, she did her best to swell the Hawkins ranks. She didn't believe in abortion and was dubious about birth control, so each of her committed relationships would yield offspring: a total of six children by four different fathers. Like everything else in her life, her childbearing decisions weren't planned or calculated. She was a working mother earning a moderate wage, and each addition to her family brought increased monetary burdens. She kept having children for the simplest reason: She loved them. But she wasn't shy about asking their fathers for support, and when it wasn't forthcoming she wasn't shy about taking them to court.

Always, always, she stuck up for herself and her loved ones.

Certainly she had lapses of judgment where men were concerned. Diane's first long-term romantic relationship was with a man named Tyrone Jackson. She met him at age eighteen and had her three oldest children by him: Tyrone Junior, Reco, and Shante. By all accounts, Tyrone Senior, was a sweet-tempered man and a well-meaning if often absent father. He and Diane would be together, more or less, for ten years, a decade marred by Tyrone's steady descent into drug abuse and petty thievery. Diane stayed with him, went to court with him, tried to change him, and finally broke up with him. Beyond a certain point, Tyrone's fate was as easily predicted as her alcoholic father's had been, and he died of AIDS in early 1993 at age forty-four. Her last long-term relationship before her death was likewise plagued. Lamar "Skeeter" Wilkinson was the father of Kiki, Diane's baby, born in 1991. He was a tall, bearded man with a deep drug dependency that he'd managed to hide from Diane until their relationship was well under way. Her patience exhausted, Diane evicted him from her house in the spring of 1993.

In between Tyrone and Skeeter came the other two men in Diane's life, men who would later be central players in the drama she left in her wake: Willie Harris and Norman Harrell.

In many ways, Willie Harris was the polar opposite of the voluble Diane Hawkins: He was as reticent as she was effervescent, and he always seemed to look as if he expected the worst the world had to offer. But somehow they found a small but fertile patch of common ground: For all their differences, they were both good-hearted and guileless. Willie was a baker like Diane, and they met at the job over cakes and pastries. When Willie acted on an ambition to go out on his own and run a small business, Diane resigned from her grocery store job to help him. Willie bought a small bakery and hired a staff. He and Diane embarked on the project with high hopes. But Willie was mild-mannered and gentlemanly to a fault, qualities not ordinarily associated with commercial success. He didn't easily exercise his managerial authority; he hated even asking, let alone ordering, anyone to do anything for him. Diane's brother-in-law Ty was a skilled handyman and repeatedly offered Willie free assistance in repainting the store. Willie never really said yes or no, so Ty finally arranged for

Diane to open up the store one night and did the work anyway, and Willie was very appreciative when he saw what had been done. He just didn't have it in him to do the arm-twisting and whip-cracking necessary to run even a home-style bakery, and soon Diane could see that his employees were taking advantage of him. The venture didn't thrive, and after four or five years, Willie and Diane abandoned it for a stand at a nearby outdoor market where they could sell baked goods and sandwiches with fewer administrative headaches.

On July 15, 1979, Katrina Denise Harris was born. She was Diane's fourth child, her first by Willie, and she had her mother's eyes and coloring and her father's smile. At the time, Willie was living with Diane and her children in an apartment. They talked about marriage but never decided on it. Diane loved him, loved the stability he provided for her and her family, and probably came closer to marrying him than any other man she was ever to know. Willie loved her as well, but they never got married. They were still living together when Diane met another man who was as imposing as Willie was unassuming, as assertive as Willie was retiring, and Diane began seeing him behind Willie's back. His name was Norman Harrell, and he would father Diane's youngest son, Rasheen, born in 1983.

Though Willie no longer lived with Diane and Trina, he still spent considerable time with his daughter and doted on her. Trina, in turn, was her father's soul mate; she rivaled her father as the quietest person ever encountered by those who knew them both. As a small child, she would avoid other children on social occasions, even at her own birthday parties, preferring to sit by herself and watch. At family functions, her aunts and uncles would try to involve her in activities, to draw her out and find out what she was thinking, but then the more boisterous children would make demands on their time and Trina would be easily forgotten. This was unfortunate, because the few people with whom she felt comfortable knew her to be an extremely bright little girl, an honor student who harbored college aspirations even at an early age. Her observations of the people and events around her may have been passive, but they were also purposeful: She didn't miss a thing. She would become remarkably self-sufficient in practical matters.

It was her mother, though, who could bring her to the surface as no one else could, and Trina seemed to follow her everywhere. In the end, Trina's fate was fused with her mother's because, like her father, she couldn't resist the pull of Diane's exuberance.

Perhaps it was encroaching adolescence, perhaps daily exposure to her mother's personality, but as she approached her fourteenth birthday her family began noticing signs that Trina was emerging a bit from her shell. She joined the school cheerleading and flag teams—not activities typically engaged in by the irredeemably bashful—and was displaying a touch of the sass, the don't-mess-with-me attitude, that lay beneath Diane's good humor. This would occasionally get her in trouble with some of her elders, Norman Harrell in particular.

Trina was still a homebody at heart. Her cousin Carlene would never forget the third Saturday in May 1993, when she sat talking with Trina on Diane's front porch. Carlene's three children were planning to join Trina's brother Rock on a school trip to Disney World. Wouldn't you like to go with them, she asked Trina. The girl's face lit up, and she said that she would. Ask your father if he'll pay for it, Carlene suggested, knowing how much Willie worried about his daughter living in the city and how he looked for excuses to get her away from it. Katrina thought for a moment. No, she said, she'd stay home to help her mother take care of two-year-old Kiki.

Which is what she was doing three evenings later.

WHAT WAS I to make of Diane Hawkins? Put aside whatever moral judgments one might apply to her as the mother of six children out of wedlock. After six years as an inner-city prosecutor, I encountered far more unmarried young mothers than married ones. One gets used to what one sees all the time, and begins looking to other standards to measure character. In so many other ways Diane Hawkins was a virtuous person, with a charismatic big-heartedness that still fired the memories of her friends. But more to the point: How was I to regard her entanglement with Norman Harrell? If he did what I thought he did, he was a brute, a beast, a monster . . . and she'd apparently loved him, slept with him, bore his child, even abandoned another man with a gentle soul to take up with him. Surely her relationship with Harrell—what the two of them brought to it, how they got into it, how each reacted when it ruptured—was the hinge on which this case turned.

I didn't expect to find all the answers. One comes at any problem from the perspective of one's own experiences.

My own parents were extremely devoted to each other. To family and friends they were a single entity—"Kitty and Larry"—not a rhyme, not really even an off-rhyme, but close. The story goes that they were out at a restaurant one night after they were engaged, before they were married. The meal over, my father left the table, returned after a few minutes, and told my mother that he wanted to show her something on the way out. He walked her to an empty room under renovation. The walls were being repainted white; the job wasn't finished yet and the workers had left behind the paint cans and brushes. My father had taken it on himself to write "I love you, Kitty" in massive white letters on the undone wall. His love was returned in equal measure. I'd seen their commitment displayed most recently under great strain. The summer before, my mother had descended inexplicably into a severe depression that had put her into the hospital and still persisted, in less serious but still debilitating fashion. For many months my father obsessed over one mission: He was committing his life to the reclaiming of hers.

But as devoted to each other as they were, my parents were almost as different in personality as Diane Hawkins and Willie Harris: my mother passionate and mercurial, my father stolid and restrained.

Usually, they complemented each other well. My father admired my mother's spunk—a word that has gone out of fashion but fit her to a T—and she was buttressed by the very reliability of his rectitude. Occasionally, they didn't complement each other, and I was given an early lesson in how wonderfully and aggravatingly mysterious relationships between men and women can be. On balance, my parents' marriage was a happy one, and I certainly had a happy childhood; the acts of love that filled our house far outnumbered anything less. But their marriage and our family weren't like any others, and no relationship is like any other, either.

THOSE CLOSEST to Diane Hawkins thought they knew Norman Harrell, and in the days and weeks after the murders, even as the evidence against him began mounting, some refused to believe that he could have done them. To understand this, one had to remember a simple fact: For the better part of a decade, before he was a defendant, before he was a suspect, before he and Diane had become so estranged that his very presence brought a brooding tension to social gatherings, Norman Harrell had been one of the family.

Years before, when Diane first began seeing him, she managed for long months to keep Harrell a secret from Willie Harris and her family. But suspicions became aroused when Diane and Danky began appearing publicly together with increasing frequency. When Diane became pregnant in mid-1982, her friends and acquaintances speculated that Willie might not be the father. Harris, as guileless in love as in business, either wasn't aware of Harrell's encroachment or chose not to acknowledge it. In any event, when Rasheen Hawkins was born on April 22, 1983, he bore a striking resemblance to Harrell. Soon, the baby boy was informally christened with the nickname Rock, a name that evoked Harrell more than the gentler Willie.

Before long, Willie and Diane's relationship ended, leaving Willie with an empty house and an unfamiliar acrimony welling up in his gut. He would never completely cut ties with Diane. She retained custody of Katrina and Rasheen, and he had to see her in order to see them. But he would also never forgive her.

Diane moved on with her life. At first, her closest friends had misgivings about the choice she'd made; no one could ever say an unkind word about Willie. But once they'd become adjusted to Norman Harrell, most began to like him, and some even thought he was a better fit for Diane than Willie had been. He was more of a physical being, and like Diane he met the world head-on. He was a man's man, a truck driver who loved the outdoors, and he had a masculine charisma that drew people to him on first meeting. Some felt that his kind of character better complemented Diane's extroverted personality. Danky's qualities also stood in stark contrast to those of the other love of Diane's past life, Tyrone Jackson Senior. Harrell was a workingman, holding a steady job and owning his own home, and he wasn't known either to take drugs or to drink to excess. On top of all that, Diane and Danky both had a great love of children. Each had offspring from previous relationships, and they were known on occasion to act on a shared impulse and gather a group of them for some horseback riding or a day at the beach.

All in all, Diane Hawkins might have been justified in thinking that she had a shot at a decent future with Mr. Norman Harrell.

In time, though, the man's coarser qualities became more apparent. When Diane and her children moved into River Terrace, her house on Eads Street became the focal point of a swirl of social activity. Harrell was a frequent visitor, and some of the other regular guests found they could take him only in small doses. For one thing, he had a habit of talking incessantly, even obsessively, about the same subjects. With Deborah Courtney, Diane's best friend, Harrell repeatedly shared his musings on Jamaican-style killings. It was a fixation that she found odd, to say the least. He was just as expansive about hunting and fishing, activities in which he purported to be an

expert. He'd stand in the middle of whatever group he was addressing and expound at length on various hunting techniques—tracking
animals, gutting and skinning them, and the like—until at some
point he would press his audience to join him on one of his outings.
Most declined, although Diane's son Reco would later recall going
rabbit hunting with Danky five or six times when he was eleven or
twelve years old. Years later, Reco wouldn't remember much about
the trips, but he'd vividly recall, as would several other witnesses to
Danky's monologues, how Harrell would easily move to another
topic that seemed to fascinate him: how much more challenging it
would be to kill a human being with a knife than with a gun, and how
much more skill and courage it required. Two of his regular listeners
were Vietnam veterans who painfully remembered the lessons of
battle, and more than once they asked him: Why would you wait for
someone to get that close? And isn't the point just to kill the other
guy, not how you go about it? But Harrell couldn't be sidetracked,
and he constantly and loudly derided the manhood of the young men
shooting each other at safe distances on the city's streets.

To Edward James, who was Diane's brother-in-law and who spent
hours in Danky's company, much of this was just bluster, the false
bravado of a city kid trying to claim a wilderness pedigree. James had
been by Danky's house and had seen no hunting trophies, no signs
that he was the sportsman he boasted of being. Admittedly, James
had serious problems of his own, including a drug dependence that
had sent his life into a downward spiral, but even in his more desperate moments he remained a charming man, capable of holding a
conversation with just about anyone on just about anything. In times
when James wasn't in jail, he got to know Harrell better than nearly
anyone else in the family. For whatever reason, Danky lowered his
guard around him, and even got drunk with him once in a while. Not
that Harrell was able to use these opportunities to raise himself
much in his friend's esteem—James decided that in addition to his
other limitations, for a man of his size, Harrell couldn't hold his

liquor. Beyond that, James found himself feeling a little sorry for him. He judged Harrell to be a man who knew little or nothing about any subject—football, politics, movies—other than hunting and fishing, and who gave no evidence of being particularly proficient at the sports he held closest to his heart.

But among the other members of Diane's "social club," as Deborah Courtney later called it, Harrell didn't evoke pity. While group discussions at these gatherings were generally loose and free-wheeling, Harrell was a stubborn and unyielding conversationalist. To keep the peace, others around him would often avoid further debate by either agreeing with him or changing the subject. But some, such as Deborah, couldn't resist challenging him, which would usually cause Harrell to sulk or worse. He seemed especially perturbed when the person confronting him was a woman.

Still, none of the Eads Street regulars ever saw him lay a hand on anyone in these situations, and Diane never reported any violent incidents in their relationship. The get-togethers were large enough to accommodate everyone's idiosyncracies, and the most important thing was that Diane seemed happy with him. If he's good enough for her, the thinking in the family went, he's good enough for us. This was the classic African-American extended family, where brothers and sisters and nieces and nephews merged with cousins and friends so close they were called cousins. Norman Harrell was with Diane Hawkins, so he was in the Hawkins circle just as surely as Carlene or Ellen, or Wallace or Magdeline, or even Captain or Sary.

The irony, of course, was that by its sheer expansiveness, its all-inclusiveness, the Hawkins family unwittingly brought danger into its midst.

One member of the family wasn't so accepting of Norman Harrell: Katrina Harris.

Trina generally held her emotions in check and was as hard to read as her father, Willie, was. Still, from an early age, it was clear to everyone that she wasn't warming up to Harrell. Perhaps this observant little girl saw her mother show affection to him and rejected him simply because he'd replaced Willie. Or maybe the reason wasn't all that complicated: Maybe she rejected Norman because she just didn't like him very much. Likewise, Harrell seemed ambivalent about Trina. True, no one ever heard them shouting at each other, and he was never seen striking her. While their dealings with each other could be strained, they didn't appear to be overly rancorous. In fact, Danky and Trina could be compatible on occasion, teasing each other around the house. Just a short time before Trina's death, an aunt had watched Harrell stop to tickle her as he went by; Trina had seemed to tense a bit. But Trina took great pleasure in standing up to him and defying him, particularly as she began to grow into herself and become more assertive. Harrell retaliated by depriving her of favors he was extending to his and Diane's other children, pointedly leaving her behind, for example, when he was taking the others on an outing. If these slights bothered Trina, she didn't say so. Others took umbrage on her behalf, and after one episode Harrell was confronted by Sherman Hogue, the father of a baby by Diane's sister Elaine. Their encounter was chilly and left Hogue unsatisfied, so he arranged to take Trina, Rock, and Hogue's own daughter on a trip to amusement parks in three states. Harrell, feeling shown up, never spoke to him again.

None who knew Danky and Diane doubted that he loved her. They remained romantically involved but lived separately for a couple of years after Rock was born. Finally, Danky decided to ask Diane to marry him. Afterward, Diane told her niece Carlene that she thought Danky was kidding: "You know Danky, he's always joking. So I laughed out loud." Danky felt humiliated by Diane's reaction, and pledged never to propose marriage to her again. But he went back on his pledge two or three times; Diane rebuffed him each time. The subject of Diane's rejection was added to Harrell's quiver of conversational obsessions, to be aimed and fired at Diane's friends when she was out of earshot. For some time afterward, words such as "I'll never forget what she did to me" and "If I can't have her no one will" were often heard from him.

Their relationship didn't end immediately, but it did change. Harrell began looking elsewhere for a wife, and Diane didn't discourage him. In 1987, he had a child out of wedlock by another woman; yet Diane continued to see him off and on. As late as 1991, Harrell felt close enough to Diane that he called on her when his girlfriend took him to court for child support, and Diane and Carlene Hawkins went out to a Maryland courthouse to provide moral support.

But now their friends noted a strong undercurrent of antagonism in the way Harrell treated Diane. Before, he would never be seen handling her roughly in front of others; now he would grab her arm to make a point, forcing her to break away from him. He grew more possessive of her—incongruously, given his own involvement with another woman—and provoked arguments with her about men he accused her of dating. She, in turn, deferred more to him than in the past, as if wanting to avoid an altercation. Deborah Courtney came to the conclusion that Diane was truly afraid of him, particularly after she declined even to ask him to return some things that belonged to her. Diane did take tentative half-steps toward independence when she began seeing a man named Lamar Wilkinson. Harrell disliked him on sight and baited him until the two had to be separated.

The tensions between Diane and Danky were made worse by their differences over money. It was this point of contention that would destroy the last vestiges of their friendship.

A combination of factors had kept Diane from rising out of the ranks of the working poor: a houseful of children, a wage barely sufficient to satisfy their needs, and recurring health problems. Her rent at the Eads Street house, which she leased from her sister and brother-in-law, Barbara and Malcolm Harwood, was subsidized by public funds. Still, she ran late every month with the payment, and at one point, over a year had elapsed between checks. In another family, this might have caused a major rift. Both Harwoods worked, and they were raising three children of their own, so they could have put the rent payments to good use. But they understood Diane's situation and knew she was doing her best with what she had. They decided not to prod her about the debt, and gradually Diane paid it all back. Diane and her children continued to live from paycheck to paycheck, and her situation deteriorated further when she was diagnosed with breast cancer. A stoic and a person of great religious faith, she felt she could endure the physical and psychological hardships of the disease, but as a provider she was devastated. The illness cost her time from work, and for the first time in her life she had to claim welfare for a period of months before finally being able to return to her job.

Her instinct for protecting and caring for her children compelled her to seek help from their fathers, with mixed results. She'd filed a child support claim against Tyrone Jackson Senior in 1980 but received little or no satisfaction; she was trying to tap a dry well. In 1989, she sought financial support from Willie Harris for Katrina. This effort met with more success, though Willie would always claim that the suit was unnecessary. True to form, Willie ended up paying *too much* child support. At the time Diane and Katrina were killed, the D.C. government had more than $1,000 in funds paid by Willie for future dispersal to Diane, and it was still holding on to the money a year after their deaths.

Meanwhile, Diane was getting no money from Danky for the support of Rock. Not that Harrell didn't give anything to his son; he'd buy him a toy every so often or take him out for a special event. This approach, calculated to exalt Harrell in the boy's eyes at the expense of Diane, rankled her even more than if Harrell had refused to provide the boy with anything. She was cast in the role of struggling provider, while he played a sort of beneficent Santa Claus. She also knew that Harrell's failure to provide child support wasn't because he couldn't afford it—he made a good salary—but rather because of the principle of the thing. If there was an issue about which Norman Harrell obsessed even more than his beloved hunting and fishing, it was child support. For as long as anyone could remember, Harrell had voiced his heated opposition to the notion that a judge could make a man pay for a child he'd fathered. By his reckoning, it was up to each father to decide the appropriate amount to contribute to his child's welfare; courts had no business meddling in personal affairs.

Over time, Harrell's views on the matter became more extreme. One lazy summer night in 1992, a group congregated on Diane's front porch. Harrell was there, along with Sharon Randle, who was Diane's close friend and niece by marriage. As usual, Harrell was standing over the group; Diane was coming in and out of the house serving guests. Several of the women began discussing men and how irresponsible some were. Someone told an anecdote about child support as Diane walked past the group with a platter in her hands. Harrell addressed the group but looked directly at Diane: "If she ever took me to court for child support, I'd kill her." Diane laughed and went inside, but Sharon felt a chill.

Diane held back as long as she could, but finally, in late 1992, she summoned the courage to raise the matter of Rock's support to Harrell directly, hoping to persuade him to contribute voluntarily. Harrell exploded and dared her to take him to court. "No matter what happens," he said, "nobody's going to make me pay more than what I think is fair. And besides all that," he added, "it's your own fault that you didn't marry me when you could have, since now you'd be living better."

Through 1992, Diane debated whether to file a support claim against Harrell. She knew that by so doing she'd be instigating what could end up being a long, ugly struggle, one that would end whatever friendship she still had with him, but she'd injured her hand on the job at the grocery store bakery and was disabled indefinitely. Worse, her employer was contesting her claim for worker's compensation, so she was receiving no salary or benefits during her convalescence. As a result, she'd been forced to go on public assistance again. Each day she felt less and less in control of her life. Her family very much needed the money.

To make matters worse, her oldest son, Tyrone, who had minor problems with the law as a juvenile, was now facing jail time for drug dealing. She suspected Reco was drifting into the same business, and she couldn't shake the notion that they were doing what they were doing because she wasn't bringing enough money into the house.

The breaking point came at Christmas 1992. Harrell didn't buy gifts for any of the children, and didn't give Diane any money to buy them herself. Was it an oversight or just another way of punishing Diane for raising the forbidden child support issue? It didn't really matter to her anymore. On January 6, 1993, after much agonizing, Diane Hawkins filed a court action against Norman Harrell.

Days went by and then weeks, and Harrell never mentioned the case. When Diane had submitted her paperwork, a clerk had told her that notice of the court action would be mailed to Harrell, but he never confirmed to her that he'd received it. He continued to drop by Diane's house about once a week, but only after he'd called in advance to find out whether Rock would be there. Harrell didn't speak to Diane during these visits.

In mid-May, she received a notice that the first hearing in the case had been scheduled for May 26, 1993. The document didn't state whether Harrell had also been notified; Diane assumed that he had, but in the days to come Harrell was silent as ever. The pending hearing was one of several developments converging upon her. She evicted Skeeter Wilkinson, Kiki's father, ordering him to seek drug treatment before returning. Tyrone Junior was now jailed in a Virginia penitentiary, convicted of a drug charge, and he'd remain there for at least a year if not longer. For whatever reason, her energy was waning, and she was uncharacteristically allowing her home to become unkempt. Sharon Randle, who in recent years had been an almost daily companion, now spent even more time with her than

usual, helping her with housework and cooking and running errands
for her.

As the hearing date approached, Sharon found that Diane's attention span was getting shorter. The only subject that Diane seemed
to focus on for any length of time was the court case and Harrell's
possible reaction to it. As far as Sharon could tell, whether Harrell
knew about it or not, he had nothing but contempt for Diane. The
last time Sharon saw them together was several days before the
hearing date, when Harrell came by for Rock while Sharon was visiting. As he entered the house, he mumbled a greeting to Sharon,
but glared at Diane with a look of pure hatred. After he left, Diane
shook her head and said, "He doesn't say a word to me anymore."
She wasn't laughing him off as she had in the past.

Sunday, May 24, was the day that Rock was going to Disney World,
the trip having been paid for by Harrell at Deborah Courtney's urging.
That morning, Harrell took Rock to the house of Carlene Hawkins,
whose three children were also taking the trip. From there they drove
to the elementary school where the buses were loading. On the way,
Carlene and Danky had a chance to talk while the children played in
the back of the van. Carlene was fond of Danky and usually felt comfortable in his presence. This day, though, he was angrier than she'd
ever seen him, over something Carlene found trivial: Harrell thought
Diane should have come out to send Rock off on his trip. Instead, he
said, he'd had to go by Diane's house himself to pick the boy up.
"Rock should be living with me anyway," Harrell said; "Diane can't
take care of him like I can." He went on like this for several minutes
and then said, out of nowhere, "You know, I would hurt a person if
they took me to court for child support." Carlene didn't know what to
say. She knew that the hearing was coming up in three days but said
nothing about it, wanting to avoid unpleasantness. Harrell went on
about how he would never pay child support to anyone for any reason,
going on in that fashion until they arrived at the elementary school
and discharged the children.

Rock and the others rushed to the bus after hurried good-byes. One of the trip's chaperones approached Harrell and asked him to give her his home telephone number in case of an emergency, but he refused. The chaperone pressed Harrell. He got testy, and Carlene stepped in, saying that her telephone number could be used instead.

Later in the day, Diane dropped by Carlene's house, and Carlene told her about how Harrell had acted earlier. Diane just shook her head. "You don't know that crazy motherfucker like I do. He's going to kill me." Carlene told her no, Danky's all talk; he'd never do anything like that. But she made a mental note to keep close watch over Diane in the next few days, and she was prepared to go to court with her on Wednesday if she was asked.

Diane's frame of mind hadn't improved by Tuesday. Sharon Randle came by to see how she was doing. She knocked on the door for more than half an hour before Diane finally opened it, looking furtively over Sharon's shoulder. On their trip to and from the store, Diane asked several times if Sharon could accompany her to court the next morning, and each time, Sharon said she would. As the afternoon went on, various friends and family came by to check in on Diane. Others tried to call, but the phone had been disconnected because she hadn't paid the bill. When he got off work, Sherman Hogue, father of Diane's niece, came by to sit for a few minutes. At 7:55 P.M., as the sun began to set, he drove to a liquor store just a block away to buy a lottery ticket before the machine was closed down at 8:00 P.M. When he got to the store, he was dismayed to see a line of people waiting for tickets, but the line moved quickly, and he bought his ticket just before the deadline. One of the people waiting on line was well known to him, but Sherman let him pass by without greeting him. It was Norman Harrell.

At about 9:30 P.M., Toi Cohen came by to see Reco. Toi had been Reco's girlfriend for two years, and although they no longer went out with each other, she remained on good terms with Reco and his family. When Toi arrived she found Reco in his bedroom and Diane in the bathroom, giving Kiki a bath. Toi stood at the threshold of the bathroom, talking with Diane while Kiki played in the tub. Diane told her she was worried about going to court the next day. "At least I won't be by myself," she said. "Sharon's going down there with me." They spoke for a while about the case until Katrina walked in. "You know, Danky's downstairs," she said. Diane made a face. When Trina asked what they'd been talking about, Diane shook her head. "Nothing," she whispered. "Just the court case." She shooed them out of the room, and Toi went downstairs.

Norman Harrell sat in the living room with his eyes closed. As Toi took the last step into the living room, he jerked up: "What are you sneaking up on me for?" She said she hadn't meant to startle him and went to find Reco. They left the house to go to a convenience store. Harrell asked when they were coming back. Reco answered, "In a few minutes." As they got into her car, Toi looked at the lighted dashboard clock. It was 11:30 P.M. Toi and Reco drove to the store, picked up sodas, and returned to the house within a couple of minutes. When Toi last saw him that night, Reco was walking up the steps to his house. She drove off, heading for her home.

Reco went inside, dropped off the sodas, and checked in briefly with his family before leaving to go down the street to the house of his friend Eric Fisher. His sister Kiki was asleep in her crib; his sister Katrina was asleep in her room; and his mother was sitting in her darkened bedroom watching television.

Downstairs, sitting alone, was Norman Harrell.

CHAPTER 5

WE ALL HAVE OUR BIASES, and we all have an innate inclination to protect those who are closest to us when we sense they're in danger. One of the first rules of any investigation is to get to a suspect's family members quickly and talk to them one on one, before they can all get together and water down the truth. And so, starting in July 1993, we began to bring in Norman Harrell's family—his brothers, sisters, children—as well as any friends, co-workers, or acquaintances we could get our hands on.

The leads seemed endless. At some point in most investigations, a prosecutor can sense that his work is nearing an end: Leads circle back on each other, the same stories and names are heard from different people and their common sources can be identified, and the universe suddenly becomes known and finite. The Harrell case was different. Leads led to other leads, which led to still others. They all had to be checked, some at the cost of much time and trouble. If five potential witnesses were asked a certain question, it seemed the fifth always raised yet another question and provided names of five more potential witnesses. Such was the business of combing through the past to find the one detail that might illuminate these unwitnessed murders. Even a matter as simple as the number of Norman Harrell's children produced confusion: Some said three, others four, still others referred to a long-lost, nameless fifth child by an unknown mother. I couldn't call Harrell in to talk with me; as a criminal defendant he had an absolute constitutional right to remain silent. So I had to rely on others around him, and not always successfully, since Harrell had trusted few people with personal confidences.

One person remained ever elusive: Harrell's present wife, Gale Tolson. In late August she contacted me indirectly and said that she would claim the marital privilege: Under the law, a person can't be forced to testify against his or her spouse. By absenting herself from the case, she would leave it with a gap that wouldn't be filled for many months to come.

As for Harrell's other close contacts, I was asking them to open doors for me that they might never before have wanted even to crack. All the questions I had for them really came down to just one: Was there anything in Norman Harrell's past that told you he was capable of killing like this?

HE WAS BORN on January 1, 1949, a New Year's baby.

His parents were Willie Bell Harrell and Montigue Harrell, and years later his childhood would be recalled as having been as normal as anyone's. He and four siblings were raised in the city of Washington, on East Capitol Street, about thirteen blocks from where he would settle as an adult. He had early problems in school; he had to repeat two grades, and he dropped out entirely after the tenth. He landed in Boys Training, a vocational school, but he took classes there for only a year before abandoning them. He took jobs as a laborer and mechanic with a construction company in D.C., then as a stock clerk at a grocery store warehouse in suburban Maryland. He also drifted toward petty crime, picking up one conviction for housebreaking at age sixteen, another for larceny at age eighteen.

Between 1969 and 1971, his record was clean; he was otherwise occupied. The military called for Norman Harrell in late 1968; he was inducted into the U.S. Army on January 23, 1969, and served until mid-1971. His service was undistinguished, to say the least; he went AWOL several times and suffered a demotion in rank. But the ironies of war worked in Harrell's favor: Many fellow soldiers, more responsible than he, saw combat in Vietnam, but he never set foot outside the United States and managed to avoid danger before being discharged in 1971.

During the same period, Harrell married and divorced a young woman named Pamela Williamson. She was more educated and sophisticated than he was. When they first met, she called him a "gentle giant" and was drawn to his ingenuousness; there seemed to be nothing calculating or scheming about him. In its early months, the prospects for the marriage seemed promising, and in 1969 they had a son, Norman Junior. But Harrell's military duty kept them apart for long periods. On those occasions when they were together, Pamela began noticing a darker side, most often where other men were concerned. His jealousy surfaced in odd ways; for example, he wouldn't allow her to use the self-service pump at a gas station because he thought it put her in a position where the attendant could look at her body. He was also a man of unpredictable moods, and when he was enraged he sometimes put his hands on her. Once he choked her to the point of semiconsciousness, and she had to be taken to the emergency room for treatment. Another time she actually had him arrested for assault. But she didn't pursue the case vigorously, and it went nowhere, though she did have a court impose a stay-away order against him for a time.

The couple remained together until 1971, when he surprised her by filing for divorce. She surprised him even more by not contesting it, and then by not asking for alimony or child support. She didn't want to be beholden to him in any way. As soon as they separated, Pamela had the strong impression that Harrell's divorce filing was a bluff, and he was sorry she'd called him on it. But it was too late. After the divorce, they continued to have contact on account of Norman Junior. These encounters were often stormy. Harrell pressed her repeatedly to let their son live with him. Their disagreement culminated in an incident in which Harrell, without Pamela's knowledge or consent, snatched the boy from a day-care provider for an unauthorized visit. Rather than taking Harrell back to court, Pamela came up with a subtler and shrewder response to his demands for custody of his son: She let him have it, knowing that Harrell wasn't responsible enough to care for a young child. Sure enough, within a month, Harrell had returned the boy to her, and his demands from then on were muted. For a long time after the divorce, Harrell seemed to carry a grudge against her. Twenty-two years later, Pamela would wryly observe that he'd only recently started calling her by her first name again. Before that she'd simply been "bitch."

In the two years after the breakup, Harrell was arrested twice more, for assault and armed robbery. He was convicted of the assault. His 1973 mug shot shows him as a man looking a decade older than his years, with uncombed hair parted low on the side and a baleful stare for the camera. In 1976, he dodged his most serious charge to date: A rape complaint was filed against him by a woman named Jane Higgins. They were atypical charges—Higgins was the mother of Harrell's second son. She chose not to go forward with the case, and Harrell was never actually arrested.

Harrell got a chauffeur's license, which enabled him to leave warehouse work behind, but the pattern of his work history was established early, and for several years he bounced from job to job, even having to go as far away as Paramus, New Jersey, to secure work.

In the mid-1970s, he began dating a woman named Glenda Barr, nicknamed Teri. All in all, Teri's memories of her years with Norman Harrell echoed those of his other women: He was jealous and possessive, had an ugly temper, and didn't know his own strength. And: He could be sweet and gentle, he was close to the daughter she had from another relationship, and he loved children. She would never have imagined him capable of hurting a child.

After Teri came Diane Hawkins. Most of Harrell's family and friends never got to know Diane well, never spent a lot of time with them as a couple, and didn't know how much he was hurt when she turned down his marriage proposal. He decided that Diane was disenchanted with him because he'd lost his job as a truck driver with an excavation company. Whether by conscious effort or coincidence, he would remain in his next job, with a trucking company called Yellow Freight, for longer than ever before. But his newfound employment stability never impressed Diane enough for her to change her mind.

Harrell and Diane continued to maintain relations through the 1980s, and Harrell held on to the hope that Diane would marry him. But in 1985, he met a woman named Gale Tolson. When Gale's old boyfriend found out that Harrell had entered Gale's life, he embarked on a prolonged campaign of intimidation and harassment of her, issuing death threats as well as the inevitable "If I can't have you, no one will." Harrell was a witness to several of the threats and the target of one. Gale became so frightened that she moved in with Harrell at his house on A Street. The matter eventually ended up in court, with the boyfriend pleading guilty in January 1987 to a criminal charge of threatening Gale Tolson. He was placed on probation and ordered by the court to have no further contact with Gale, and she would have no more problems with him.

On February 12, 1987, just a month after the criminal case against the old boyfriend was resolved, Gale gave birth to a son named Torey. Norman Harrell was the presumptive father, but the boy's birth didn't bring his parents closer together. In fact, once the threat posed by the old boyfriend had passed, Gale moved back to her mother's house in suburban Maryland, where she was to live for the next five years.

Gale wasted no time in going against Harrell for child support. On April 29, 1987, barely ten weeks after Torey's birth, she filed a paternity suit and asked for financial support and medical insurance. On May 19, 1987, Harrell was summoned by the court to appear in person at a hearing to be held on June 24, 1987. It would be his first appearance in what would end up being a long court battle.

At the hearing, Harrell demanded a blood test to establish whether he was in fact the father. Though the test indicated that there was an overwhelming probability (99.26 percent) that Harrell was Torey's biological father, Harrell nonetheless demanded a jury trial on the issue of paternity. The trial was held on December 4, 1987, and ended in a verdict as predictable as the blood test result. A judge promptly ordered Harrell to pay Gale $200 a month for Torey's care, beginning January 1, 1988. Harrell just as promptly appealed the order, stating that because of his other financial obligations he was unable to pay Gale more than $150 a month. Harrell specifically claimed to be supporting two other sons already living with him—a lie, since Harrell was neither housing nor supporting his other children. No matter; Harrell's appeal was still denied and the original order upheld. Harrell would have to pay $200 per month to Gale. As an additional indignity, he was ordered to reimburse the state for the $200 cost of the blood test he'd demanded.

But Norman Harrell wasn't going to let the matter rest. He filed another appeal, and on July 25, 1988, Harrell and Gale once again appeared on opposite sides of a courtroom. Harrell reiterated his earlier claim of insufficient financial resources—living expenses for himself and "two sons" and a mortgage payment of $200 per month, against an annual salary of $22,000 to $23,000—and once again challenged the paternity finding. On September 15, 1988, a judge denied Harrell's appeal and imposed, once again, the original order. The $200 monthly obligation was to be considered binding retroactively, dating back to January 1, 1988. Harrell already owed Gale an accrued amount of $1,600.

The dispute was over, at least for now, and Harrell and Tolson picked up the pieces of their relationship. During the months to come, they would again become intimate, although they would continue to live apart. Harrell would also see Diane Hawkins on occasion.

Likewise, Norman Harrell's affiliation with his employer, Yellow Freight, was plagued by contentiousness but persisted. From the point of view of company management, this was a shotgun marriage, with the weapon being the union contract, which protected Harrell from being fired for anything but the most serious violation. And so Harrell and his bosses coexisted for nine long years, each of which was marked by numerous allegations of dereliction and insubordination on Harrell's part. All of his direct superiors shared the same impression of him: He was a lackadaisical worker who didn't take direction well; he only did what he was directly ordered to do and no more; he refused to admit he was ever wrong about anything; and he constantly complained that he was being discriminated against because of his size. Overall, Harrell was among the least productive employees in the company, and he was written up for so many violations that his disciplinary file was hundreds of pages thick.

Harrell's medical file was even thicker. Some in management considered him either the most injury-prone employee they'd ever known or the most malingering. Harrell once claimed to be unable to work for weeks because he'd cut his right index finger while cleaning his windshield wipers.

Still, he was capable of intimidating coworkers and supervisors when he was angry. He was respected among other drivers for his physical strength. He was also well known for his temper, which surfaced more than once when he was confronted about his job performance. No one ever saw him strike another person at work, but some felt the threat was ever present. One of his supervisors, a woman, was particularly cowed by him. One account had Harrell storming into her office, screaming at her, and then throwing a coat rack through a wall. Generally, the managers and other drivers tended to steer clear of him. As far as anyone could tell, he didn't socialize with anyone from work, and when he did talk with his coworkers he avoided anything personal. Later, even his closest friend—or, more accurately, acquaintance—at Yellow Freight could only recall two subjects that Harrell discussed frequently: hunting and child support.

If Harrell was focused intently on child support in early 1991, it was for a good reason. On January 3, the county child support enforcement office, acting on behalf of Gale Tolson, filed with the court a motion to cite Harrell for contempt of court, alleging that he was delinquent in paying over $5,000 in support to Tolson. The court agreed to hear the matter and summoned Harrell to appear on January 24, 1991, or risk being jailed for contempt of the court's 1988 order. On the appointed day, Gale appeared before the judge, but Harrell didn't, and a bench warrant was issued.

On May 29, 1991, Norman Harrell was arrested on the warrant and appeared involuntarily in court. While Gale Tolson didn't attend the hearing, two other women who had a long history with Harrell did: Diane Hawkins and her niece Carlene, who'd come along to offer moral support. They watched Harrell tell the judge that he would have to be thrown in jail before he would ever pay child support. The judge took Harrell up on his offer and had the bailiff take him back into custody. Not surprisingly, the disagreement was resolved within a matter of hours. At Harrell's request, he was taken back to the courtroom. There he pled guilty to contempt of court and received a suspended sentence and one year probation. More important, as far as plaintiff Gale Tolson was concerned, was the judge's ruling on support payments. From then on, the matter wouldn't be left in Harrell's hands; a lien was placed against his wages and the amount of $200 would be deducted automatically and sent to Gale directly by the county.

Harrell had secured his freedom by convincing the judge that he was contrite about his past sins, but it had all been a show. Defiant as ever, he strode straight from the courtroom to the clerk's office and filed a motion of his own, naming Gale Tolson as respondent and seeking a regular schedule of visitation. Her written response not only disparaged Harrell's parenting skills but hinted at deeper, more ominous issues between the two of them: "Our relationship has not been one where I visit his house under any circumstances." The judge reading these exchanges in December 1991 could only conclude that these were incompatible people, incapable of engaging in the ordinary give-and-take of child rearing.

Just nine months later, in September 1992, Norman Harrell and Gale Tolson became man and wife.

There was no elaborate wedding; some of Harrell's friends were unaware he'd gotten married until they noticed him wearing a large gold band studded with small rhinestones. This was how Deborah Courtney, mutual friend of Harrell and Diane Hawkins, found out about it, months later. Deborah teased him when she saw the wedding ring: "You know, Danky," she said, "I still think you never got over Diane." Harrell exploded. "If that was so," he said, "I wouldn't have gotten married." "Besides," he said, "now I'm all set up to take custody of Rock from Diane. She doesn't need that stress right now." Deborah Courtney listened for Harrell to express any affection for his new bride, but he never did. To others, too, he was just as unemotive, saying to one acquaintance with a shrug, "I had to get married to someone, didn't I?" But whatever Harrell's motives were for embarking on a second marriage, outward signs indicated that he and Gale were going to try to make it work. Gale moved into Harrell's residence on A Street in autumn 1992, and soon set about redecorating it.

Only one piece of business remained before the reconciliation was complete: Gale's withdrawal of her child support claim against Harrell. But as 1993 began with Harrell's forty-fourth birthday, the case was still pending.

Gale Tolson had been married to Norman Harrell for only eight months when he was arrested for the murders of Diane Hawkins and

Katrina Harris. The government's investigators wouldn't be privy to her thoughts in the aftermath of her husband's arrest. People who knew her said she was committed to support him to the end.

If so, she joined others among his family and associates whose voices were raised in united chorus: He couldn't have done this; he's not capable of such violence; he isn't clever enough to cover his tracks as the murderer did. On many details in Harrell's life they were stingy with information. Even as simple a matter as finding out the identity of the woman in the pictures on Harrell's bedroom dresser—the ones that had been studiously cropped to mimic decapitation—proved to be impossible. All anyone could say was that it wasn't Diane—the skin tone and the body type didn't match—but my other questions also remained unresolved. For that matter, no one could say for sure that it was Norman—rather than, say, Gale—who'd taken scissors to the pictures. But on one point they were expansive: The Norman Harrell they knew may have been many things, but he was no killer.

HIS PARENTS WERE long gone, his family circumspect about his childhood. He'd given no indication that he'd be using an insanity defense in my case; maybe he just didn't want any doctor peering down the corridors of his psyche. So I looked to other sources. I read books about domestic murder, about serial killers, trying to get a clue. I read one book about mutilators. The book included a montage of photographs of the mutilators and the mutilated. I found I wasn't able to tell which was which without looking at the captions.

I went back and forth, checking myself, checking the case: Let's assume he didn't do it, then who else did, and why does so much of the evidence point toward him, in an amazing array of coincidences? Well, let's assume he did. If this was done by Norman Harrell—a man who had a weird bent on child support, some bubbling hostility toward women, but no prior history of violence like this—could it just as easily have been done by anyone? When I first took the case, he'd looked normal, ordinary. By a reasonable measure, it seemed well within the range of the ordinary to be a conversational bully, an indifferent worker, an eccentric obsessor. Talk about an obsessor—I was one myself, obsessed with *him*. If Norman Harrell's traits, taken on their own, qualified as suspicious in the context of a double homicide, the police had their work cut out for them in eliminating all the suspects.

I finally realized that I was getting it all backward.

The killers among us don't walk about like Beelzebub in a horror movie, with dragging tail and dripping fangs. They don't lead with their evil; they lead with their blandness and keep their evil hidden. How many times have we seen it on the news? The police go into a house and find a guy in the basement sitting next to a headless corpse. Neighbors are interviewed, and one by one they say, "He was very quiet" and "He kept to himself." Why? Because the guy *was* quiet, and he *did* keep to himself; he never let the world get a peek at the anger and fear and insecurity and rage and who knows what else that was searing his gut. Hannah Arendt got it right when she looked at the everyday grayness of the executors of the Holocaust and said they embodied the banality of evil.

All that matters are the results.

Assume, again, that Norman Harrell did these murders. He didn't do them because he was evil. He was evil because he did them.

A PROSECUTOR CAN never go wrong by going back to basics: the tangible evidence, the objects seized from the crime scene or the suspect's house, the things you can touch and feel and imagine in the hands of predator or prey. One day in August 1993, I asked an officer to bring to me all the evidence recovered in the case so far, and we would go through it, piece by piece. What if Norman Harrell, like so many more careless killers before him, had left something of himself behind on this murder scene—a button from a favorite shirt, a distinctive key chain, or some such—and we'd just missed it?

This wasn't a project for the squeamish. The first objects out of the box were the clothes Diane and Katrina were wearing when they were killed. They were folded in transparent plastic bags with twist ties that ensured the smell of death remained intact, but the once-crimson bloodstains they bore were now a faded brown. For all their emotional impact—and it had to be remembered that these were the last items of clothing Katrina and Diane had chosen to wear, at a time when they were blissfully unaware of what was going to happen to them—they apparently had little or no forensic significance. They had been examined for foreign hair, fibers, and blood; none had been found. The same was true of all of the objects seized from the Hawkins house: the sheet from the living room sofa and pillow cases from the back bedroom, which were blood-smeared but otherwise unremarkable; the knives that were recovered from the kitchen and appeared unstained to the naked eye; the gun that had been under Diane Hawkins's mattress and seemed to have no relevance to the case.

In separate parts of the box were two bags of articles the police had taken from Norman Harrell's truck and house on the morning of May 26. Some of the items appeared to have been haphazardly chosen for seizure: a ring and spare change from the truck, a set of keys and a clear plastic bag from the house. Nothing in that package looked particularly important. I lingered over the bag of evidence recovered from the Ford truck, having forgotten for the moment that it didn't include Harrell's blood-speckled cooler, the dashboard cutting, and the armrest; all of those items were undergoing further DNA analysis at the FBI laboratory.

We were about to reseal the box when I noticed a book wedged against the side.

It was entitled *Maryland Hunter Safety Student Handbook,* and it bore the insignia of the Maryland Natural Resources Police. Above the title was the name "Norman Harrell" pencil-written in script. Detective Stanton had seen the book in Harrell's bedroom closet and picked it up, thinking that it would confirm that Harrell was a hunter and had access to heavy cutting weaponry of the type used in the murders. On the book's cover was an illustration of a happy family on a hunting trip: a father with his young son and daughter, all dressed in outdoor gear and toting rifles. On page four was a table of contents, listing chapters headed "Hunter Responsibility," "Firearms and Bowhunting," "Survival and First Aid," and "Game Care and Wildlife Identification." Under the last chapter was a subchapter: "Game Care in the Field." I'd never hunted and had no interest in starting. But I had a vague sense of what "game care in the field" entailed and had a thought that made me turn to that section, which began on page fifty-eight.

Down the right side of the page ran a series of drawings diagramming the skinning of a dead squirrel. To the left was text:

> Just how tasty your venison and other wild game will be depends almost entirely on the field care you give the animal after it has been killed. Dirt, heat and moisture are the three main causes of meat spoilage.
>
> To insure returning home with good table meat, proper equipment to combat the heat, moisture and dirt is necessary. Game care equipment must be carried into the field, so plan your list carefully before your hunting trip begins.

Suggestions were provided as to what equipment was necessary:

> Basic gear includes a belt or folding saw, skinning knife, 10 or more feet of strong cord or rope, a whetstone, and a light cloth bag. Many types of hunting knives are on the market. However, a butcher's skinning knife is one of the best. It can be used in dressing the animal and is most efficient for skinning.

I looked again at the drawing of the squirrel on the bottom right corner of the page. There was a gaping hole in its midsection, and its entrails were lying to its side. I turned to page sixty, headed "Field Dressing":

> The best way to get most of the blood out of the carcass is by prompt field dressing. This will cut all of the major blood vessels and permit the flow of blood. In field dressing big game, the animal should be hung up, or positioned on a slope with the head up. The first cut is made by slitting the skin and belly muscle tissue, beginning at the breast bone and cutting to the pelvis. It should be done slowly and with care.

The text was accompanied by three diagrams that showed a man straddling a deer and cutting into its midsection with a small knife:

> The heart and lungs lie within the chest cavity. There are two ways to enter the chest cavity. Some hunters prefer to cut around the diaphragm close to the ribs and others prefer to open the chest by cutting through the breast bone. Sever the windpipe and esophagus as far up in the throat as possible.

Here, a diagram showed the hunter reaching into the deer's midsection with his right hand.

> The carcass can now be rolled onto its side so the entrails can be removed. In order to pull out the heart, liver and lungs it is necessary to reach deep inside the chest cavity. Don't be squeamish, just roll up your sleeves and get to it. Most of the entrails will pull away without difficulty but may require a bit of cutting at the back. Drain all blood from the cavity.
>
> The heart and liver are excellent eating and should be washed and placed in a plastic bag for carrying.

I'd read enough. Curtis Lancaster's photographs of the body of Diane Hawkins came to mind: on her back, with a wound around her throat, a gaping hole in her gut, her insides spilling onto her dining room floor. And Katrina Harris: also on her back, heart missing. Here was a how-to manual, the property of Norman Harrell, found in the man's bedroom, describing the same methods for skinning hunted prey.

Norman Harrell had left something of himself on the murder scene, after all. The bodies bore his mark, just as surely as if he'd carved his own signature into them.

CHAPTER 6

THE HARRELL CASE WAS ALL-CONSUMING. It could easily have filled all of my work hours for weeks on end. But I didn't have the luxury of devoting all my efforts to only one case. Among those that occupied the balance of my time in the summer of 1993 were two other murders that, coincidentally, had arisen out of passions engendered in the placid environs of River Terrace. For reasons that wouldn't be completely clear until much later, the name of Reco Hawkins would be raised in connection with these deaths, too.

The first to die was a young man named Michael Graham.

From an early age he sold crack cocaine on the streets of River Terrace with the single-mindedness of a business school graduate. As a juvenile he served other dealers as a lookout, sneaking around corners to watch out for the "rollers," the police. Before long he was a runner—the first contact with buyers, directing or taking them to a dealer—and then a juggler, shuttling drugs and money back and forth. Michael Graham was a good enough go-between that he was given more responsibility, moving more dope and maneuvering others around with the skill of a born leader. He started looking outside his neighborhood for his own sources, and from the contacts he made, he began to develop his own business.

Crack dealers in D.C. enjoyed a sellers' market, and Graham's business thrived. River Terrace had a small but faithful band of addicts, and Graham brought in more customers from outside. The business featured a staff of youthful runners and lookouts supervised by a core of lieutenants named Harvey Newman, Chauncey Turner, Lloyd Johnson, and a young comer named Andre Brown. By his early twenties, Graham was a man of swaggering, athletic physique and commanding insolence, inspiring respect and even fear among those who worked under him or knew of him. He was a hip-hop Gatsby with vague rumors of past violence attached to him. Some said he'd killed a man once, but nobody had been there to see it. Graham's manner and look seemed to confirm the worst. His persona helped him reach the measure of true success in his profession: By 1992 he was able to keep himself at arm's length from the day-to-day transactions of the business.

Hand-to-hand drug sales were handled by his minions, and he had different agreements with each of them, depending on how close he was to them. To members of his inner circle, he distributed supply in exchange for a cut of the revenue. He dealt with others as if they were independent contractors, taking more money from them up front but not demanding a kickback. This was Graham's arrangement with Charles Turner, brother of his lieutenant Chauncey, and with Reco Hawkins, son of Diane.

Graham was also able now to distance himself from the brutality that was a necessary evil in his line of work: preserving his territory, intimidating rival dealers, going after deadbeat "pipeheads" for back debts. For this kind of dirty work he looked to Andre Brown. Brown was small and stocky, with a low forehead, a trace of peach fuzz on his upper lip, and lazy eyes that looked as innocent as Bambi's. But his appearance belied his true nature. Brown was Graham's enforcer: too young to drive but not too young to know how to wield a gun. By age sixteen he was a grand master of street violence, a deft manipulator, a plotter of elaborate intrigues which he then acted on with swift cruelty. There was nothing in his life that he didn't regard with callous disdain, even those things that a normal person would cherish: His nickname for his infant son was Little Killer. With Andre Brown by his side, Michael Graham could move about in a cocoon of safety, at least as long as he kept Andre happy. And so he took pains to do just that, taking him under his wing, treating him like family, even introducing him to friends as his flesh-and-blood cousin.

But the benefits Graham was enjoying didn't go unnoticed by Andre and the others. Like them, Graham was a young man with a limited education and no legitimate job prospects. Unlike them, he headed up a drug business that brought him cash wealth with little risk. Graham was far from the action when his underlings hit the street, jeopardizing their freedom at the hands of the police and their lives at the hands of street robbers who knew they could be shaken down and never report the crime. All of them—Harvey, Chauncey, Lloyd, and Andre—were doing well. They were all making far more money than they ever could have by doing something legal. But Michael Graham's riches and lifestyle set him apart, and his friends began to resent him for it.

Graham, his girlfriend, Eloise Hill, and their young son divided their time between River Terrace and an apartment in a fashionable area in Southwest D.C. far removed from his home turf in every way. Eloise was two years older and more worldly than Michael, and she decorated the apartment in the lavish style of a young mogul. The apartment became Graham's headquarters, containing the safe in which he secured the thousands of dollars worth of rock cocaine he was getting from his supplier and the thousands of dollars in cash he was getting from the sales. The crack and the currency never stayed long in the safe. Graham made sure to get the drugs to River Terrace as soon as they came in and was just as quick to spend the profits.

But during its brief residency in the safe's steel sanctuary, the money made a gaudy showing: crisp, shiny twenties, fifties, and hundreds, green and fresh as a country club fairway, neatly stacked in foot-high piles. Graham's closet was a museum celebrating ill-gotten gain: dozens of pairs of shoes and more shirts and sweaters and leather coats than the eye could take in. Graham could never wear them all, never even took the store tags off of most of them. Sitting among them were a .25-caliber pistol and Mac-10 semiautomatic firearm, poised as if waiting to be put to use to protect them.

Graham came to recognize how his wealth was causing a rift between him and his friends. He moved to fill the gap with generosity, feverishly spreading gifts, loans, and favors among his subordinates. Andre Brown took full advantage, borrowing $8,000 from him to put toward the purchase of a $30,000 Acura that he would someday be able to drive legally if he took the time to get a license. But it wasn't enough for Graham's young protégé, who looked at everything his mentor had and wanted more for himself.

As Christmas 1992 approached, Brown began plotting to kill Michael Graham.

The murder of Graham wouldn't be easily executed. Earlier in the year, he'd been shot by a rival, and since then he carried a gun wherever he went. He also spent more time with his girlfriend and his son and less time in situations where he might be vulnerable. When he did go out to a club, he always traveled with his crew. Andre Brown knew he'd never be able to catch Graham by himself.

The only solution was to turn Graham's friends against him, playing on their lust for a bigger piece of Graham's business and the money it would bring them. Working on them for weeks, honing in on Harvey Newman and Chauncey Turner, Brown proceeded to do just that, until finally he wore them down, stoking their sense that for as long as Michael Graham was alive they would have to settle for second best. It was no great challenge for Andre Brown to persuade the likes of Newman and Turner to join in heart-stirring violence for financial gain. To paraphrase the old saying: In the kingdom of the greedy, stupid, and weak, the cruel and conniving man is king.

A few days before Christmas 1992, Brown gathered Turner and Newman at Chauncey Turner's house. Chauncey's brother Chuck was in and out of the room but never joined in the meeting. He eventually left to visit a baby he'd fathered by a girl who was a blood relative to River Terrace resident Diane Hawkins. The plan was simple: They'd kidnap Michael Graham, torture him to get him to reveal his secret stash of wealth, then kill him and dump his body. They went to a nearby mall and mixed with holiday shoppers as they stocked up on the implements of their coup: shovels, a flashlight, and an ice pick, their chosen weapon of torture.

On December 26, Graham accepted Brown's invitation to go out to a club. But first he had to tend to some unfinished business: moving $50,000 in crack cocaine from River Terrace to the Southwest apartment, where it would go into his safe with the cash. Graham called Eloise, and she drove over to River Terrace to take care of it, carrying the two kilos of crack in the backseat next to their five-year-old son.

Graham and his friends then went to the Eastside Club, a gang hangout known for regular melees and a clientele that was armed to the teeth. Brown felt at home here. They left the club about 2:00 A.M. and piled into Chauncey Turner's car. The plan called for Graham to be killed on the way to River Terrace, but Graham complicated matters. Unexpectedly, he directed Turner over the line into Maryland to visit a girl named Robbin Lyons, whom he'd recently started seeing behind Eloise's back. The stop wasn't part of the script, and Brown was dismayed that an outsider would see him and the others in Graham's company so soon before they intended to kill him. After a brief visit with the girl they left to drive back to D.C. It was now about 3:00 A.M. on December 27.

On the ride back into town, Graham was sitting in the front

passenger seat, Brown directly behind. Graham had drunk too much and began to nod off. Prodded by Brown, Newman disarmed Graham by sliding Graham's gun out of his coat, and Brown then grabbed Graham by the neck, yanked him into the backseat, and shot him in the head and body with the gun Brown always carried. Graham died almost instantly, though Brown didn't know it at first; he duct-taped Graham and slapped him repeatedly, berating him for "faking it," before realizing that he was beating a corpse.

In short order, the rest of the plan came to fruition. Brown took Graham's keys from his coat, told Chauncey Turner to stop, and then ordered him and Newman to help him dump the body into a trash can (after Brown had pulled Graham's pants around his ankles as a final show of disrespect). After that he had Turner drive to Turner's house, where another car was picked up; told Turner to drive the bloodstained car to a remote location in Maryland, where it was set afire; then had Turner drive him back in the other car to Turner's house, where Brown calmly made a telephone call to a girl he knew so as to establish an alibi for the time when the car would be observed ablaze. In a matter of hours, Brown and Turner would enter Graham's apartment with Graham's key, steal and empty the safe of its cocaine and money, then bury it in marshy land by the Potomac, all without being seen or leaving a fingerprint.

Graham's body wasn't discovered until almost two days after the murder. MPD homicide canvassed Graham's neighborhood and learned who his associates were, and within hours Brown, Turner, and Newman were at headquarters, being questioned about what they knew about Graham's death. They all stuck close to Brown's concocted story: that they'd last seen Graham at about 11:00 P.M. on the night when they were all together in River Terrace. They weren't particularly concerned that anyone at the Eastside Club could contradict them—the club wasn't exactly a spawning ground of cooperative government witnesses. But one of the detectives mentioned a name that did raise a problem: Robbin Lyons, the girl Graham had visited in Maryland shortly before the murder.

Brown didn't know exactly where Robbin Lyons lived. Graham had been the one who gave directions to her apartment; none of the others knew the area. Only one person in Brown's circle would know: Lloyd Johnson, who'd worked for Graham and had visited Lyons with Graham in the past. Lloyd Johnson had been too loyal to Graham for Brown to consider approaching him with the idea of killing Graham. Now, predictably, Johnson was devastated by Graham's murder, believing it to be the work of drug rivals.

Brown went to Graham's mother's house at River Terrace, ostensibly to console the family, but knowing that Lloyd Johnson and others in Graham's crew would be there. Brown loudly proclaimed that he thought Mike's new "bitch" must have set him up. Eloise didn't need to be prodded to believe the story; just days earlier she'd caught Graham running around with this other girl, and now he'd turned up dead. Brown spun out his theory so convincingly that his listeners became enraged. Brown sidled over to Johnson: You know where Robbin lives; let's go out there. It was just about midnight when Brown, Turner, Newman, and Johnson struck out for Landover, Maryland. Johnson knocked on Lyons's door. When she opened it Brown rushed in, stabbing her twelve times and then shooting her twice in the head for making too much noise. The only person outside the crew—Brown's now, not Graham's—who might have been able to hurt them was now dead.

ANDRE BROWN'S PLAN might have succeeded if he'd been able to commandeer three other Andre Browns to help him execute it. But the very qualities that made Brown's partners bend to his will were the same that made them susceptible to police pressure. When no other leads implicating others outside River Terrace surfaced, MPD homicide decided to turn up the heat on Graham's associates. Within weeks, detectives had it all figured out.

In February 1993, MPD homicide arrested Andre Brown for the murder of Michael Graham, and I took over the case. The arrest warrant, which was presented to Brown when he was apprehended and brought to court, was based primarily on the word of a single witness, identified only as "W-1," who claimed to have heard of the plot of Brown and his confederates to kill Graham. Within weeks, Chauncey Turner and Harvey Newman would also be arrested for the Graham murder, and Lloyd Johnson for his part in the Lyons murder.

Andre Brown spent the time awaiting trial trying to figure out who in River Terrace had given him up and planning how he was going to get his revenge.

ON THE MORNING of Thursday, September 21, 1993, I prepared to go into the house where Diane Hawkins and Katrina Harris had been killed.

I'd be joining three FBI technicians whose task was to read the patterns left by the life blood of the victims on the walls and floors of their home. They were the experts; I'd be peering over the shoulders of scientists as they went about their work.

When I'd first heard about blood pattern analysis a few months before, it had sounded bogus to me. How could blood's random markings, spread about a crime scene as if by a child's spin-art toy, tell us anything about a murder? I did some research and became a believer. Because it's thicker than other liquids, blood behaves more predictably when it strikes a surface. Dripping straight down from a wound or a stationary object onto a flat surface, it creates a circular stain. Being cast from a wound or an object in motion—a fleeing victim, a plunging knife—it creates an oblong stain. Moreover, the speed of the motion can be determined from the length of the oblong, the direction from its shape. The angle of impact of blood on a surface can be calculated by a trigonometrical formula; knowing the angle, one can determine the height of the source of the blood and infer whether a victim was, say, standing or prone when struck. Blood being transferred by contact with a surface creates a pattern different from the one it makes when it's cast or dropped on the same surface. A pattern of contact stains can chart the progress of a victim or a bloodstained assailant through, say, the rooms of a house. Blood is highly durable and can be typed even when dry; determining whose blood was left in what areas of a crime scene can establish the sequence of a particular series of events.

Everything in a murder mystery is connected with everything else. The *how* of this case—who was killed first—was connected with the *why*. All of the motive evidence that pointed to Harrell related to his relationship with Diane Hawkins, not with Katrina Harris. Presumably, he would have killed Diane first and attacked Trina for other reasons: Maybe she saw her mother's murder and had to be silenced. If bloodstain analysis were to suggest that Katrina was the first victim and her mother the second, it might make me think again about the *why*—and then once again about the *who*.

The Hawkins house had been sealed since the murders. When 3461 was last lived in, the spring air had carried traces of the coming summer; the calendar now said summer was over and a bracing breeze confirmed it. I stood at curbside under sullen skies and stared at the house we were about to enter, looking up at it as if it might let me in on what it knew.

My main job that morning would be simple: to stay out of the way. One of the FBI experts was Robert Spalding, the leading blood-pattern authority. I trailed behind him at a respectable distance as he proceeded methodically through the house, photographing and measuring each stain, making notes that he would later memorialize in his formal report. We started in the kitchen, at the back door.

In the kitchen of the residence there is blood around the knob and on the adjacent frame of the rear-entry door. The stains are contact-type stains. No blood is noted on the screen door outside. Sufficient volume of blood is transferred to allow draining of the blood down the door.

I'd thought the house might carry the stench of death, but it didn't—only the musty odor of a space kept shut through sweltering summer heat. Like Spalding, I noted the blood on the doorknob and frame. Unlike him, I didn't pause to think about where it came from but moved on to the kitchen.

Blood is present on the doors of the kitchen cabinet above the counter with the dish drainer and below on the counter itself. The blood on the cabinet doors is of a contact nature. The stain on the counter apparently was formed by a simple dropping action where a single drop of blood fell vertically to form a single round spot on the counter.

Vertical drop-type stains are also on the floor of the kitchen at the entry doorway from the dining room. Also observed on the kitchen floor are three partial footwear impressions, to be preserved for possible future comparison with any footwear which might be recovered.

Time and heat and humidity had drained the color from the blood scattered around the room. It had been captured at peak crimson by the crime scene photographs that were taken just hours after it had burst from bodies still in the flush of life. Now the drops and stains appeared dark brown or even black. They had an aura of permanence. In the sink and on the drainboard sat the dishes from what had probably been the very last meal eaten here.

I took two or three steps to cross the room, almost tripping over pots and pans that had been left out on the floor because there was nowhere else to put them. In front of me to the left was the door leading downstairs, only a few feet from the sink. To the right was an olive green refrigerator dotted with magnetized note boards and pictures, including a small school portrait of Katrina Harris.

I stepped around a square on the linoleum floor, inches from the threshold leading to the dining room. The square was marked with police tape. The analysts had seen what they thought might be a bloody footprint on it. As hard as I looked, I had no idea what they were talking about. All I saw were faint smudges that, to my eye, could just as easily have been a part of the floor pattern. They wanted to save the square for analysis; if the smudges were a footprint, they'd have lab technicians compare the pattern to shoes and boots the police had recovered from Harrell's truck. We had no other choice than to take up an entire section of the floor. We called in some firefighters for help, and they arrived with power tools to pry up the flooring. The drills kicked up an enveloping smoke cloud that spread throughout the house and followed us from room to room.

Moving into the dining room, bloodstains in the immediate area of where the victim was include an impact spatter pattern on the wall near where the victim's left leg was resting. Stains in this pattern range in size from fine to medium and are generally below two feet six inches from the floor. Many of the stains indicate a directionality downward and those near the top of the pattern indicate a nearly ninety-degree impact of the blood on the wall. Above this stain pattern is a light, smeared contact pattern, which exhibits irregular movement by the object which deposited the blood on the wall.

In the dining room, I saw a child's hobby horse, standing still on corroding springs. On the faded turquoise rug were two black splotches, one larger than the other. Here had lain Diane Hawkins. I thought back to the crime scene photographs. The smaller splotch appeared to be where her head had been, the other at her midsection. Sitting on top of the smaller stain was a low plastic table scaled down for a child. On either side of the lower stain was a small plastic rabbit and an old lottery ticket.

> *On the door frame and wall above the location of the victim's head and just over six feet above the floor is a contact stain with an adjacent cast off stain pattern which extends to the north wall with small spots vertically impacting that wall. This stain pattern indicates a bloody object contacted the door frame with enough force to cast off blood to hit the west and north walls. The specific identity of this object is not indicated.*
>
> *Significantly absent in the area surrounding the location of the victim is impact spatter on the white table, the underside of this table, and on the walls in the corner.*

Spalding told me that the stain at the top of the entranceway was a "contact stain." Did the killer steady himself with a bloody hand in the midst of the attack? Did the height of the stain suggest the height of the killer? Other stains, what looked to be hundreds of drops, were at a low level on the walls around the area where Diane Hawkins's body had been outstretched. I asked Spalding what it all meant.

"Too early to tell," he said, preoccupied with his camera work, "but it looks like the woman wasn't lying flat when she was being attacked." He pointed to the height of the drops. "She was eviscerated while lying down, but she stayed up for a very long time, through a great deal of stabbing and hitting."

"Doing what?"

"Probably just trying to stay alive."

The living room is in some disarray, with the couch, a table, and a lamp being overturned and/or lying on the floor. The couch bears contact bloodstains. There are stains typical of impact spatter on the curtain behind the couch. One of the stains on the front of the couch exhibits a drain track showing that at the time it was made, the couch was upright. Blood was also noted on the light-switch plate at the bottom of the stairs, on the inside of the front door around the knob, and on the screen door outside.

Two giant steps took me through the dining room into the living room. Before this moment, I'd only seen the rooms in two-dimensional photographs. Ordinarily, a photo tends to flatten and reduce an interior space; here, reality was even smaller than it had been depicted. On the floor to my left were the table and lamp that had been upended during the murders, still sitting where the police first saw them. In front of me was the sofa, which was also toppled over but was now upright. Near the sofa was a small table. On the table was the photograph of Katrina Harris and the Mother's Day card she gave Diane a few weeks before the murders. Looming above was a hanging plant, now dead and disintegrating.

One of the cushions from the sofa was propped up against the television. Spalding picked it up and examined a stain that trailed down the cushion's edge. He replaced the cushion in the open space on the sofa and then rotated it until the stain on the edge matched a stain on the sofa's front section: almost a perfect fit. I watched as he pushed hard on the cushion and released, then pushed hard and released again. Out came the camera and the tape measure as Spalding moved behind the sofa and scrutinized an array of dried droplets on the white curtains.

"What do you see?" I asked.

"It all started on the sofa," he replied after several seconds, not looking up. "The killer hit her more than once: That's where the spray on the curtains came from. She was bleeding a lot: That's the contact stain on the sofa."

> *An envelope on the landing two steps up from the living room floor bears two bloodstains, which exhibit a directionality to indicate when they hit the envelope, the drops were moving towards the wall to one's right. Contact stains with enough volume to allow draining are present on the iron railing at the foot of the stairs and at the top of the stairs in the second-floor hall. Present on the west wall going up the stairs is a cast-off pattern, which exhibits an upward movement of blood.*

This was the same staircase Mike Harwood climbed in the first moments of May 26, oblivious in the semidarkness to the trail of blood drops to his right. Even with the room well lit, the stains were hard to see against the royal blue walls. They were more easily seen at step level, where the white molding made for a better background. The stairs were carpeted, but frequent footfall had rubbed the fabric threadbare and exposed each step's hardwood edge. Over the course of an hour, Bob Spalding's knees touched every step as he photographed the many droplets speckled across the walls and molding. I wondered how they got there, whether they were cast off from a victim's wounds or a murderer's bloody hands, but Spalding was too focused on his work for me to bother him for a theory.

At the top of the staircase was a bathroom, the same one Harwood was using when he heard Kiki crying. I turned and started toward the front bedroom. To my right was a bedroom with bunk beds; I continued on. I thought: Before the murders, Katrina Harris was asleep in this bedroom. She was found dead in her mother's. As I walked toward Diane Hawkins's room, crossing the threshold and moving around the bed in the middle of the room, I was now retracing Trina's steps.

How many times as a young girl had she come down this same hall, startled out of sleep and seeking solace from her mother, blanket and bear in hand, leaving behind a nightmare or maybe an imaginary monster beneath her bed?

The northeast bedroom is in a state of disarray, and large bloodstains consisting of spatter, contact smears, and a linear smear pattern are present on the east wall between the bed and a large Huggies disposable diapers box. Original photographs depicted the victim, Katrina Harris, supine, with her head against the wall at the base of this pattern. Pooling and saturating bloodstains are visible on the carpet beneath where the body was positioned. Impact spatter peripheral to the main pattern indicates that impact(s) to a blood source occurred approximately twelve to eighteen inches from the floor and close to the east wall between the bed and the diaper box.

Linear and generally parallel light blood contact smears are present on the wall above the victim's head.

Here is where it all ended.

This wasn't her fight. She had had no part in the private animosities of her mother and Harrell. All she did was answer her mother's screams, and here is where she fell.

I'd had enough.

But as I backed out of the room, I had to ask Bob Spalding a final question about the four long smears on the wall above where Trina had been found—they didn't make sense to me. It appeared from the other stains that she was close to the floor when she was attacked. *What was it that left these stains a full four or five feet above floor level?*

"Let me show you something," Spalding said, taking one of my hands and measuring the width of one of my fingers. Without a word, he then held the tape measure against each of the stains. They were about the same width as my finger.

"She had her back to him while he was stabbing her, and all she could do was to claw at the wall with bloody fingers."

I WASN'T SURPRISED when the first rumors about the Eads Street murders reached me: that they had to have been connected to drugs, that they somehow went back to Reco's doings, even that Diane and Katrina themselves might have had suspicious alliances.

The fact is, most of Washington's violent crimes are committed by black offenders against black victims, and many are drug related. So pervasive are drug murders in D.C. that my fellow prosecutors and I look for a drug connection in just about every case. There also was something about the gruesome nature of these particular crimes that almost invited greater speculation. For some, they were too horrific to be attributed to a seemingly ordinary workingman approaching middle age; better to put them on nameless figures in an underworld where violent excess was more the norm.

A conspiracy theorist could find encouragement in a few facts. What about that loaded gun that police had found between the mattress and box spring of the bed in the room where Katrina was found? Or the fact that, on the night of the murders, the 911 caller told police that the bodies had been discovered "in the house you've been watching for some time"? Or that the name *Reco* was written above Trina's body? Did she scrawl it as her killer bore in on her? Was it left there by enemies of Reco sending a message to him after killing his family members?

Conspiracy theories are usually wrong and sometimes downright irrational, but I couldn't ignore the questions and still go home at night thinking I'd done my job honestly.

At some stage in an investigation, before asking a grand jury to indict a defendant or a trial jury to convict him, a prosecutor has to have an epiphany, a moment when he becomes absolutely convinced of the defendant's moral culpability. In this case, I'd had my epiphany. I had an abiding belief that Norman Harrell had gutted two innocent people as if they were animals and taken a girl's heart, and I hated him for it. It was no longer possible for me to look at him with dispassion in the face of the blood in his truck, the testimony of Deborah Courtney, the accounts of the victims' family, and the black-and-white text of the hunting manual.

But moral culpability is different from legal guilt. Every defendant, even the most unappealing, is entitled to due process under law. I had an obligation to be just as vigilant as before in following up on evidence that Harrell could use in his defense—not an easy task, but a necessary one.

In just a few weeks, we shook down River Terrace. We talked to anyone who might know of a drug link to the murders. We found nothing—nothing, that is, except what we already knew, which was that Reco Hawkins had sold drugs before the murders and used poor judgment in choosing some of his friends. Did he owe anyone money for drug debts? Did he carry a gun or any other weapon? If so, had he ever used it against anyone? The answers we received convinced me that the murders had had nothing to do with Reco Hawkins. But I still needed to face the young man himself.

In the first days following the murders, he'd stayed at the house of his friend Eric Fisher right there in River Terrace. Every night he'd slept with the lights on; every day, he'd moved about in the neighborhood as he always had. Now he was staying with family, and I reached him by phone on the first try. He wasn't exactly acting as if he felt endangered by killers on the loose. He agreed to come in and speak with me. He was a rangy young man with braided hair, high cheekbones, and impenetrable eyes with a slight Asian cast. In a family full of broad faces and open features, he stood out. In the early days of the investigation he'd talked to us about Harrell. Now he had to talk about himself.

He didn't shy away from any of my questions. Yes, he'd sold drugs. He'd sold them in his neighborhood, where he grew up, where his mother, his younger brother, his younger sister, and his baby sister lived—right across the street from his house, in fact, though never from inside it. No, none of his family was involved with him; he worked alone. "I was never no high roller," he said. I eyed him up and down: T-shirt, worn baggy jeans, and standard-issue playground Nikes—not the look of someone who was living large.

I asked him, "Why did you ever start dealing dope?" The question hung in the air for a moment before he spoke.

"It's not like all that," he murmured. "You've been in our house; you saw how we were living. It's been a long time since we had much money coming in, and just about all of that went for Trina and Rock and the baby. I got no job and nothing's coming up. Anything I got from hustling just went to my food, basically. That's just the way it was."

Maybe I was naive, but I believed him. What he said was what we heard from other sources. He was a small-timer, not turning over the volume to draw fire from anybody. The only imponderable was what he'd make of his life. Other family members had told me he was racked with guilt and tormented by questions after the murders: *Why didn't I stay? Wouldn't they still be alive?* He wasn't being fair to himself—it wasn't as if Harrell had been telegraphing his intentions as he sat in Diane's living room that night—but the fact that Reco's first instinct involved self-reflection spoke of a strong conscience, which, I suspected, would stand him in good stead.

As for the gun under the mattress, it belonged to one of the friends of Reco who went into the house with him on the night of the murders; the friend took it with him for protection but panicked and stashed it under the bed when the police rushed into the house. We interviewed the 911 caller. She offered nothing solid to support her opinion that Diane Hawkins's house was being used for drug dealing, only that "people came and went all the time." MPD narcotics investigators in the area contradicted her claim that the Hawkins house had been under police surveillance. As for the word *Reco* on the bedroom wall, an innocent explanation surfaced: Years before, it had been neatly inscribed in pencil by a young boy learning to write his own name.

In the end, I was satisfied that there was nothing to the rumors that the murders had been drug related. But I knew the matter wasn't closed. There were still four people that we couldn't talk with, people who knew more than anyone about drug dealing in River Terrace. All four were beyond our reach. They'd been indicted for murder and were sitting in jail, represented by lawyers, keeping mum and awaiting trial.

Their names were Andre Brown, Chauncey Turner, Harvey Newman, and Lloyd Johnson.

CHAPTER 7

The attack on Diane Hawkins was likely to have begun on or in the vicinity of the couch in the living room, with her being beaten and significant bleeding taking place to stain the couch in various locations. The violence of this activity is indicated by the overturned furniture.

I was meeting with Bob Spalding in a windowless forensic laboratory room. In front of us were the FBI's reports on the patterns and DNA compositions of the bloodstains found in Diane Hawkins's house.

We began with basics. I asked him: "How can you be so sure that the assault on Diane began in the living room and ended in the dining room?"

"Well, let's look at the photos that the police took on the night the bodies were found. They show that the body ended up on the dining room floor. Now if we go to the photos that I took at the house later, they show several things. First, there's blood on the living room sofa and the curtains behind it. Second, there's much less bloodstaining in that part of the house than on the dining room floor, where the body was found. Third, there's no blood trail between the living room and the dining room. And fourth, there's human flesh and tissue visible around the body in the dining room but none in the living room."

"All of which means . . ."

"All of which means that there was an assault in the living room, but it wasn't the fatal assault. She wasn't cut up in that room. And Diane was still ambulatory after she was assaulted; she wasn't dragged prone into the dining room."

"What does the bloodstain pattern in the living room tell you?"

"Well, it tells me that even though she could still move around afterward, she was hit very hard, more than once. The blood drops sprayed on the curtains are very small—that's consistent with what we call a high-energy impact."

"And how do you know she was hit more than once? Couldn't a single blow have caused the same pattern?"

"No. Think about it. The first impact opens up a wound"—he smacked his left hand with his right fist—"but it takes a second impact to transmit blood from the wound"—he smacked his left hand again and spread his fingers outward to mimic blood spray.

I looked at the crime scene photographs of the cushion sitting apart from the overturned sofa on the living room floor. The seat of the cushion bore a reddish blotch that trailed into another stain on the edge. At the Hawkins house in September, I'd watched as Spalding put the cushion in its proper place on the right side of the sofa. The pattern of the stains on the edge of the cushion and the bottom of the sofa had seemed to come together like matching jigsaw pieces. Spalding now flipped through his own photographs and brought out two. They showed the cushion and sofa edge in a tight close-up.

"Look here," he said. "When we were at the house, looking down at the sofa from a few feet away, it looked to you as if the stains came together perfectly. But if we look closely at the first photograph here, you can see that there's a straight line of fabric that's unstained. The line only disappears if you press down hard on the sofa cushion, harder than if you were sitting or lying down on it."

I looked at the second photograph, taken when pressure was being applied to the cushion. Sure enough, the stains were now truly one. "But what's the significance?"

"Just this: The large blotch is a contact stain, with the source presumably being Diane's wounds from the assault, and the combination of the two patterns tells us that when the source was coming into contact with the sofa, great pressure was being applied to the sofa cushion. The cushion and the sofa had to have been pressed together when the stain was being made."

I thought back to other facts I knew about that night, and a story began coming together in my mind. Reco brought sodas back to the house. Harrell was sitting in a living room chair, Katrina was in her bedroom asleep, and Diane was in her bedroom watching television with the lights off. Reco left, and at some point Diane came downstairs—maybe on her own, maybe because Harrell called for her. She sat as far as she could from him: across the room and at the far end of the sofa. They began to talk about the next day's hearing, and they began to argue. He left his chair and sat next to her on the sofa. They continued to argue, and she defied him: *No*, she said, *I won't drop this, no matter what you say.* And so he punched her, again and again, and she fell to the side with her bleeding face against the cushion, and he leaned over and held her down as hard as he could and pressed her over and over to drop it, drop it. And she wouldn't give in. Instead, she broke free from him, and he sprang after her.

At this point, the victim may have tried to escape to the rearentry door of the residence, leaving blood on the door and door frame. Not escaping, she would have been returned to the location in the dining room adjacent to the north wall in the

northwest corner of the room, where additional beating took place. Impact spatter on the wall described above indicates the blood source was roughly thirty inches above the floor. She fell or was pushed to the floor, and the neck and chest wounds were inflicted, to include the attempts at evisceration.

I looked at the photographs of the rear kitchen door. When the police arrived on the murder scene in May, they found the outside screen door locked, the inside door slightly ajar. On the inside door frame, about shoulder high, was a red smear, from which ran a tributary of blood that ended close to the door frame's base. Presumably the smear was left by whoever had touched the door frame while trying to leave the house. Spalding had concluded that this person was Diane. I was skeptical.

How can you be so sure that the killer didn't leave the blood there after the murders, trying to go out the back of the house?

"I can't be *sure* of anything," Spalding replied patiently. "All I can do is make my own observations, look at the crime scene photographs and the police reports to put things in context, and then give you my opinion as to what is most *likely* to have happened. Now if all I had to go on was my own observations of the bloodstain pattern on the door frame, I couldn't really come to an opinion as to who left it there. But remember, an officer swabbed that stain, and the lab was able to type it. That bloodstain was all from Diane."

I looked through my file and found the FBI report analysis of the swabs taken from the house. All of the blood samples taken from surfaces upstairs had been Katrina's. All but two of the samples downstairs had been Diane's—including the sample from the door frame.

"So," Spalding continued, "if the killer had been the one who tried to get out the back door after the murders, the blood he left there would most likely have been a mixture of Diane's and Katrina's or all Katrina's—not just Diane's. Which makes it more likely that Diane left her own blood on the door frame in trying to escape. Then, presumably, she was caught and taken back to the dining room."

At some point during these events, Katrina Harris became aware of what was taking place and fled or was pursued to the northeast bedroom on the second floor of the residence.

I asked Spalding how any bloodstain pattern could possibly tell him all of this.

"Not just the bloodstains," he replied, "but also reasonable inferences drawn from the crime scene photos and police reports."

He brought out a series of enlarged pictures of the stairwell leading from the main floor to the upstairs. The railing was to the left of the stairwell, the royal blue wall to the right. The photographs showed numerous stains along the entire expanse of the wall.

"These are cast-off stains," said Spalding. "They were flung from a blood-bearing object. With this kind of stain you can tell two things: directionality—which way the drop was moving when it hit the surface—and the speed at which the blood-bearing object was moving when the blood was cast off."

Each of the stains consisted of a single drop with a long tail.

"Now," continued Spalding, "the elongated end of each of the stains points upstairs, right? That means the source was moving upstairs when the blood was cast off. And the length of each of these streaks tells us that the source was moving very quickly."

"So if the source was a knife . . ."

"Then these stains would have been cast off from a knife, held in the right hand of someone running fast."

Spalding's scenario now made sense. Harrell would have had no reason to run upstairs if he hadn't been pursuing someone, no doubt Katrina, who'd last been seen by Reco asleep in her bedroom but who was later found in her mother's room.

And I knew from my witness interviews that Harrell was right-handed.

Katrina was cornered in the bedroom next to the bed and the east wall, where she was stabbed and cut with her back to the attacker. It is likely that the large chopping to the back of the neck took place at this time. She then turned around or was turned around, and the attack continued with facial stabs and cuts and the chopping to the left side of the neck taking place. The chest wounds and attempts to eviscerate would then have taken place at this time as well.

On the table before me was another set of photographs showing the narrow space where Katrina Harris had been found. I asked, "Do you see any indication that the girl ever faced her attacker to defend herself?"

"No," Spalding answered. "On the contrary, I'd say that she had her back to him and was crouched down low. First, I showed you before how the blood streaks on the wall behind her are all of finger width, as if she was clawing at the wall during at least part of the attack. And second, look at the impact spatter on the diaper bag to the left of the body and on the bed to the right. You can see that all of the drops are roundish—no elongated shapes. In this case, that means that when it was hit, the blood source was roughly at the same level as the point where the stain resulted—no higher. And if we assume that the blood source was the girl's neck and head, we can see that it was no more than"—he glanced at his report—"eighteen inches off the floor at the time of impact."

"And there was no sign that she was attacked elsewhere in the house and dragged or carried into the back bedroom?"

"None. No blood trail, nothing like that. She was definitely assaulted and killed on the spot where she was found."

The attacker would then have left the room, leaving blood on the bedroom door and bedroom light switch.

I had another question. When Reco had left the house at about 11:30, his mother had been watching television in this room with the lights off. When Mike Harwood entered the room and found Katrina's body some forty-five minutes later, the lights were on. According to Spalding's theory, the murderer would have to have deliberately turned the lights on as he left the room, after killing the girl and then partially covering her. This made no sense to me.

Spalding paused. "You're right. Maybe he turned them on as he entered the room—maybe he was looking to see where the girl was hiding."

"No, that couldn't be the way it happened, either. The lab was able to type the blood on the light switch. It was Katrina's, not Diane's. The killer already had Katrina's blood on his hand when he touched the switch."

"Well, then," Spalding replied. "There's only one other logical alternative: He must have paused in the middle of his work to turn on the light, you know, so he could see what he was doing."

"And then when he was finished he left the room without turning the switch off . . ."

"Maybe his hands were full."

"And then headed back downstairs . . ."

"And left more stains in the stairwell." Spalding handed me two crime scene photographs. They showed blood draining from two scarlet blotches on the wrought-iron railing on the right side as one descended the stairs. "Those are contact stains," said Spalding. "They were made by a blood-covered object coming into contact with the railing in those two places."

At some point after Katrina Harris was bleeding, blood exhibiting her serological characteristics was deposited on the kitchen counter and cabinet doors.

I said: "Let's assume that the killer went straight into the kitchen after coming downstairs. What was he doing?"

"Well, as he walked through the kitchen he was leaving a trail of small blood drops on the floor—you can see them in the crime scene photos. Those drops weren't big enough to be swabbed and typed. But this one was." Spalding brought out a picture of a single drop on the kitchen counter. The lab had determined that this drop was Katrina's blood.

"What can you tell about how it was left there?"

"It's not a contact stain, and it's not an impact stain. It's perfectly round; it fell to the counter from directly above. I'd say it's most likely that it dropped to the counter from an object bearing the blood of Katrina Harris."

"And what about the blood smear on the kitchen cabinet to the right and above the drop on the counter?"

"That was also Katrina's. And it's clearly a contact stain. It appears to have been left there by someone going into the cabinet for something."

"So if the killer was holding something in his left hand—something that fit softly in his palm and was covered with Katrina Harris's blood—and reached with his right hand to get something out of the cabinet . . ."

"This would be consistent with that. Although," he added, holding the photograph closer to his face, "it doesn't look like he would have found what he was looking for in there, does it?" The cabinet door was slightly open, behind it a row of full peanut butter and preserve jars. "When the police searched your defendant's truck did they find any kind of Tupperware pot, anything like that?"

No, they didn't, but I now had a hunch that I needed to discuss with a member of the Hawkins family.

I returned to my office and made some calls. "Who," I asked, "would be the best source of information about what sorts of things Diane kept around her kitchen in the days and weeks before her death?" A name came up: Sharon Randle, Diane's niece by marriage. Sharon had spent almost every day with Diane in the last months of her life and had regularly helped her with housecleaning. I called Sharon and set up a meeting for the next day, then called Detective Dean Combee to ask him to sit in with us. If I was right about what I was thinking, this was a meeting Combee wouldn't want to miss.

WE STILL HAD no usable eyewitnesses to the murders and never would. We had no eyewitnesses to Harrell leaving the Hawkins house, to his ditching his knife or his clothing. The FBI laboratory hadn't completed its DNA analysis of the bloodstained items from Harrell's truck or the serological analysis of the knives taken from the Harrell and Hawkins houses, or the imprint analysis of the footprint left in the Hawkins kitchen, or the fingerprint analysis of any of the evidence seized from the Hawkins or Harrell houses. We had no murder weapon and no tangible evidence to confirm our theory that Harrell had changed clothes after committing the murders and before being stopped by the police.

It wasn't as if we weren't trying. But sometimes hard work isn't enough. A case can be worked every which way for months on end, with every lead bird-dogged and every theory explored, and there's still no substitute for stupid, simple luck.

I learned the lesson early in my career. I was in my second day of a drug trial, watching my case unravel. Police had seen the defendant selling tinfoil containers of PCP and marijuana on a street corner; he'd fled the scene when the marked car entered the block. Before the police stopped him, he'd managed to rid himself of all but one of the tinfoils, which he then threw over a fence and onto a freshly painted red patio, where police recovered it. An easy enough case, until my officers actually had to testify and face cross-examination, which twisted each of them around like a plastic Slinky. Desperate, I sent an officer on a mission during a break: Find the guy who owns the patio, maybe he saw something. Half an hour later, the officer miraculously reappeared with an old man who looked as if he had no idea why he was there or where he was. The judge gave me no time to talk with him before he hobbled up to the witness stand.

"Do you remember anything unusual happening around your home on the afternoon of June 15?"

"No, nothing."

I tried again: "Did the police ever come around your house some-time last summer?"

"No, not that I remember."

A bad experience was becoming humiliating. A last-ditch gamble: I took the tinfoil package in the plastic evidence container to him. "Have you ever seen this before?"

He looked at it for what seemed like an hour, until his face bright-ened as if illuminated by strobes. "Look here, look here!" he shouted. "See that red dot right there? That's from my patio." And with that, he turned and looked at where the defendant was sitting, and his eyes widened. "And that's the dude who threw it over my damn fence!" Smiles all around; the case was saved.

In the Harrell case, we were to the point where we could use a break like that.

When the call came, I was in my office, staring at undone work sit-ting on my desk. The caller was the manager of Norman Harrell's trucking company. She'd heard something she thought we might be interested in. "One of the drivers," she said, "was saying that a friend of his knows Norman real well. He heard that Norman had gotten locked up for a murder, and something stuck in the other guy's mind—that earlier that same morning, sometime after midnight, he'd seen Norman at a car wash off Walker Mill Road—he was hosing down his truck. He also saw him take a bundle and throw it over an embankment into some tall grass and shrubs. This other guy tried to talk to Norman but he didn't say anything, just drove off."

I took down every fact she could tell me. She mentioned a wooded lot near a twenty-four-hour car wash a couple of miles from where Harrell was spotted by Corporal Mike Hunt when he was driving along in his pickup truck.

Twenty minutes later, I had the car wash in sight, through the fogged windshield of Detective Tony Duvall's car. Duvall was a burly African-American man with a full head of curly black hair, an ingratiating smile, and an interviewing style so smooth that prosecutors knew to bring him into any case with recalcitrant female witnesses. He also had a photographic memory about his cases; it seemed as if he'd had a case on every street corner in D.C. and could call up all the details in an instant. In the past, I'd worked with some investigators who couldn't have been moved to action if I'd told them that the victim had returned from the dead to identify his killer. The Harrell case had been blessed with a different breed; Duvall had jumped at the chance to join the chase. We were headed for a coin-operated car wash at the intersection of Walker Mill Road and Richie Road.

A heavy rain pelted us as we parked near a row of stalls and got out of the car. An attendant was on duty, but he was occupied with a customer requesting change for a machine. Incredibly, someone was paying to have his car washed in a rainstorm. We decided not to approach the attendant right away, but instead went straight to the lot next to the car wash. The downpour slackened as we mounted a small hill and looked down on a vast expanse of overgrown foliage, out of which poked random items of discarded trash. "Well, let's pitch in," I said to Duvall, with more enthusiasm than I felt. I took a step down the slope. The next thing I saw clearly was the sky. I had slid down the hill like a toboggan rider, and my suit sported a racing stripe of mud. Our search had begun well.

Time and time again, we came across plastic-wrapped packages of the right size and shape, nudging each with a foot to see if it had weight, then picking it up gingerly by an edge to avoid contaminating it. After an hour, we'd gathered nothing but a Dumpster's worth of empty beer cans and liquor bottles. As the rain pounded us harder and the day began to fade into smoky twilight, we called it quits for the night. Trudging to the car, I decided that morning would bring us success.

But it didn't, not for us or for a troop of fifty police cadets, the plebes of the force, who were recruited to comb like Boy Scouts through every inch of the lot. A second location—another wooded area near another all-night car wash a few miles away—was searched as thoroughly and as futilely.

We were lost in the forest without a compass. Still, we had a list of four truck drivers who were said to have been in the chain of information that had led to the company manager. Certainly by following the chain backward we would find the source and our evidence.

Three were easily located and came in to be interviewed. All were taciturn and wary, workingmen off their turf. All were Teamsters, and all said they thought Harrell was innocent, though none knew anything about the case. As for the rumor about Harrell and the mysterious bundle, they either said that they didn't know anything about it, or that they'd heard about it and passed it off.

Finally, we singled out a fourth driver as the original source and decided to focus our efforts on him.

His name was James Ballard. He was a dour man in his late forties, with a trim mustache. Three detectives were with me: Eric Gainey, Dan Whalen, and Herman Johnson.

I started with the perfunctories—name, address, work history: thirty years as a truck driver.

"You know Norman Harrell?"

"Yes."

"Is he a friend of yours?"

He paused. Several seconds went by. "No. I just knew him when we shared the same building."

I asked a series of questions about his dealings with Harrell over the years. His answers were terse and unrevealing. I leaned toward him. "You know he's been charged with two murders, don't you?"

"I've heard something about it. That's only a charge, right? I haven't thought much about it, to tell you the truth." Millions of people never met Jeffrey Dahmer, yet he had occupied their thoughts for a time. Here was old Jim Ballard telling us that a man he knew had been charged with slaughtering two women and he'd given it no more thought than the late-night ball scores.

I got to the point: "You remember how you first heard about Mr. Harrell getting stopped by the police?"

He nodded.

"Well, Mr. Ballard, we've talked to a lot of people in this case, and we're going to talk to a lot more. Some very credible people have told us that earlier that night, before he got stopped, you saw him doing something near a car wash. Would you care to tell us about that?"

"I don't know what you're talking about." He knew exactly what I was talking about. "I remember seeing him, but I don't know what day it was. All I know is it was daylight, and I saw him on Brooks Drive, not far from where I live. But he wasn't doing anything special. He was with his truck. I stopped to see if he needed help, and he said no. That was it. I didn't think any more about it until you guys all showed up."

"He wasn't doing anything unusual?"

"No."

"Wasn't washing his truck, dumping anything, nothing like that?"

"No."

"Nothing to make the moment stick in your mind from that day to this one?"

"No." Now he hesitated, not as confident. Maybe he'd seen where I was going.

"So you're telling us that this random meeting on the street, some time a while back, which you can't remember as being special in any way, was something that you thought was important enough to tell a bunch of your coworkers about?"

He should have said: "I didn't tell anybody about anything." Or "How'd my name get put in this, anyway?" Or "Whoever told you about me got it all wrong." But he said something else: "I told them I'd seen the man on the day of the murders, that was it. That was the only reason I remembered it."

"I thought you just said, not even two minutes ago, that you didn't recall what day you'd seen him. Now you're telling us it was the day of the murders. Which one is it?"

"That's what *you're* saying, that's what you want me to say, but I don't know what day it was. You want me to tell you a lie, and I'm not going to do that. I'll never tell a lie about anything."

We went around and around for hours. I went after him as hard as I would a defendant at trial, pacing the room, probing inconsistencies, circling back to weaknesses in the story. The detectives took their turns. Jim Ballard changed in front of us, sinking in his chair, moistening his lips, adjusting and readjusting his shirt collar. Repeatedly we scored points, but our triumphs were hollow. He wasn't budging.

In the end, no lie is harder to expose than "I didn't see it," no vow harder to wear down than "I don't want to get involved."

He tried to stare me down, and I stared back. But we were unequals; he had the advantage. I needed to get the truth from him more than he needed to give it to me, and he knew it and I knew it. I had no claim on him. He could walk away without giving me anything, and only I would be the lesser for it. I'd already stoked his insecurities by implying that we knew more than we did and trying to bluff him into telling us the truth (he was unimpressed) and appealed to his logic by exposing the inconsistencies in his story (he was oblivious). It was time to appeal to more primal emotions: guilt and fear.

"I want to show you something," I said. "It's something that will give you some idea of why we're taking this so seriously, why we're pressing up on you so hard, why we won't let this go."

He looked at me blankly. I pulled out a file marked "Crime Scene Photographs," carefully removed the rubber band from a stack of color eight-by-tens, and began leafing through them. The backs of the photographs were to him. I caught him straining slightly to see them, and I brought them closer to me; he eased back. I drew from the pile one photograph of Diane Hawkins and one photograph of Katrina Harris. I held them up for him to see.

"This is what someone did to somebody's mother . . . and this is what someone did to somebody's daughter." I waited as he looked. "We know who did it, and we know you know who did it. And there's one other thing that you may not know. You see the opening in the girl's chest? Well, that's where her heart was, and we still haven't found it. We think maybe it was . . . Well, I think you know where I'm going with this. And all I'm saying to you now is, when you look at these photographs, do you really want to hold back on telling us what you know?"

He kept staring at the pictures.

"Do you really want that to follow you around for the rest of your life, when you're going about your business, doing something with your family, or whatever . . . Do you have kids?"

He nodded.

"Maybe you're out at a ball game, and you think of how these people died and think maybe you could have done something to put him in jail for what—"

"They don't bother me."

"What?"

"These pictures don't bother me in the least." I thought I saw the corners of his mouth turn up. "And they definitely don't make me tell a lie to you."

That was it.

"You are one cold son of a bitch," I heard myself say to him. "And you're a lying motherfucker. I'm going to put your ass on the stand, and you can sit there and tell that lie; you can tell it just like you just told me, and make sure you throw in that part at the end about not being bothered by those pictures, and I'll have your ass indicted for perjury so fast it will make your head spin. And you can take your ten-year felony rap and go straight over to D.C. jail, and you and your buddy Norman can rot over there together for the rest of your lives for all I care."

I walked out of the room and paced. When I returned, Detective Herman Johnson asked me to step outside.

"Listen, he told us something. Well, maybe you should know it before you go at him anymore."

"What's that?"

"He says he hasn't been himself lately. He's been . . . preoccupied. He just found out he has lung cancer."

"Is . . . Do we . . . Have you . . . Oh, Jesus Christ, do you believe him?"

"Well, yeah. I mean, why would he lie about that?"

"Oh, okay, I get it. 'I got my own problems, buddy. I don't need to get involved in somebody else's!' Right?"

Johnson shrugged.

I walked back to face Ballard again, but I'd lost any leverage I had over him: The threat of a perjury prosecution would mean nothing to a man facing a possible death sentence. I could go back to him again on another day and then another, trying to wear him down, but it seemed pointless; he'd never waver. So I cut my losses and left him, telling him that I'd be calling him again but knowing that I never would. I started to wish him well with his illness, but then I thought better of it and said nothing.

I had no doubt that I'd go back to the woods again and again, but the chances were slim that I'd ever find what I was looking for. The woods were deep and thick, and my only guide was turning his back on me.

Norman Harrell had been caught red-handed by the one person in a thousand who would keep his secret for him. To anyone who believes in divine intervention in worldly events, it's the eternal paradox: The same God who is said to love justice, choosing to smile upon the lowest of his creations in the wake of a terrible sin. But to a sportsman such as Harrell, who'd spent time at the mercy of nature's whims, this was pure random luck, good one day and bad the next: The whitetail comes close in a clearing as the rifle is raised, the wind gusts or the foot stumbles or the rifle slips, and the whitetail escapes.

As much as human malevolence or folly, sheer good luck or bad luck plays a role in every murder case. Take one of mine: A young man joins his family for a barbecue and is hit in the backside by a bullet fired by a stranger who's caught up in a neighborhood gang war that the young man doesn't even know about. A minute or so later, the young man is sitting up talking with his family, the victim of an embarrassing but nonlethal wound. Unbeknownst to all of them, the bullet has severed a major artery; five minutes later the young man is dead. Or another case: Two friends stand on a street corner, and a rival fires at them from a car. One is hit in the head and lives; the other is hit in the arm and dies. Or this scenario, one that you're already familiar with: A girl is offered the richest opportunity of her young life—the chance to join friends on a trip to Disney World—but declines so she can help her mother at home and pays for the choice with her life.

I knew all about good fortune. Before my parents met, they'd traveled in different circles; if they hadn't converged by chance on a D.C. street in 1952, I would never have existed. A chain of serendipitous events had likewise preceded my meeting the woman who eventually became my wife. But it wasn't until I started handling homicide prosecutions that I saw so vividly how the difference between bad luck and good luck can be the difference between death and life—or between spending the rest of your life in jail and getting away with murder.

And what about the case of the PCP tinfoil on the freshly painted patio? No sooner had fortune walked in on the arm of our surprise witness, the old man who hobbled into court to identify the defendant and his drugs, than it had gotten up and left in a hurry. Our next witness fumbled a crucial point in his testimony, and the judge dismissed the case. Minutes later, the defendant walked out of the courtroom, a free man with a smile on his face.

PATRICE AND I had an annual October ritual: Columbus Day weekend in Philadelphia, visiting her family and observing the birthdays of her mother and sister. In 1993, because my mother continued to suffer from serious depression, we couldn't plan the trip too far in advance. But two days before we left, my father, ever her vigilant guardian, told me he saw no reason why we shouldn't go; there were no signs of an imminent crisis. And so we took our trip as scheduled, though I was bothered by a strained sound in my father's voice when I spoke with him on Friday afternoon. At first I wondered if he was holding something back from me, but then dismissed the idea. He and I had been partners for a year in trying to bring my mother back to health, speaking by phone every night and meeting with doctors together. He was a private man whose family was his life. I was the only person he really talked with about this ordeal; he never wanted to burden anyone else. I was sure that if anything were going on with my mother, he would tell me.

Still, I tried to call my parents several times on Sunday and got no answer. Monday morning was the same. When we came home Monday afternoon I called again: no answer. I went outside to distract myself and mow the lawn for the last time in the season. The tall, sparse grass was now flaked with crackling russet leaves. I went to get gasoline for the lawnmower. When I returned, my wife came out to me. My father had just called, she said. Nothing was new with my mother, but something else was going on, and he wanted to talk with me before anyone else. I knew whatever it was, it wasn't good. I went to a telephone upstairs and called. My mother answered the phone herself, for the first time in months: "Hold on, son, I'll let your father talk to you." He came on, and I asked him what was going on.

"Well, Kevin, I might have a problem." He'd been having chest pains all week, and they'd gotten worse on Sunday. He and my mother had gone to the emergency room, where an electrocardio-gram was taken: normal. They were about to go home when my mother insisted that he get a chest X-ray, which he did. Minutes later a young doctor came out smiling: Everything looks fine. "Your mother and I, oh, we were *jubilant*," he told me. It was an odd word coming from him about anything having to do with himself; it told me how worried he must have been at the hospital.

Then the doctor said, "Let me get someone to take a second look." This time the wait was longer.

Another doctor came out, not smiling. "Here are the X-rays," he said, handing over a manila envelope. "Get them to a pulmonary specialist as soon as possible."

"I got an appointment for Thursday," my dad continued, "and we'll know more then."

"What do they think it might be?" I asked, even though I knew what the answer was.

"Well, you know, they think it might be lung cancer," he said, as calmly as if he were reporting a problem he was having with one of the family cars.

I drove over to see them, along roads I knew well. They lived in a Virginia suburb of D.C., in the house they'd bought thirty-four years before, when I was a baby. On a normal day the drive between my house and theirs took twenty minutes. This day it took longer; I didn't hurry. As I pulled into my old neighborhood, I passed the ballfield where my dad had taught me how to hit, drove down the street my mom had walked with me to my first day at kindergarten, to the house that held a thousand memories but now looked small and fearful.

Entering the house, I hugged my mother. For the time being, at least, she seemed to be bearing up. My father took me upstairs and showed me the X-rays. "This is where they say the problem is," he said, pointing to something on the right lung. I couldn't read the X-ray, couldn't tell the difference between the area that was supposedly healthy and the one that supposedly wasn't. I actually drew some consolation from my ignorance. For the rest of our conversation he spoke only of my mother: whether this could push her over the edge, whether she even was quite aware of how serious this illness could be. I carried the thought one step further and looked ahead a year. What was to become of them if this was as bad as I feared it was?

A lifetime passed between Monday and Thursday. I tried to keep my fears from my wife, Patrice. "It's probably a lung infection," I told her several times, "I'm not going to jump to conclusions." But in my own mind, I'd already made the crossing. From the time I was a small boy, my father had been a heavy smoker and my mother and I had nagged him to quit. He'd always been a worrier; smoking eased the tension. Besides, it was the only vice in life he enjoyed. But I didn't have to be a pulmonary specialist to know where it might one day lead.

Thursday brought no definitive news, only a bleak preliminary diagnosis from a doctor who'd had many such talks with people sitting where my father was. More tests had to be done, he said, and we should return the next Tuesday for a final diagnosis, but all signs pointed to lung cancer. As we walked from the doctor's office, my father tried to be jaunty and brave; my mother was very quiet. Later he called me: "What's the difference, really, if somebody just lives to seventy or gets to seventy-five? The most important thing is that you not let this get in the way of your life or your job." To make him feel better, I told him it wouldn't, but thought, *How could that ever be possible?*

I spent the rest of the day driving around by myself. The Beltway forms a misshapen fifty-five-mile circle around Washington; over the months to come I would know its every turn. I ended up at a bookstore. A year before, I'd gathered a small library on depression, then another on baby care. Eight years before, my dad had been diagnosed with colon cancer, and my reading on that subject had encouraged me to be optimistic. But I found no comfort in the statistics on lung cancer. Some estimates put the survival rate as low as 5 percent, depending on the type of malignancy; certain types were terminal even at diagnosis.

By the time we arrived in the doctor's office the next Tuesday, I'd prepared myself for the worst. Instead we heard a classic bad news–good news report: definitely lung cancer but with no sign of spread to other areas, and treatable, at least in the short term. Sometimes, the doctor said, there's even a cure.

My mother had brought with her a writing pad and was taking notes. She looked up. "So is there hope, doctor?"

"Yes, there's hope."

So deep had been our pessimism that when we left the doctor's office, Patrice and I took my parents out to lunch to celebrate the news. We'd heard the four-letter word we wanted to hear. And something else had happened as well: At lunch, for the first time in almost a year, my mother was fully engaged. In the weeks to come, she would take responsibility for bringing my father back to health. With jarring suddenness she'd renounced the role of sufferer and claimed the role of caregiver. Faced with the possible loss of her husband, she was rallying.

The next week, my father began chemotherapy treatment. An oncologist likened my father's cancer—called small-cell carcinoma—to a voracious predator, devouring healthy cells in rapid succession. It was an inoperable disease; it moved too quickly to be cut out of the body. But chemotherapy could be effective in containing it— trapping the predator, so to speak—by confronting the cancer cells with cancer-killing chemicals. If it could be contained within the lung, it could possibly be eradicated with radiation. But if it escaped from the lung, the patient was doomed; it almost always moved to a site such as the brain or the liver, and little more could be done.

The treatment plan sounded too simple to work, but the doctors told us it had before—in about 20 percent of the cases. If we'd had the numbers on our side, we would have banked on the numbers; not having them, we had to try to ignore the reasoning side of the brain. *If out of every five there's a one, why can't my dad be the one?* Besides, maybe a medical breakthrough is around the corner—hold this sucker off long enough, keep all our options open, and maybe my dad can be the beneficiary of it. There's no more optimistic phrase in the language than "Something will turn up."

WHEN I WAS A CHILD, my mother taught me how to pray. She was more devout than my father, who was an observant but more detached Catholic; he liked our pastor's sermons because the man's sonorous cadences were conducive to a nap. At age five or so, I learned that a prayer is like a private talk with God; to me, this meant I could take Him to one side and ask for anything I wanted. Later in childhood the petitions became more mature—no more prayers for a Davy Crockett coonskin cap for Christmas—and my nighttime ritual generally involved pleading with God to continue to prop up various members of my small, aging family. As an adult, I no longer believed in a micromanaging God manipulating every event on earth. The caprice of such a deity—deciding that Kevin in Annandale should get his cap on Christmas morning, but Bobby in Arlington, say, should die in a car wreck the next day—didn't fit my concept of a loving and merciful God. Instead I thought of Him (or Her, or It) as a spiritual presence whom one could approach for strength and solace in time of need, with the catch being that He would be most responsive to those whose lives best served Him. God didn't create the cancer in someone's chest, I reasoned, just as He didn't cause the devastating rumbles in His earth or the homicidal impulses in His people. Those were the manifestations of a physical world and a human will unfolding on their own, under God's benign, unobtrusive watch. But He understood, I thought, how anxious and fretful we could be in a universe of such confounding unpredictability, and He could be counted on at least to stand by and cheer as we tried to make our way through it. I didn't pretend to have all the answers, but for more than a decade or so this had been my creed—or, more accurately, the end result of my modest efforts to Figure It All Out—and I'd stuck to it.

But I now found myself hearkening back to the simpler faith of my youth, wishing I could simply pray in good conscience for Dad's cancer to go away. I struck a compromise of sorts, inspired by some advice that a friend of mine gave my father. The friend had lived half his life with cancer, and was a medical marvel; the disease was still in him but cowed into retrenchment. He despised doctors— "They'll kill you as quick as they'll cure you"—and generally disdained conventional treatments. He was skeptical about support groups—"They're great until everybody starts dying on you." But he deeply believed in the power of mind over matter, the force of a steadfast spirit in the face of illness. He suggested, among other things, that my father meditate daily and visualize the "good" cells in his body vanquishing the "evil" cells. As medical theory it sounded eccentric, to say the least, but it had its proponents, and my friend was a walking advertisement for the benefits of eccentricity. My father's desperation was boundless, and he went along. Taking the cue, I would pray not only for the infusion of God's sustaining spirit into myself but into my father as well—vicarious inspiration, so to speak.

At work and at home, I felt myself engaged in a Manichean struggle on parallel courses: confronting evil in two different forms and attempting to confine it so it would do no more harm. The only difference between the two: No matter how much I would try to convince myself to the contrary, it was only at work that I had any control.

————

MEANWHILE, the Harrell trial loomed.

I received daily calls from members of the Hawkins family—usually from one of Diane's sisters, sometimes from Willie or one of Diane's friends. They called to pass along information, a tip here or there that they'd just thought about or heard about. Sometimes they called just to talk; I was a centering force for a family reeling and disoriented. Usually they called because they were getting impatient, eager to see the case in court. As the trial grew closer, their voices sounded more purposeful; soon they might again have something to rally around. Not long before, they'd all congregated at the house on Eads Street, and at the midpoint of memory they could still conjure visions of Diane bustling in and out with dishes and drinks and Trina lingering inscrutably to the side. Now, with Diane's children scattered among relatives and everyone else driven into private corners of grief, they congregated only in court or in my office. Each day that passed with the case unresolved prolonged their pain and delayed their coming to terms with their loss. Again and again I told them to separate the grieving process from the court process. Inside, I knew it was easier said than done.

I had my own reasons for wanting the case to go forward as soon as possible. I needed the enveloping experience of a trial to take me away from my father's ordeal. Maybe once I was standing in court, framing questions and making arguments when every word mattered, stoked by the juice of competition, the world would slow down and for a few hours I could grab hold of a manageable slice of it.

I also wanted my father to see the trial. My memories of the public stages of my past—everything from Cub Scout talent shows to high school track meets—placed my parents' faces always in the audience, and sometimes not passively: Family lore had my mother jumping out of the stands and onto a basketball court to protest when a misguided referee had the temerity to call a questionable foul on her son. When I became a lawyer, my father took a special interest in my work—mostly out of parental pride but partly, I suspected, because he was a retired government engineer who'd felt thwarted in his job and privately wished he'd gone to law school. Now, for all I knew, he was dying. By some projections, if the chemotherapy and radiation proved ineffective, he might have as little as a few months left. This would be the most significant trial I might ever handle, and I wanted him and my mother to be there for it.

Months before, the judge had set the date for the beginning of trial: December 1, 1993. If the FBI laboratory finished its DNA and fingerprint analysis before then, we'd be ready; if not, we wouldn't.

I was in a position I was already becoming familiar with: sitting around waiting for lab results.

ONE WEEK BEFORE we were supposed to go to trial, the FBI came through with its DNA report on the evidence seized from Harrell's truck: the cooler, the piece of fabric from the dashboard, the paper bag, the armrest. The blood on the cooler and the fabric cutting was of the same DNA type as either Diane or Katrina or both, and not of the same type as Harrell. The victims shared these types with only about 3 percent of the African-American population. A statistician might quibble, but it made sense at least to me that this meant there was a 97 percent chance that the blood on these items came from the victims. If the laboratory had had larger blood samples to work with, it could have used a procedure that offered the highest degree of DNA discrimination known to science: comparisons on a scale of millions or even billions, not hundreds. Still, the DNA numbers gave me something more to work with; they were definitely more impressive than those yielded by the conventional serological test done in May.

But what about the blood on the bag and the armrest? The DNA recovered from the two specimens had come from more than one individual—not only Diane or Katrina but also Norman Harrell himself. How could this be?

I confronted the FBI analyst: "Under the serological test, the bag and the armrest were found to contain only the blood of the victims, but under your DNA test, they were found to contain a combination of the victims' DNA and Harrell's too. What's that all about? Does this mean Harrell had bled on these items too?"

"Not at all," he said. "The serological test only discerns blood. DNA testing discerns any sort of bodily fluid. What my test picked up were most likely some cells from some other fluid secreted from the other source."

"What sort of fluids?"

"Possibly perspiration," he replied.

Suddenly it made sense. The armrest was on the driver's-side door. When Harrell left the Hawkins house he was pumped with the adrenaline of murderous exertion. He had the blood of the victims on his shirt sleeve. Sweat soaked through his shirt and mixed with the blood of the people he'd just killed.

And another thought. If he'd tried to clean himself up before his arm touched the armrest, this was the one place on his body he couldn't have seen: the underside of his elbow.

FROM THE DNA UNIT, the evidence went to the laboratory's fingerprint section. There was no point in analyzing the knives and other materials taken out of Harrell's house and truck. They were his property, he'd had his hands all over them, and they'd be covered with his fingerprints. Instead, we wanted the FBI to focus on the ten knives from the murder scene: the seven from the box beneath the sofa and the three from the kitchen that completed the set. And one more thing: the hunter's manual, even though it had been taken out of Harrell's bedroom and had Harrell's name on the front. If his fingerprints were on the inside pages he wouldn't very easily be able to claim ignorance of the book's contents—and especially the lesson on gutting hunted game.

On November 19, the analyst called. "I'm not getting anything off of the knives," he said, "but I pulled two of the defendant's prints from the hunter's manual. I don't have my report in front of me, but one was from a page in the 50s and the other around 115." I went to my copy of the manual to see where the discussion about gutting animals began: page 60. There hadn't been any usable prints on that page. "But I took one from the page before it," the analyst said. "Page 59."

Close doesn't count, I thought to myself.

"Do you have your book in front of you?" he continued. "Page 59 is on the right side. The print was a left index finger, down at the bottom right edge of the page." He paused. "Is there something about page 60 that makes it important to show that he looked at that page?"

I said, "You might say so."

"Well, this proves it. This print is from about one quarter of the whole index finger. It's down at the bottom right, and it's slanted slightly toward the right."

I took my copy of the manual and placed my left index finger at the bottom right edge of page 59, at an angle. "It's an awkward way to hold your hand," I told him.

"Not if you're turning the page to look at the next one."

I turned the page and saw the outline of my index finger pressed against page 59, in the same position and at the same angle as the print that the analyst found.

Before me was page 60: "The heart and lungs lie in the chest cavity . . ."

CHAPTER 8

By November 1993, Norman Harrell had gotten himself a new lawyer: Michele Roberts, a prominent local attorney with a compelling courtroom style and a background in high-profile, complicated cases. For years she'd been employed by D.C.'s Public Defender Service—an organization of idealistic defense lawyers with a decided antiprosecution bent—and now she was on her own. I didn't know how Harrell had hooked up with her, but he'd made a good choice. I had more than sixty-five jury trials to my credit, a pretty large number even for a seasoned prosecutor, but my experience paled next to hers. For other reasons, too, she was ideal for him. Like the victims, she was a black female. She was long and lithe, with close-cropped hair. She wore matching gold bracelets and hoop earrings that rattled with her stride. Everything about her—her voice, her dress, her posture—radiated self-confidence and empowerment. Some jurors would naturally identify with her, and in their eyes, Harrell would be enhanced by her association with him. Some might even ask themselves: How bad can he be if Michele Roberts is willing to take up his cause?

A few years before, she'd been profiled in a local magazine; the article circulated widely around my office. The title: "Her Life Is Her Job." The first scene: a karate class where Roberts was squaring off against a male opponent, letting him tire himself out with flailing punches and kicks, then pouncing on him and forcing submission. Later in the piece, she related how she'd encountered virulent racism as a girl, and the experience had made her suspicious of white people.

When I heard she was coming into the case, my first thought was: *Maybe we'll get along okay. I'm suspicious of a lot of white people too.*

Whether it was due to martial arts or trial training, she evidently knew she had to take a step back to mount an effective defense in the Harrell case. The DNA and fingerprint results had come in before the December 1 trial date, but too late for her to be able to prepare adequately. She asked for more time, and the judge gave it to her: The trial would now start on February 15, 1994.

FOR THE FIRST time in six months, I had no pressing responsibilities in the Harrell case. The trial was many weeks away, there were no fresh leads to follow, and the rest of the world was preoccupied with the holidays. My work schedule in December looked depressingly manageable: no trials, two legal briefs to write, an appellate argument—nothing so absorbing as to be a real distraction.

In memory, I returned repeatedly, obsessively, to the previous December and its promise of better things to come. My son, Connor, had been born ten days before Christmas. Flushed with the joys of fatherhood I wrote a rhyme for him that included the line "No pleasure ever gained by human striving / Could match the joy you brought by just arriving." Two days after the delivery, Patrice was walking around hospital corridors that sported twinkling red and green lights. A new course of treatment and the birth of a cherished grandchild had sparked a rejuvenation in my mother; she would falter again in early 1993, but we didn't know that then, and my father was thrilled by her resurgence. He came to the hospital one evening to see the baby, and as I said good-bye to him at the elevator I thought: *He's won.* He'd defined his goals narrowly, to be sure: the physical and emotional well-being of a circumscribed set of people, his family. But he'd kept it intact, he had his first grandson, he had his wife back, and Christmas was on the way. Now a year had passed, and we would all live out this Christmas under a shadow—not the shadow of a loss already suffered but one feared to be imminent. My father's change in circumstances summoned dark thoughts in me that didn't befit the festive season.

It was Patrice who gave me perspective. She wasn't one for philosophical self-flagellation. She'd lost her father to cancer ten years before. She'd been just as close to her father as I was to mine. "Each day that goes by," she told me, "you just have to remember—your father's alive." Where there's life, there's hope, was the message. Better still to be holding on to something, however tenuously, than having to do without it.

My daily conversations with the family and friends of Diane Hawkins and Katrina Harris brought fresh reminders of the value of hope. They had none, at least as far as ever seeing their loved ones again. As Christmas approached, they called me more and more often; it was a new experience for me. Growing up, I saw only a couple of grandparents, a few aunts and uncles, and a couple of cousins with any frequency. One cousin had a baby girl when I was twenty-five years old; she was the first baby born into my family since . . . me. Now, day by day, I was being drawn into the populous Hawkins clan by Diane's sisters and brothers, nieces and nephews, cousins.

Time and time again, I heard the same phrases from the family: God must have known what was best for them; Diane and Trina are in a better place; God must have had a plan for them. Over and over I heard a simple proscription, uttered like a mantra, for handling adversity: "Let go and let God." These were the same sentiments that had abounded at the wake and funeral, and the words now gave the family something to hold on to in the dark nights that seemed never to end. Intellectually, I didn't necessarily agree with their view of God's workings in the world. I preferred a more aggressive approach to invoking God's mercy, if only because I still wanted to hold on to the notion that I could partner with the Almighty and will my father back to health. But this is a quibble. Their credo was rooted in devotion to something bigger than themselves. To me, in times of crisis, that message beats a faithless one every time. We were looking to the same source for help; who was I to say that my vision was better than theirs?

In whatever form it took, though, spiritual comfort seemed beyond the reach of two parents who'd lost children on May 26, 1993. Magdeline Hawkins was the seventy-five-year-old mother of Diane Hawkins, grandmother of Katrina Harris, matriarch of the family. Before the murders she was in good health; at the funeral she needed a wheelchair and a nurse; four months later she was dead. She went into her final decline on what would have been Diane Hawkins's forty-third birthday, and everyone in the family knew this was no coincidence. Willie Harris, father of Katrina, lived on and actually was able to return to some semblance of a normal daily routine. But he bore his grief as if it were a physical pain, and he showed no sign of being sustained by religious conviction. It was during December that Willie started calling me at my home—not often, maybe only once every few weeks, and always with apologies. He spoke haltingly, as if he had to gather strength through long silences to form another sentence. He never delved into details about the case; he only asked, "How does it look?" He didn't talk much about how he was feeling; he only said, "It hurts so bad." He said he blamed himself for Trina's death: "I should have gotten her out of there. I never wanted her to live in the city." In all of our conversations, he never said that he thought God knew best or that God had a plan for his daughter.

Two days before Christmas, Willie took a few hours off from his bakery job and came to see me at my office. He was a round-faced man with soft, guileless eyes. His features settled naturally into a grimace, having had seven months' practice. We spoke about familiar subjects. I pictured him as a young father, and I pictured myself where he was now. One year before, just hours after our son, Connor, was born, I'd looked at the baby and said to my wife, "Yesterday we didn't even know who he was, and today, if anyone harmed a hair on his head, I'd kill them with my bare hands." This day, after Willie and I parted, I would go out and do last-minute shopping for my little boy. Willie, for the first time in fourteen years, had no child to bring a Christmas treat home to.

IN AUGUST 1979, the body of a forty-four-year-old woman was discovered in a park overlooking San Francisco Bay and Golden Gate Bridge. Over the next ten months, six more young women and one young man were killed in the same area and the same general fashion. All were outdoors enthusiasts in the prime of life. Through the joint efforts of local police and the FBI, the so-called Trailside Killer, a fifty-year-old industrial arts teacher named David Carpenter, was identified, caught, and convicted.

On May 29, 1979, the body of a twenty-two-year-old woman named Betty Jane Shade was found in a dump site in Altoona, Pennsylvania. She'd been severely beaten, sexually assaulted, and stabbed numerous times. After death she'd been mutilated. Through the joint efforts of local police and the FBI, Betty Jane Shade's killers, two brothers named Charles and Michael Soult, were identified, caught, and convicted.

Between 1980 and 1983, the bodies of four young women were found in remote wooded areas around Anchorage, Alaska. All had been either prostitutes or topless dancers. All were unclothed when found. The murderer had taken each into woods, stripped her, let her loose, then stalked her and killed her. Through the joint efforts of local police and the FBI, the killer of the four women, a baker named Robert Hansen, an avid hunter, was identified, caught, and convicted.

Thousands of miles separated California, Pennsylvania, and Alaska, the states where David Carpenter, Charles and Michael Soult, and Robert Hansen lived and where they took the lives of others, but these killers, and many others like them, had one thing in common: The fact that all were brought to justice was largely due to the work of a small group of FBI special agents comprising what was called the Behavioral Science Unit. The unit was world-renowned for its psychological studies of serial killers and had a subspecialty in other variations of depravity. In late 1993, I decided to ask for its help in the Harrell case. We might not be able to get the monster to tell us what had been in his head, but we could do the next best thing: talk to people who knew a lot about monsters.

On January 27, 1994, a caravan of cars carrying our investigative team traveled thirty miles south through snow flurries to Quantico, Virginia. It was here, at the FBI's National Training Academy, that the unit worked in subterranean offices that never saw the light of day. It was an appropriate setting for a group devoted to the study of the mind's dark corners.

A few weeks before, I'd sent to Quantico a package of materials about the case. For the benefit of anyone in the group who hadn't had the chance to read them, I planned to begin with a brief introductory presentation, but I was barely five minutes into it before I was peppered with questions from my audience:

"What did Harrell do that day? Have you tracked his movements?"

I replied: "He punched in at work at exactly eight A.M. He punched out at four twenty-eight P.M. A friend tells us he saw him at a dry cleaner at about six P.M. Somebody else tells us they saw him in River Terrace at a liquor store at eight P.M.: He was getting a lottery ticket. He went over to P.G. County to see his wife and son, and he was back over at Diane's house at about nine thirty P.M."

"Any idea why he was over at River Terrace at eight? He could have gotten a lottery ticket anywhere, right?"

"Maybe he was casing out the Hawkins house, seeing if he could get Diane alone."

"Where do you think he got the murder weapon?"

"He might have used one from the house. More likely, he brought one with him—though he managed to hide it from Reco and his girlfriend before they left."

"How do you think he took the heart from the house?"

"Well, his cooler had bloodstains in it; maybe he used that."

"Do you think he brought it in the house with him, or did he go to his truck after he killed them?"

"I don't know."

"Where do you think the heart is now?"

I don't know, I don't know, I don't know, I thought. *Look, I don't know all the answers. That's why I'm here.*

"You say," one asked, "that you think Katrina was in bed before the murders, but she was found in a T-shirt and gym shorts. Do you know for a fact that's what she wore when she went to sleep?"

"That's what a family member told us."

"Did you get any foreign hairs or fibers from the victims' clothes?"

"No. The lab did a sweep of the clothes—nothing came up. Same with the comparison of the knife tip from Katrina's skull and the broken knife from Harrell's house: no match. Same with the bloody footprint from Diane's house and the boots seized from Harrell's truck. The print could have been left there by any number of people who ran through the house before the scene was sealed off, but the defense will still make a big deal out of it, say it was left by the real killer."

"Are you sure that the telephone in Diane's house wasn't working, or is there a chance that the wires were cut by the killer when he entered?"

"Sources from inside and outside the family told us that the telephone was disconnected because Diane hadn't paid the bill."

"Was Reco known to be in the habit of being around Diane's house at the hour when Harrell dropped by?"

"Family members told us that Reco's schedule was unpredictable. Both he and his sister Shante were in and out frequently."

"Where did Harrell usually leave the truck when he came over? Did anyone see it there that night?"

"He usually left it out front because he said he was nervous about the neighborhood and wanted to keep it in sight. And no, no one saw it in front of the house on the night of the murders."

"Why don't you think Harrell was telling the truth to Reco and the police when he said he'd walked to Diane's house that night?"

"Harrell's house and Diane's house were several miles apart. No one in Diane's family ever knew him to walk there before. And if he was lying about walking, you have to ask yourself why. Maybe he hid the truck nearby—he didn't want anyone outside the house to know he was inside—and he was trying to explain to Reco why the truck wasn't in its usual place."

I saw a couple of the experts nodding.

"Can you prove for a fact that Harrell knew that the court hearing on Diane's child support claim was scheduled for the next day?"

"Well, we can show he was sent several notices by the court but not that one was served on him in person. One was mailed, another was left for him at his house. But the morning after the murders, he told his supervisor at work that the case had been scheduled to go to court that morning. That certainly implies he knew about it beforehand."

"Yeah," came the response, "but you know what he'll say: Some police detective told him that when he was being interviewed the night before."

"True enough."

Another question: "What was the relationship between Harrell and Katrina? It was her heart that he took."

"Tense, with an undertone of hostility. But we don't know of any physical violence."

"Was she ever touched sexually by him?"

"No, not that we could ever say for sure, but we did hear a rumor that we couldn't substantiate. One of Trina's friends told somebody that she'd come upon the girl in the bathroom a short time before the murder. Trina was crying and saying that she'd been sexually abused by her stepfather. But the school friend would never admit to saying anything like that to anybody, and all we were left with was hearsay."

"Did Harrell really have any Jamaican friends? Or was he just puffing when he talked to Deborah Courtney about them?"

"We asked around and couldn't find any."

"Has there been any talk of a plea?"

"No. From what we can tell, Harrell is going to say he's an innocent dupe, in the wrong place at the wrong time."

"What about insanity?" There was an exchange of glances around the FBI table.

"I don't know for sure. Harrell's lawyer could test the waters, even have a shrink take a look at him, and I'd never even know about it unless they decided to use that defense at trial. All I know is that it's getting pretty late in the game for that."

"What about Harrell's childhood? Was he ever abused, anything like that?"

"Not that we can tell. His brothers and sisters made it sound very ordinary. Who knows, though; they're hard to figure, and come to think of it, one of them seemed a little off."

"Did Harrell belong to any video clubs? Do you know whether he was renting any weird stuff?"

"We haven't checked."

"Were there any reports of animal slaughters in the area before the murders? A lot of times these guys do a few things like that to warm up for the big event."

"We haven't checked that, either."

"Did you do an off-line records check on Harrell's truck for the time between the murders and the stop to see if any officer might have seen it under suspicious circumstances and called it in to see if it was stolen or something? It's a long shot, but it might be a way to track where he went."

I made a note. My list of questions was getting longer, not shorter.

Now it was my turn: "If any of you had come on this crime scene, would you have been able to tell whether the murders had been committed by a stranger or by someone who knew the victims?"

All eyes turned to John Douglas, who was sitting at the center of the table. He was a pleasant-faced man in his late forties with gray at the temples, a twenty-five-year FBI veteran who'd become legendary among his colleagues for his pursuit of the likes of the Atlanta child murderer and the Green River killer in Seattle.

"Well," he began, "just looking at the photographs of the crime scene, it's not impossible for the murders to have been done by a stranger. I've seen this sort of carnage in stranger-on-stranger murders. But looking first at the mother, I'd say it's more likely that she was killed by someone who was extremely angry with her. And the mutilation is consistent with that as well. That can be looked at as a way of depersonalizing her. Also, the way she was left— completely exposed, with her shirt up and her pants undone—it's clear he didn't have any remorse, and he didn't want to leave her with any dignity."

"What about the way Katrina, the daughter, was left?"

"That one's a different story," Douglas replied. "It's clear he did have some remorse about what he did to the girl. He immediately wanted to cover up what he did. It's almost as if he wanted to act as if it had never happened."

"What does this tell you about who was the killer's primary target: the mother, the daughter, or both?"

"The main target was the mother. The daughter was incidental."

This fit with our motive evidence: strong proof of Harrell's motive to kill Diane, no strong proof of his motive to kill Katrina, only a theory that he did so because she was a witness to her mother's murder. I thought for a moment about Bob Spalding and his bloodstain-pattern analysis: It indicated that Diane had been killed first.

"If Harrell planned Diane's murder in advance," I asked, "why would he have been so stupid as to carry it out in exactly the same way as he'd described to Deborah Courtney just one month before? Didn't he realize that this would be horribly incriminating?"

"Remember what you're dealing with," John Douglas replied. "These murders were the product of a tremendous rage. He might have been so angry that he forgot what he'd said to anyone."

And in his rage he'd followed his obsessions: killing the way hunters killed, the way Jamaicans killed. The thought really is father to the act.

Douglas turned back on me: "Has his lawyer given any indication about what his defense is going to be?"

"Nothing directly, but we've heard of talk around the neighborhood that would have the murders be drug related. None of the rumors checked out, and we've got no suspects other than Harrell, but his lawyer might use the rumors as the starting point for a defense."

"What sort of crime is common in the neighborhood where the murders occurred?"

"Mostly drugs. Some street robberies, robberies of drug dealers, that sort of thing. It's a fairly quiet area, not a lot of murders. When they happen they tend to be over dope, but these never looked like drug murders to me."

"No, they're not," said Douglas. "For one thing, drug murders are usually done with guns, quick and impersonal. These murders took time: killing the two people, mutilating them, taking one heart and trying to take the other. A stranger in a strange house, doing a murder over drug business, wouldn't want to take that much time. These murders were personal, and they were done by somebody who was comfortable in that house."

"What about robbery?" someone else at the FBI table asked. "Have you eliminated that as a motive?"

"No, no!" A voice resounded from the end of the table. I turned toward the sound. It was one of the analysts, feverishly flipping through a pile in front of him. "Look at the pictures. There's no ransacking. And look at the girl. Look at her finger and around her neck: gold jewelry. If this was your classic burglary-robbery murder, there's no way they'd have left that there." The group was soon passing around all of the crime scene photographs, and their comments overlapped with each other until I changed the subject: "What problems do you all see in our case?"

Douglas chimed in: "He didn't have any blood on his clothes when the police stopped him, right?" I said that he'd had enough time to change clothes and wash himself, and the outfit that Reco Hawkins saw Harrell wearing before the murders didn't match what he was wearing later, but we had no other proof that Harrell had changed, only Reco's word—and Reco, as we knew, posed some problems as a witness.

One of the FBI experts asked if we had any video footage of Harrell. I brought out the tape we'd received of the television newscast of May 26. I'd seen the video once, months before. It included a glimpse of Harrell being escorted to the police cruiser in P.G. County. A call was made for a video machine; during the delay I called my office.

The video tape was cued up. I was half-watching, half-listening to my phone messages. Only one message really mattered—my parents were meeting with my dad's oncologist that day for a progress report. Only one question really mattered: Is the cancer shrinking or growing?

"On Eads Street early this morning . . ."

Out of the corner of my eye I saw the news film taken outside the Hawkins house after the murders.

"The victims were forty-two-year-old Diane Hawkins . . ."

The face of one of Diane's nephews appeared.

I listened to all my messages: no word from my parents.

I looked over at the video screen. There was Harrell, walking open-shirted to the police vehicle.

"Family members said that Diane Hawkins's ex-boyfriend was known to be at the house that night."

"Wait a second," I said. "Go back to where Harrell is walking to the police car."

The tape fell silent, and Harrell and the officers walked backward spastically.

"Now roll it forward and pause it."

There on the screen, captured in freeze frame, was Norman Harrell with his shirt unbuttoned and his bare chest exposed. I thought: *How did I miss that?* Then: *Reco was right after all.* Harrell changed clothes after leaving the Hawkins house, was even in the process of changing them when the police first saw him, and just didn't have the chance to finish fastening himself.

One by one, we were closing off Norman Harrell's escape routes. You say this had to have been a drug killing? Well, it didn't fit the pattern, and here's why. You say this must have been a stranger-on-stranger murder, a burglary gone wrong? Well, how do you explain the jewelry on one of the victims? And what difference does it make that your clothes were blood-free when you were stopped by the police? We know you had changed them after you left Diane Hawkins's house, and we'll show you a videotape that proves it.

Two DAYS LATER, under sunny skies, I drove over thawing roads to my parents' house. Thursday's winter storm had moved along, and the snow it had left in its wake was vanishing. This Saturday would be devoted to an outing. For years, my mother had a standing Christmas gift request: tickets for the two of us to a show downtown. For the last two years, because of my mom's depression, the tickets had gone unused. This year, the ritual was being renewed.

Before I could knock on the door, my father opened it. In his hand was a piece of paper that set out, in medical language, what he'd been told in layman's terms by his oncologist on Thursday and related to me later that evening. He wanted me to read the report.

I protested: "I'm no doctor; I won't understand what it means."

"Just read it," he said with gentle insistence.

Even the most resolute pessimist could find no ominous foreshadows in the language. The treatment was working, even better than expected; almost all of the cancer had disappeared from my father's lung. Other scans were showing that the cancer hadn't resurfaced in another part of his body.

As Mom and I drove from the house, I looked back at him, framed by the doorway. In my eyes, almost overnight, he'd lost the pallor of a victim and assumed the glow of a survivor. He was regaining the hair and the weight he'd lost to chemotherapy. He would spend this Saturday as he'd spent most in the more placid intervals in his retirement: padding around the house and fixing everything in sight.

On a day such as this, it was easy to believe that life was going to go on as it always had.

I knew that the true test of his treatment wouldn't come for several months. I knew that if any of the cancer broke through the body's line of resistance at the boundary of the lung, it would run free.

But I still believed.

EVERY DEFENDANT has the right to know, before he goes to trial, the nature of the charges against him and the facts and physical evidence that the prosecution will be bringing out in court to prove those charges. The process by which the government discloses these matters to the defense is universally known as "discovery": an oddly whimsical choice of words, implying an open-ended, adventurous quest, when in fact the ritual usually amounts to little more than exchanges of letters between lawyers. These exchanges, and the face-to-face negotiations that sometimes follow, can be formal or informal, contentious or casual, depending on the nuances of the relationship between the prosecutor and the defense attorney. I've had cases with lawyers whom I've known and liked for years, and our discovery conferences have usually devolved into friendly banter and, too often, indiscreet revelations about the government's case. And I've had my share of telephone conferences that have gone something like this:

"My client is entitled to know the names of your witnesses."

"No, he's not."

"Well, I'm demanding to know who they are and where they live so I can talk to them."

"You mean, so you can tell your client and he can have somebody go out and kill them? Go pound sand." (Click, dial tone.)

In the months before our trial, the dialogue between Michele Roberts and me was careful and proper, but with an undercurrent of mistrust. We were like two college roommates who'd been thrown together at random, awkwardly stepping around possible issues of conflict. Almost all of our communications were in writing, and our personal interactions were strained. There came a point when I had to show her and her colleagues—a junior lawyer serving as her assistant, and her investigator—the hundreds of items of evidence the police had gathered and the hundreds of photographs they'd taken. I reserved a room in my office building, recruited a police officer to do the honors, and stayed as far away as possible. The displaying of all the evidence would take hours, and the dead intervals would be filled with questions about subjects that I didn't have to, and didn't want to, talk about.

After the defense team left, Dean Combee appeared at my office door, asking if Ms. Roberts had seen me. I said no. Dean scratched his mustache and said, "That's funny; I thought she might have something to say to you. I just saw her about five minutes ago. She was sitting outside your office here, looking at all the photographs of Diane and Katrina. She was crying."

"She was *crying*?"

"Yeah, bubba," he said. "No doubt about it."

A YOUNG BLACK WOMAN stood before me. Her head moved spasmodically from side to side and her voice shook as she pointed a finger at me. "Some of us," she said, "wanted to take care of this the night it happened, but we followed what our elders said, and we held back." She stopped and took a breath, then spat out the next sentence: "Now we're wondering if we should have gone ahead and did what we wanted to do."

She was a niece of Diane, and she'd inherited more than a niece's share of Diane's pugnacity. Her ire had been raised by an event in a courtroom earlier that day, an event that had taken less than ten minutes to play itself out: the Harrell trial being delayed again.

Michele Roberts had called me two days before, saying she wasn't prepared for a February trial. Suspecting this was just a delaying tactic, I'd gone into an uncharacteristic rant: "I'm going to be ready to go, why can't you be? I'm not going along with this, and the judge won't, either." We'd gone back and forth with escalating vehemence, until finally I'd hung up on her loudly when she was still midsentence. At the time, I hadn't known or cared how that act would affect our dealings with each other over the weeks or months to come. All I'd been thinking was: *We can go to trial now. We have to go to trial now.*

We both went before the judge to plead our case: Evelyn Queen, a black female in her forties, a native Washingtonian with a prickly temperament. She'd listened to Roberts, brushed off my objections, then moved the trial to mid-July.

Before the hearing, the Hawkins family had filed into the courtroom quietly. Afterward, they'd left it grumbling audibly among themselves.

Later that night I convened a family meeting at the house of Ellen Neblett, one of Diane's sisters. I'd expected a group of about twenty. When I walked in, at least fifty people were there, and more came in as the meeting went on. For the next two hours, nine months of frustration boiled over. They treated me like family, sort of—maybe someone who'd married in, someone they'd started to have their doubts about because he wasn't quite pulling his weight. I told myself: *Don't take it personally. They're disenchanted with the legal system you represent, and they're taking it out on you.* But I knew there was more to it than that. They'd seen Michele Roberts have her way at the hearing. She and the judge were on a frequency I wasn't tuned into; it wasn't even on my dial. The family had to have wondered if the trial would go the same way. I was now in the position of having to defend myself without seeming too defensive.

"This is a big case," one of them said. "Maybe you should get yourself an assistant."

Meaning: Wouldn't it be a good idea to have a sister in there?

"I don't need more help," I answered. "Just watch."

I understood why they were impatient. For them, each day seemed endless and the nights offered no relief; a trial would give them something to focus their energies on and maybe offer some measure of resolution in the end. I tried to give them some perspective: "Every criminal case has its own clock. Compared to most cases, this one is moving pretty quickly."

What I didn't tell them was that I was as disappointed as they were to see the trial pushed off into the ominous future. Looked at from the fringes of winter, July was a distant landscape fraught with imponderables. I didn't tell them about my father's clock, ticking silently for however much longer.

One man wasn't at the meeting: Willie Harris. I called him the next day to tell him that the judge had rescheduled the trial for July 15. His first response was a groan. I said, "What's so bad about July 15?"

"Trina would have turned fifteen that day."

MOVING ON A parallel path was the case against Andre Brown, Harvey Newman, Chauncey Turner, and Lloyd Johnson, charged with the murders of Michael Graham and Robbin Lyons. It was now in its second year and heading toward a trial in late May 1994. Earlier that spring, the police had searched the jail cells of Brown, Turner, and Johnson and uncovered evidence of further criminal plotting. With nothing but time on their hands, Brown's crew members were writing to each other regularly, with Brown's letters revealing his twin fixations: obsessing over who his mystery accusers were and playing his fellow gang members against one another. Brown's missives featured a shifting cast of antagonists, but they had a common theme: Let's find out who's snitching on us and kill them.

He was increasingly concerned about losing control over his friends.

He was confident that Chauncey Turner had remained loyal to him, less confident about Lloyd Johnson and Harvey Newman.

And he still didn't know the identity of W-1, the witness outside Brown's immediate circle who had told the police about the meeting at which Brown, Turner, and Newman had plotted Michael Graham's murder.

AFTER ALMOST A YEAR and ten months of investigating Norman Harrell, I felt I knew more about him than many people know about their friends—his hobbies and prejudices, his romantic history and family background, his personal finances and employment record—the thousand and one shaded dots that make up the picture of a person.

But in one respect Harrell was remaining ever elusive: He still hadn't revealed exactly how he planned to defend himself at trial. He had left it to me to ponder his next step.

Finally, in late March 1994, came the first sign: a letter from Michele Roberts, requesting any and all information we had collected about drug dealing at the Hawkins house. I responded: No, you can't have it. We'd investigated this angle thoroughly and we were sure—as sure as you can be about anything—that there was no connection between drugs and the Eads Street murders. Some of the sources we had interviewed were confidential; we didn't want to turn their names over to the defense unless we had to. We wrote a letter to Judge Queen, declining the request and giving our reasons. She agreed, calling the defense's request "a fishing expedition." In essence, she was saying the defense can spend their time going off on such a trip if they want to, but the government doesn't have to supply the boat, the rods, and the reels.

The drug issue had now been raised and confronted, but surely not for the last time. Harrell was trying to find an enemy of the Hawkins family to blame the murders on—the more reprehensible the character the better, since the defense would compare him with the responsible workingman that Harrell would be portrayed to be at trial. Their search had brought them to the same path we'd already traveled: tracking down rumors of drug activity in and around the Hawkins house. Harrell's attorneys and investigators would be following our trail.

It's a strange feeling, after chasing a man for the better part of a year, to realize suddenly that he's coming up behind you.

IN JUNE 1994 Andre Brown was tried for the murders of Michael Graham and Robbin Lyons. The trial was handled by another

prosecutor in my office; I was occupied with the Harrell case and
other assignments. Sitting in a borrowed suit in court, wearing fake
glasses in a desperate effort to look fey and innocent, Brown finally
learned the identity of the mysterious W-1 referred to in the warrant
for his arrest—the person from River Terrace who'd told the police
everything he knew about Brown's plot to kill Michael Graham.

The witness was Chuck Turner, River Terrace hanger-on and
brother of Brown's codefendant Chauncey Turner.

Reco Hawkins had no part in the Andre Brown trial. He never
testified, never was even subpoenaed.

If Chuck Turner's appearance as a government witness surprised
Andre Brown, he didn't show it. He was just as stoic when another
familiar figure took the witness stand, dressed in blue prison garb:
Harvey Newman, now cooperating with the government under an
agreement that called for him to plead guilty to reduced murder
charges in the Graham and Lyons cases. The price for the plea offer:
testimony against Andre Brown.

If Andre Brown and Harvey Newman had both been on the street
leading up to trial, Brown would have sensed Harvey's disloyalty and
killed him without a moment's thought. But in jail, ironically
enough, Newman was able to free himself from Brown's hold; soon
he decided to cut his losses and accept a plea deal. The government
tucked him away in a jail outside the D.C. system. Newman's new
home catered to a unique clientele: cooperating defendants in violent cases from various states. He was now far outside the reach of
Andre Brown or any of his cohorts.

There was little that Andre Brown could now do to defend himself. The courtroom wasn't his territory, and his talent for creative
violence was useless away from the small piece of the streets he had
ruled for a few weeks one winter.

At the close of the weeklong trial, Andre Brown was found guilty
of the premeditated murder of Michael Graham, as well as conspiracy to commit the murder of Robbin Lyons. He still faced Maryland

charges for the actual murder of Lyons. He'd spend the rest of his life in jail. In the ensuing months, Chauncey Turner and Lloyd Johnson—tried separately from Brown—would likewise be convicted and sentenced to life imprisonment.

The case had exposed an ugly side of River Terrace. As settled as the community appeared, it had still spawned a gang of young men as dangerous as any that society had seen—youths animated only by the pulse of self-preservation and the thrill of the kill, whose minds wrapped easily around the idea of murdering a best friend over money and a young girl on a hunch and a whim. Anyone who observed the trial had to be taken aback by the eagerness with which the young men embraced violence as the solution to all their problems.

Michele Roberts was nobody's fool. Her team had had a front-row-center seat for the Brown trial. They hadn't missed a thing, and the wheels were turning.

MONTHS BEFORE, I'd defined a simple mission in the Harrell case: talk to everybody who knows anything. We'd done the best we could in the time we had. Now, with trial just over the horizon, there was just one more person to talk to: Harvey Newman. If there were any connection between the Andre Brown gang and the Hawkins murders, he'd know about it; he knew about everything the gang had done.

Reco Hawkins had dealt drugs in River Terrace, Newman said, but he was a small-time seller of "dime bags, twenties, fifties": ten-, twenty-, and fifty-dollar bags of crack cocaine, nothing bigger. Reco never sold drugs out of his house. Newman knew Reco's mother and sister Katrina from the neighborhood; they hadn't sold drugs or even used them. Reco had never worked with Newman, Brown, or Turner, and he had never worked in Michael Graham's gang. Newman knew of no reason why anyone would have wanted to harm Reco or his family—"He didn't owe nobody, didn't mess up nobody's money, didn't do nothing to nobody, didn't know nothin' about nothin'." Reco had never been in on the plot to kill Michael Graham, and none of the plotters had ever had a reason to think of Reco as a snitch.

As we left the jail, Newman's lawyer told me that Michele Roberts wanted to set up an appointment to talk with Newman. "I can't see how he can possibly help her," he said. I agreed.

As the July 15 trial date approached, the pace of our efforts accelerated. Much of what we spent time on were the mundane details of organizing and coordinating a trial presentation involving more than forty witnesses and many more exhibits. I called Diane's sister Ellen Neblett, my main contact in the Hawkins family, and told her to spread the good news: There would be no more delays. Travel arrangements were finalized for the witnesses and other family members who would appear for the trial.

Only one person with an intense interest in the proceedings would miss the first day: My father, who'd been given a clean bill of health in June but had a nagging numbness in his right foot. His doctor told him it was a side effect of chemotherapy, but he still wanted to have it checked. He had scheduled a test for Thursday the fourteenth and a doctor's appointment for the next day, but was looking forward to attending the next Monday. He wouldn't miss much; the first day of trial was usually like the first day of the school year: Everyone was there to get reacquainted and nothing really happened.

As for our case preparation, only one thing was left to be done.

Every few weeks, through summer and fall, winter and spring, Tony Duvall and I had piled into a car for a road trip. We traced Norman Harrell's escape route through D.C. and Maryland so many times that I knew the roads as well as some in my hometown, and I even knew the distances from point to point. We'd drive past River

Terrace to East Capitol Street, over the Maryland line to Route 202, where we would turn right, as Harrell said he did, and then to White House Road, where we'd turn right again. To our left would be the county landfill; to our right, dense forest extending along White House Road to a more developed area that included a car wash and several gas stations. Soon we'd be on Richie Marlboro Road and then at the point on Walker Mill Road where the P.G. County police officer first saw Harrell's brown and tan Ford truck coming toward him.

Whenever we drove from Eads Street to this point, usually in afternoon traffic with no stops, the trip would take twenty to thirty minutes. It took Norman Harrell almost two hours.

We knew that Harrell's mother-in-law lived just beyond Walker Mill Road. Maybe he was heading there, where his wife was staying, when the police stopped him. If so, Harrell went miles out of his way by turning off Central Avenue, taking Route 202 and White House Road.

We kept going back to the landfill; surely it had something to do with Harrell's detour. P.G. County police had canvassed it the night Harrell was stopped but hadn't seen anything suspicious. Even if they'd missed something, within a matter of days it would have been buried under mounds of garbage; any search we mounted would be futile. But on our last visit we did see a small sign we hadn't noticed before, posting the landfill's hours: CLOSED, MIDNIGHT TO 7:30 A.M.

Harrell couldn't have gotten into the landfill; the gate was locked.

And so, we were compelled into the deep woods just across the road. Just days before trial I returned to those woods, this time by myself.

As I turned off Route 202 onto White House Road, I thought: I've just killed two people, my clothes and boots are covered with blood, I have a bloody knife and a human heart in my truck. What do I do? I went to the entrance of the landfill. I was there at midday and the gate was open. I imagined it closed, as it would have been after midnight on May 25. I turned back onto two-laned White House

Road. In the dead of night it would have been unlighted. It had no shoulder, and on the right side there was a sharp slope between where it ended and the thick woods began. About a quarter-mile from the landfill, the fringe of land between the road and the forest briefly widened and flattened. I pulled onto the small piece of turf and descended into the woods.

I hadn't thought to change clothes before leaving my office. Now I was sweating through my dress shirt and the cuffs of my slacks were snagging in the brambles. I cursed old Jim Ballard, the man who saw Norman after the murders but couldn't bring himself to tell us. He could have saved me from all this.

I walked over the edge, under hanging vines and evergreens holding pinecones clustered in pairs like staring eyes. The sun flickered through the trees, and I entered a world of alternating light and shadow. Fifty feet in began an endless dark green. I walked farther. There at my feet was a cooler speckled with a brownish sludge.

I nudged the cooler with my right foot. It opened to reveal . . . a container of motor oil that spilled out on my shoe.

I emerged from the woods a short while later and got into my car. My hands were dirty and my shirt was stained and the fenders of my car were grimy from the dirt kicked up from the side of the road.

No matter; up the street was a car wash that I could use if I wished and a gas station where I could wash up.

I came out of the woods empty-handed. I hadn't expected to find anything, really; the dense forest would have consumed what I was looking for. But I'd still gained something.

Now I knew where he'd gone and what he'd done: first to the landfill, which he'd found locked; then to the woods across the street, where he'd made his drop; then to the car wash, to clean his truck; then to the gas station, to clean himself.

Driving back home, I couldn't help thinking: *I've finally got you.*

CHAPTER 9

SHORTLY AFTER 9:30 A.M. on July 15, 1994, Judge Queen called the lawyers in the Norman Harrell case to the front of the courtroom, and I took my place at the government's table.

Michele Roberts had to walk behind me to get to her table, but she didn't acknowledge me as she passed by. We'd had little personal interaction since our heated telephone conversation in February, the one that had ended with my hanging up on her. After that, almost all of our communications had been in writing. I couldn't blame her for still being resentful; she had no way of knowing that my frustrations at the time had had little to do with her. But I hadn't been particularly inclined to expend any emotional energy on an explanation, either.

The judge asked if the government was ready for trial, and I said we were; Roberts promptly interjected, "We certainly are too, Your Honor." The judge told us that she was finishing another trial that morning; our trial would begin in the afternoon. Finally, we'd be under way.

Outside the courtroom, I looked for Willie Harris and didn't see him. Then I remembered: Trina's birthday, of course.

I walked back to my office, expecting to find a message from my father about his doctor's appointment. I dialed my parents' number. My mother answered the telephone. I asked, "How did it go today?"

A long silence followed.

"Son, they found cancer cells in your father's brain."

I CALLED Judge Queen's clerk and told her that I wouldn't be able to return to court that afternoon because of a family crisis; I started to describe it in more detail but couldn't get the words out. Then I called Michele Roberts and went into more detail; I was already getting better with practice. She was gracious and offered to have the trial delayed, even if just for a short time. I said I'd have to think about it. I called Ellen Neblett and told her to spread the latest news: There might be a delay in the trial after all. Next I called my father's doctor; my parents had been told that my dad's cancer had spread, but they didn't know any other details. The doctor offered no encouragement. My father could undergo another round of radiation treatments, he explained, but the treatments would probably do him no good in the long run. In the doctor's experience, virtually every case in which a malignancy had proceeded to this stage ultimately proved terminal. I pressed him: "What does 'virtually every case' mean? Has any patient ever survived after the disease has gotten to this point?"

"A few," he said. "Maybe five, out of thousands."

Dad was waiting to hear about my conversation with the doctor. He'd faced his illness unflinchingly, but he didn't need to hear these numbers, and neither did my mom. I chose to tell him that some people had been in his position and survived. I didn't tell him how few.

It was early afternoon when I left my office, got in my car, and began driving around aimlessly: the illusion of action without commitment. After a couple of hours I remembered: I had to decide whether to ask for a delay in the trial. As devoted as I was to the Hawkins family, my first obligation was to my own. Besides, I thought, the case deserved better than to be handled by a distracted prosecutor. On the other hand, the doctor had said there was little I would be able to do in the near future to help my dad. He would go through the radiation treatments each day for several weeks; they would slow down the progress of the cancer and his condition would stabilize, if only for the short term. He'd been through them before and endured them well. If the trial were moved to another date, there'd be no guarantee that the prognosis would be any different then; it could be worse, and he could need me even more.

In late afternoon it began to rain and when the rain moved on it left behind a fog and through my windshield I could see steam rising from the blacktop. Driving toward my parents' house as evening fell, I passed the church of my youth: a white stone octagon set back from the road, topped by a stained-glass dome that I'd viewed with awe as a child. Once, gazing up at it from inside, I'd asked my parents: "Is that where heaven is?" On this evening, the dome was unlit and the church could barely be seen through the mist. I didn't stop in.

As I came up the walk at their house I could see my parents through the blinds in the recreation room. They were in their appointed places, as always, watching television: just another night, but so much different. I hadn't seen my dad for a week; suddenly he had a limp. We talked in the living room. He'd regained some of his familiar stoicism. "Actually I'm glad," he said. "I knew there was something wrong. Now I know what it is, and we can do something about it." His voice was rough.

My mother was holding up remarkably. I recalled a summer night in the same room nine years before, after my dad learned he had colon cancer. She'd drawn me aside, out of his earshot, and said: "I've got to be strong for you. You've got to be strong for me. And we've both got to be strong for him." Our world was triangular then; I wasn't married, and my job wasn't demanding. Now our world had more sides to it; it was richer but more complicated, and her message this night was accordingly different: "You've got your own family to worry about, and you've got your trial. Your father wouldn't want any of this to get in the way of that. You go ahead—we'll be all right."

When I got home, I left messages for Judge Queen and Michele Roberts, then called Ellen Neblett. "Pass the word to the family," I said. "We're on."

My son was at the age where he was becoming more attuned to me. He didn't need to have me around the house, so I spent most of the weekend at work. Ostensibly, I was preparing for trial; mostly, I was brooding. Now I recognize that my father's predicament shouldn't have been viewed as particularly unique or even unexpected. His suffering—unlike, say, Job's—hadn't been imposed whimsically. If a man smokes for thirty-eight years, the laws of cause and effect will eventually work to his detriment, with no help needed from a divine force. But thrashing around for two days in solitude in a hot office, I didn't have that perspective. Instead, I felt as if I'd been set up. Years before I'd decided I favored a compassionate God over an omnipotent one, and I'd settled into a detached but comfortable relationship with Him. Then my dad got sick, and in the depths of despair I'd reached out to God to do just a little bit more than I'd asked for in years, and this was what I was left with. If God was everything that the true believers around me were saying that He was, surely He knew of the grand irony that existed in the convergence of the events of July 15: Trina's birthday, the first day of trial, Dad's doctor's appointment.

If He let all this happen, how is that fair?

If He couldn't stop any of it, what's the point of talking to Him at all?

To a friend, I confided the news about my father with an observation: "Well, it looks like God has quite a sense of humor." To myself, I held more bitter thoughts. I recalled a quote that had once inspired me: "God," said a theologian, "is our silent friend at many distances."

Over the days and weeks and months before, during glorious intervals of myopic hope, this had seemed an apt description of something that was comfortably close by. This weekend, the phrase was still evocative.

My silent friend was far away indeed.

As I LEFT my house early Monday morning, I could hear the faint chirping of crickets that had outlasted the night. In the backyard of my house is a ridge and then a steep, grassy slope that ends abruptly in a forest. On July nights, the crickets own the woods, but only the most hardy or desperate among them are still trying to mate at sunrise. I locked the front door to secure my wife and son, still sleeping in the house, and turned to face a humid and heavy summer day, dressed in a suit my father had bought for me a month before. I could still feel his fingers on my shoulders and back as he assessed the fit. "Looks good," he'd said softly, then gave me a light push, as if to propel me into the world. He and my mother had given me a harder shove on Friday night. My place, for the moment, was away from them and the clenched fear that had moved stealthily into the house of my youth like a thief of the spirit. "Let go and let God" was a phrase I'd heard over previous months. Well, I wasn't willing to let God do too much of anything about then, but I did have to let go, at least enough to do what I had to do.

Not that it was going to be easy. My personal and professional lives were intertwined, and my entire reason for embarking on this career had its origins in my upbringing. I'd been drawn to public service by the example of my parents, both of whom spent years working for the federal government. While my father's idealism was worn away by daily contact with the bureaucracy of the Department of Defense, my mother had a prolonged break in service after I was born, and for those years her optimism remained uneroded. She passed on to me the belief that civil service was a great and noble path. Reminders of both of them were unavoidable: in my office, in photographs of my infant son, whose features favored my father's from birth; in the courtroom that I entered that Monday, as my eyes wandered to the back row where my parents once watched me in trial.

Fortunately, Monday's agenda was straightforward. A murder trial is like a heavyweight boxing match, with the fighters circling each other warily in early rounds while they feel each other out. The first day or two would be devoted to hearings on preliminary matters: first, a hearing on a defense motion to bar the government from using Harrell's statements to the detectives in the hours following the murders, as well as any physical evidence that the police later recovered; then, a government motion to admit into evidence the threats that Harrell had made about Diane to Deborah Courtney and others.

On the statements issue, Michele Roberts had filed papers with the judge charging that her client hadn't simply been "stopped" by the police; he'd been "arrested," and on insufficient evidence. In criminal law, the difference between the words "stop" and "arrest" is significant. Under a Supreme Court case called *Terry v. Ohio*, if a police officer has a "reasonable articulable suspicion" that someone has committed a crime, he can stop and then detain that person for a reasonable time while he investigates further. But the officer can't arrest the person without "probable cause"—he's required to have more than a mere suspicion. An arrest on less than probable cause is illegal, and the judge can suppress any statements or evidence obtained by the police under those circumstances.

The defense was claiming that because Harrell was ordered out of his truck on Karen Boulevard, handcuffed, then taken to the Prince George's County police station, he was in fact arrested. Roberts's motion argued that the police didn't have enough evidence against Harrell to justify arresting him at that time, thus the prosecution shouldn't be able to use against him any of the statements he made that night.

I'd already filed a written response: Yes, Harrell was handcuffed and detained by the P.G. County police, but the officers were allowed by the law to take safety precautions in stopping someone who'd been linked to a double homicide. Harrell wasn't read his Miranda rights by Detective Eric Gainey while on Karen Boulevard, but this was still just a stop and not an arrest; besides, Harrell didn't say anything there anyway. When Harrell got to the police station a short time later, Gainey told him he was free to leave if he wanted to; Harrell stayed. At that point Gainey erred on the side of caution and read him his rights before starting to interview him; Harrell agreed to answer questions without a lawyer being present. I didn't write this in my response, but what was in the back of my mind on Monday as I sat waiting for the judge to come on the bench was that it wouldn't matter that much if we lost this one. Nothing Harrell said in the police station interview could be interpreted as a confession, nor did it lead to any fresh leads or evidence. To be sure, the interview was helpful to our case; Harrell had admitted that he didn't know why bloodstains would be in his truck; he'd shown no reaction when Gainey had brought up the murders; he'd almost broken down under further questioning. But if the judge threw it out, it wouldn't devastate us.

The case was called, and I stood before the judge: "Kevin Flynn for the United States." The words meant as much to me then as they do now. It's a privilege, not to be abused, to be able to cloak yourself in the flag with the first words out of your mouth in a courtroom. Michele Roberts glided to her desk and smartly introduced herself; she was ready for action. Harrell, too, looked ready to go: "Good morning, Your Honor," he said with a smile. He looked like a man who knew something nobody else knew.

There's a division of responsibility in court cases: Judges handle the law, juries handle the facts. Since this hearing just dealt with legal issues, today my only audience would be the Honorable Evelyn Queen: too preoccupied with papers on her desk to acknowledge my introduction; subject to no one's clock or calendar but her own; knowing that in this space and for the foreseeable future all power emanated from her. If she said to stand, you stood, and if she said to keep quiet, you silenced yourself, at the risk of having her rule that you were in contempt of court. If she didn't like what she heard from me or the police officers at the hearing, she could take a piece out of my case without much thought. Fortunately for me, she was a former prosecutor and, just as important, an African-American female not much older than Diane Hawkins had been. As prickly as she could be in the courtroom, her profile didn't suggest that she'd be predisposed to give this defendant the benefit of the doubt.

In stressful times one clings to the routine. Even for a comparatively junior prosecutor in 1994, a hearing like this was familiar territory. Most criminal cases rely to some extent on evidence and statements obtained by police officers, and just about every murder case involves a challenge by the defendant to law-enforcement conduct. I knew the officers in the Harrell case, knew how well they'd performed on that chaotic first night, knew that we'd survive this preliminary challenge even if it didn't matter that much. For the first day or so, I could take refuge in the commonplace.

The government's usual strategy at such a hearing places a premium on brevity: Put on as little of your case as possible, and don't give the defense a shot at too many of your witnesses.

I called to the stand Michael Barnhardt of the Prince George's County Police Department. He entered in full uniform, a husky white male with a crew cut and stolid bearing. When I asked him his name and title, he said, "*Corporal* Michael Barnhardt"; in his department, military nomenclature was used. The judge turned slowly and peered at him over her glasses.

Barnhardt's role at the hearing was simple: to explain why and how Norman Harrell was stopped in P.G. County. I played a tape of the county dispatcher's lookout for the truck, then asked him about how he'd chased Harrell and then stopped him on Karen Boulevard:

"How many officers were present in vehicles at the time that the truck pulled to a stop?"

"I don't recall exact numbers. I would say three or four."

"What did you do then?"

"The man was commanded by voice commands to exit the vehicle and come back. He was then kept outside. He was not placed in a police car immediately. He was taken to the side of the roadway. I kept visual—I kept him in my sight the whole time we were there."

"Did all of the officers have their firearms drawn at that time?"

"Yes, they did."

"What was your understanding as to what this individual's status was at the time that you were stopping his truck?"

"Considered a suspect in a homicide."

Detective Whalen's transmission from D.C. had only sought Harrell as a possible suspect or witness, but the P.G. County dispatcher had unequivocally tagged him as suspect. Not that it mattered to me; the dispatcher's message had given the county police officers a reasonable articulable suspicion to stop the truck, and the officers had relied in good faith on the message.

"How soon after he got out of the vehicle was he handcuffed?"

"Once he was placed on the ground into a prone position, immediately."

"And why did you handcuff him?"

"For officer safety."

"What happened next?"

"He was patted down for weapons and held on the scene until notifications could be made to proper authorities who were investigating the incident."

At the end of his testimony Barnhardt put two large hands on the desk in front of him, pushed himself up from his chair, and strode out of the courtroom as purposefully as he strode in.

Judge Queen stared at him as he walked out the door, then looked at Roberts and smiled.

The hearing went on for the rest of the day and featured methodical testimony from Detective Gainey about his interview with Harrell. All I now remember of the afternoon is wishing that it would be over soon and hoping I'd regain my focus when the main event began.

AT THE END of the first day of trial I walked out to the corridor, looking to gather the Hawkins family and friends and tell them about the day's developments. More than twenty people filed into the anteroom just outside the courtroom. I closed the door behind me.

"I think there are a few more outside who want to come in," said Wesley Hawkins, an adopted son of Diane Hawkins's mother. As an orphan child, he'd been befriended by one of Diane's nephews and welcomed into the family. He was a huge man with a soft voice, close-cut hair, and skin so pale he could have been Caucasian. For all I know, he was; the family never said one way or the other. I opened the door, and several more people came in. "Now," Wesley said to me, "we'd like for you to join us in prayer." I grappled briefly with conflicting feelings, not wanting to intrude on a family matter. But I was drawn in by outstretched hands on both sides of me, and the circle was unbroken. I heard Wesley begin, "Lord God Almighty." I'd never held hands and prayed with anyone; I couldn't even remember the last time I'd held hands on both sides. Everyone had their heads bowed; I seemed to be the only one stealing glances at others in the room.

"We've come together to pray to you today," Wesley said. I looked down and thought: *that you'll give us the justice we seek, in this case that means so much to all of us.*

"We've come together to pray to you today," Wesley went on, "for Kevin's father. He's very sick, and he needs your help. Please bless him and keep him, and please help his family in what they're going through."

All together: "Amen."

Their points of origin weren't the same as mine, but our paths had now met at a junction of hope and despair. Collectively, they were the older brothers and sisters I never had. When they'd first come to the courthouse fourteen months before, I'd addressed them awkwardly in another small room. In many conversations over the ensuing months, with increasing ease and intimacy, I'd tried to instill in them a sort of secular faith: to believe in the system of man-made laws to which I'd devoted my working life, to believe that in this case the system would bring out the truth and mete out justice. I don't think I ever completely convinced them to believe in the legal system, but I do know this: They believed in me. On this day, I'd lost my faith in the God that I'd talked to since childhood, in many different voices. But I believed in this family—God's surrogates, standing in front of me—and for the foreseeable future I would think of them in the intervals I'd formerly filled with prayer.

SEVERAL TELEVISION TRUCKS were parked at the curb when I left the courthouse that day, and a couple of the usual crime-beat reporters slouched to one side sharing a smoke break. The news that night gave prominent coverage to the Harrell trial. I watched with ambivalence. My general feeling about reporters at my trials was that they could only get in the way; they couldn't make my evidence any stronger or my witnesses feel any more secure or testify any more persuasively. In this case, though, I was almost grateful for the press attention, for selfish reasons. My parents would get a kick out of seeing their son on TV, at a time when they needed a kick the most.

I saw no sign of the press at the courthouse the next morning. Either I'd beaten the reporters there or they were deployed elsewhere, to return for opening statements and the government's case-in-chief. At the courtroom, I was greeted at the door by a throng of Hawkinses. More family members had arrived, from as far as North Carolina, as the word had spread that we were finally under way. I spent time with them—a surprisingly buoyant group, under the circumstances—then commandeered the cart that carried the boxes of Harrell case files and set up my table for the day. It was some time before I remembered to be preoccupied by thoughts of imminent doom.

We had one witness remaining in the suppression hearing: Detective Herman Johnson, who'd almost gotten Harrell to break down during the interview at the P.G. County police station. Johnson described how he and his partner, Detective Dwayne Stanton, had encountered Harrell outside the station, then how Harrell had once again waived his Miranda rights and consented to be interviewed.

"Now, at any time during the conversation with Mr. Harrell in the interview room, did he ever indicate that he wanted to see a lawyer?"

"No, he did not."

After Roberts questioned him briefly, Johnson left the stand, and I rested my case on the statements motion. The defense called no witnesses. The record, simple and straightforward, was now closed.

Now the judge said she'd hear arguments, first from me and then from Roberts. There was no real dispute about the facts, and the case law on the issue was well known to any competent criminal lawyer; the only point of disagreement was over interpretation. After the arguments I expected the judge to rule immediately; this wasn't exactly the IBM antitrust trial. I was surprised when she instructed Roberts and me to return to the courtroom in two hours.

Eight minutes after the appointed time, Judge Evelyn Queen took the bench and issued her ruling.

"The case before us has a man driving in P.G. County, stopped by P.G. County police, handcuffed, and put on a curbstone without explanation. The explanation, more than fifteen minutes later, was you're not under arrest. But the handcuffs remain, at least an additional ten minutes, as he was transported to a P.G. County station for questioning. It is inescapable that the P.G. County police arrested Mr. Harrell without probable cause."

Okay, I thought. *Not entirely expected, but I can live with it.*

The judge went on: "It was an arrest that was not cured by the cuffs being removed at the station in Landover. He was taken from his vehicle. He was placed in handcuffs. If it were an investigative stop, what was being investigated? P.G. County police had nothing to investigate. When MPD arrived on the scene, they did not say what needed to be said, which was take the handcuffs off, you are free to go, sir, but we would like to talk to you. There is no indication in this record at all that anyone gave him this third option—you can go home—until after Detective Gainey told him he was free to go home after the first, initial interrogations. Accordingly, the motion to suppress is granted up and through anything related to or gleaned from the interrogations of Detective Gainey. That is the ruling of this court."

I flashed back through my notes. Hadn't Gainey told Harrell that he was free to leave before the interview at the P.G. County station even started? For a moment I doubted myself: Had I forgotten to ask the question? No, I hadn't forgotten. Well, at least the ruling only seemed to apply to the interview of Harrell by Gainey and Whalen. I rose and asked the judge to clarify: Would I still be allowed to introduce into evidence Harrell's statements to Johnson and Stanton?

The judge had been looking down at a sheet of legal-sized paper. Now she looked squarely at me. "Yes. But your physical evidence, you have a problem. Because Detective Gainey was illegally in a position to view the interior of the truck, and that is an issue we must deal with. If you are not legally standing where you should be standing when you see something that is evidence, which later is developed for trial, are you able to use that? And that is your project for the night. Tomorrow we will go through the evidence that may be affected. The statements are simple. The statements to Whalen and Gainey are suppressed. The physical evidence is really another quagmire. Because we must trail it back, as it were, to see where it originates. Okay. We'll take that up tomorrow morning about ten thirty."

The judge's last comment troubled me. Was she saying that she might suppress the blood evidence from the truck simply because she believed that Harrell had technically been arrested when he was stopped in the county?

The next morning, my worst fears were confirmed.

The judge began: "Yesterday I said that all statements and evidence seized as a result of the illegal arrest at Karen Boulevard by the P.G. County police, up and through the release and excusing of Mr. Harrell by Detectives Gainey and Whalen, on the parking lot or outside of the building in Landover, would be suppressed. The issue has become one of whether or not this would possibly include the truck. Now, this means there has to be an item-by-item evaluation. And if you're prepared to put on evidence that shows that in fact the truck, its seizure, and any evidence gleaned or taken from it is *not* related to the arrest on Karen Boulevard, fine."

I was dumbfounded. We'd spent two days on how Harrell had been interviewed by the police: What was said to him, and when, and by whom. Now all of a sudden, the judge was poised to strip us of evidence that hadn't even been the subject of the defense motion or the hearing. The motion had never mentioned the blood evidence seized from the truck, only other evidence recovered by the police in search warrants that had been approved at the time by other judges. As for the hearing, out of hundreds of questions posed to three witnesses, less than ten had related to the truck or anything inside, and none had been posed by the defense. The law didn't allow the judge to give Norman Harrell something he hadn't asked for by way of the motion, but she seemed to be going out of her way to do just that, and I told her so.

Roberts rose. Judge Queen was giving her an opening; she moved to exploit it. "I really can't believe," she said, "that Mr. Flynn is suggesting that he misunderstood what Mr. Harrell's papers were seeking to suppress. There can't be any question but that we were challenging the legality of his seizure and anything that stemmed from that."

Indeed, the defense motion had requested that the judge suppress "all evidence" seized by the police following Harrell's alleged arrest. But without more elaboration, this was an empty phrase, a legal cliché, the last sentence in every motion filed by every defendant. Of course, the defense would now want the judge to rule that the evidence from the truck was connected with the purportedly illegal arrest; it included the blood of the victims, the evidence that we couldn't do without. But wishing doesn't make it so.

Roberts pressed on, as if she thought that if she took a breath this precious gift might evaporate into thin air. "It's my understanding that Mr. Flynn should be prepared to present evidence of an independent source, or something that would suggest that the evidence in the truck was not the fruit of the—"

The judge finished her sentence for her: "Poisonous tree."

Ah, the fruit of the poisonous tree: a Biblical reference in an old Supreme Court case called *Wong Sun v. United States*, requiring the suppression of evidence—the "fruit"—produced by "poisonous" illegal police activity. But the defense had never referred to the case, or invoked its colorful analogy in its motion.

"There was no confusion in my mind that this was *Wong Sun*," the judge continued, "even though the defense never said the word." She raised her eyebrows at Michele, smiled, and went on. "From the day I picked up the pleadings, I knew this was *Wong Sun*. It's old law. We all had it in law school, and we've got new and nice cases that refine it. But it's the same old stuff that we all got in Criminal Procedure class. *Wong Sun*, 'poisonous tree,' 'fruit of the tree'—it's *gone*."

Now I saw where this was going, but it was too late to stop it. I'd never thought of the evidence from the truck as being connected with the question of whether Harrell had been arrested or merely stopped by the police. These were two separate matters—not even apples and oranges, but more like apples and elephants. Nobody, not the judge and not even the defense, was saying that the P.G. County officers didn't have grounds to conduct a traffic stop of Harrell's vehicle. But the judge seemed to be suggesting that because some officers saw the blood inside Harrell's truck at a point in time after other officers had, in her view, illegally arrested him, the evidence in the truck was therefore the fruit of the arrest. It was a novel legal theory, to be sure: the defense hadn't advanced it, the government disagreed with it, and the law didn't support it. Under the law as I'd known it for years, the officers had a right to view the inside of Harrell's truck from the outside regardless of whether he'd been arrested or merely detained. But the judge held fast to her position with a fervor that seemed to increase as she marshaled rhetoric to explain it:

"The illegal activity by the police commenced when the P.G. County police took the man out of the truck, had him out on the ground and in handcuffs. That's when he was arrested. And that's when the poisonous tree got planted. When they put those handcuffs on him and put him on the curb. And I said it didn't stop until Gainey and Whalen released him on the parking lot of the P.G. County station. And if I said it once yesterday I said it ten times. That the P.G. County police acted illegally. And that the detention, the cuffing by the P.G. County police, was the arrest that created the illegality. And anything between that point and that point on the station parking lot, and anything that flows from that, or is in or under that umbrella, is suspect.

"Now, if you didn't understand that, I'll give you ten more minutes to understand it. Because right now we are going to go through the evidence. The issue is the evidence, the physical evidence. I found the poisonous tree, and I found how far its roots went. Now, I want to go through the evidence and determine which evidence either is on the tree or off the tree."

"Well, Your Honor, if I could—"

"If the officer is illegally in a position to see what he sees, the evidence must go down. If the officer is illegally in a position to see, what he sees cannot be used because his eyes are part of the illegal conduct. His view is part of the illegal conduct. I am here today to entertain whether or not there's any way that this evidence can be used by the government because it's under this umbrella or because it springs from that time period. Everything and anything that flows from P.G. County stopping this man and illegally arresting him is tainted. That's the presumption at this point in time. You must overcome it by showing me that with or without the illegal conduct this evidence would have come to light. Am I correct in that understanding, Ms. Roberts?"

"Absolutely, Your Honor."

"All right, then. Ten minutes."

I escaped to the hallway, leaving behind me a lingering cloud of mixed metaphors filled with umbrellas and roots and trees and poisons.

But one thing was clear.

The main event had started and was close to ending, and I hadn't even known it.

I HAD TEN MINUTES to figure out what to do.

Journalists have sources they call on in tight situations, omniscient characters whom they meet in dark alleys or parking garages and to whom they attach rakish nicknames like Deep Throat. My source was a fellow prosecutor who only handled criminal appeals, never trials. He was the picture of academic dishevelment: By 9:15 every morning, his shirt sleeves were up, his tie was down, and his hair was askew. In spite of this—or maybe because of it—he had a secret society of female admirers in the office, a fact to which he was entirely oblivious. He rarely socialized with coworkers and was known to be truly devoted to only two things in life: his family and the law. His memory for Supreme Court and D.C. cases was encyclopedic, and his mind worked so rapidly that it was an exhilarating feat, an occasion for self-congratulation, just to keep pace with it.

He traveled in rarified intellectual circles; he and his wife named their daughter Miranda, not after the famous case but after their favorite character from a Shakespearean play. The incandescence of his brilliance was exceeded only by the ingenuousness of his self-effacement. Our conversations were generally by telephone, usually rushed, and always in legal shorthand.

I took a minute to explain the fiasco I was living. Nine minutes left. He went first.

"Can you go forward without the blood?"

"I could, but I can't. It's our best evidence. And if I don't have it, the defense will have a field day. To the jury, it will seem as if Harrell left the scene that night and then the police locked him up a few days later with nothing more on him than they had to begin with. Besides, if she's screwing me on this evidence, what's she going to do to me on the closer calls? So . . . am I right on the stop?"

"Yes. There's no doubt that, depending on the circumstances, the cops can draw their guns and cuff a guy and still have it be okay under the *Terry* case: still just a stop, not an arrest. There's another case—"

"Well, she's not buying it. What about the truck? Say for a moment she's right and this wasn't *Terry*. She thinks that under *Wong Sun,* I lose the truck and everything inside. Right or wrong?"

"Well, did Harrell say anything about the truck after he was stopped?"

"No."

"They stopped him, got him out of the truck, and that was it?"

"Yeah."

"And how long was it before the cops saw the blood?"

"Fifteen minutes. Maybe more but not much."

"You're okay. When officers make a traffic stop they can get the driver out of the vehicle. There's a D.C. case from last year—it's *Turner,* it's at 623 or 624 A-Second, it starts at about page eleven something—and after that, *Michigan v. Long* lets them search the inside of the passenger compartment before they let the guy go on his way, to make sure there are no weapons inside. Officer safety. So they would have seen the blood anyway, and held on to the truck. There's something in the cases called 'inevitable discovery' . . ."

"I know that. You know that. But that didn't happen here. She's stuck on the fact that in her view, they'd already arrested Harrell when they found the blood. Every goddamned thing that came after that arrest, she thinks is a fruit of it, I guess up to and including this conversation. I don't see changing her mind on that. I'm having a hard enough time convincing her of what did happen—I can't imagine trying to convince her of what could have happened."

I hesitated, then asked the question I didn't want to have to ask. "If I can't move her on this, would you guys take it up there?"

"Yeah, we would. We'd take it."

This was my new reality: Not yet two days into trial, and already I was plotting an appeal. It's like this—You're driving home from work, and your reality is: I'll get home, eat dinner, see the family, watch some TV, and go to bed. Then you get blindsided and you're by the side of the road with a broken-down car, and your reality has become: I'll call the police, wait on the shoulder for two hours, get a tow, catch a ride home after midnight. Your reality has changed and you've adjusted, with barely a thought. The day before, my reality was: I'll go to trial. Now it was: I'll go back to court, make a few more arguments. Then, I'll tell the judge we'll be appealing her ruling on the evidence issue, and that the trial will have to be put on hold for many months while the appellate process grinds along. Then, I'll listen to Michele Roberts ask the judge to release Norman Harrell in the meantime because, after all, the government's case isn't that strong and he's a workingman with a family and a pretty clean record. Then, I'll listen to the judge agree, because . . . well, because she's been agreeing with everything else Michele Roberts has been saying. Then, I'll go home and hope Norman Harrell doesn't go out and start killing more people. Then, I'll call the phone company and unlist my number.

"There's something else you might think about."

"I— What?" I was now down to a couple of minutes.

"Did you try to argue at all that the police actually would have had probable cause to arrest him?"

"No. It seemed like a long shot. I thought my safer bet was to say they had reasonable articulable suspicion, not enough for PC."

"Well, at the time P.G. County pulled Harrell over, what did the police know?"

"Just them, or everybody?"

"Everybody."

I saw where he was going. There's a doctrine in the law known as "collective knowledge": In assessing whether the police had enough evidence to arrest a suspect, a judge is required to consider everything that all of the officers in the case knew about it at the time. Here, the knowledge of the MPD detectives would be imputed to the P.G. County officers who made the stop. "Well," I said, "the MPD detectives had talked with one victim's son. He told them that Harrell had a child support case with the mother and the case was going to court the next day. He said Harrell came around the house on the night of the murders, that he was acting real strange. The son said that when he left, Harrell was the last one there with the victims. Oh, and he described what Harrell was wearing, and it was different from what he had on when he was stopped."

"How'd the cops on the scene of the stop know that this was the same guy who was last seen with the victims?"

"The son said his name, and the guy identified himself by name after he was stopped."

"That could be enough for PC. You've got nothing to lose. The worst thing that happens is you lose in front of Queen, but you give the Court of Appeals something else to hang their hat on."

He didn't say what a harder man would have: Why didn't you bring all this out before? If the testimony was potentially relevant to the issue of whether the police had probable cause to *arrest* Harrell,

it was definitely relevant to whether they had a reasonable articulable suspicion to *stop* him. The answer was: I didn't think of it. I
didn't think a judge could hear the tape of a dispatcher describing a
fleeing homicide suspect and then find fault with the police taking
steps to protect themselves when they stopped him. But I'd broken
a cardinal rule of trial work: Don't assume that what's self-evident
to you is self-evident to anyone else. It would be the last time I'd
take anything for granted in this case. For the moment, though, I
couldn't look back. "Any other ideas as to how we might be able to
keep this out of your shop?"

"Well . . . you could try talking to the other officers—maybe Harrell
committed some other traffic offense while they were chasing him—
something they could have arrested him for."

"If they had PC to arrest Harrell anyway . . ."

"Then they would have impounded his truck regardless of what
MPD had on him. That would untaint the blood evidence."

With a minute to spare, I had a strategy. If my appellate guru was
the fox, knowing many things, I was the hedgehog, knowing one thing
well: how to keep my options open. The judge had challenged the
government: put on witnesses to show that "with or without the illegal conduct, the evidence in the truck would have come to light." On
its face, this made no sense. She and I disagreed about whether Harrell had been stopped or arrested, but there was no doubt about one
thing: If he hadn't been pulled over by the police, the blood in the
truck wouldn't have been discovered. Surely she could figure out
that if I had any other information in my back pocket—say, a 911 call
from another witness telling police that there was a truck full of
blood driving down Walker Mill Road—I would have mentioned it.
But I would accept her invitation, such as it was, and use it to reopen
the hearing. I was now playing to two audiences: the unreceptive
judge on the bench in front of me and the as-yet faceless, chimerical
group of appellate judges who someday would probably be reviewing
the cold record I was creating.

And while I stalled for time, I'd try to figure out what had made this judge react so viscerally against my case.

I RETURNED TO the courtroom, told the judge that we wished to reopen the hearing, and a short time later—after a rushed conference with my witnesses—called Detective Whalen to the stand. Whalen testified about everything that Reco Hawkins had told him on the night of the murders. None of what he said should have been new to the judge; the facts had been mentioned in other documents that had been filed in the case. But words spoken by a witness in court have a resonance that words printed on paper can't match, and I found myself glancing occasionally at the judge to gauge her reaction. Was there some glimmer of recognition, some sign that she recognized what I was doing, that perhaps I might even be able to move her to change her mind: a nod, maybe, or even one of the sly smiles she regularly cast toward the defense table? No, nothing. *Well*, I thought, *at least she's letting me go on*.

Detective Gainey was my next witness, making a return appearance. Before, I'd only asked him about his interview with Harrell; now I needed him to elaborate on the events that led up to the interview. He testified that when he arrived on the scene, P.G. County officers immediately directed him to the Ford truck and he saw the red stains inside, all of this happened before he approached Harrell on the curb. The point: Harrell had endured only a comparatively minor degree of confinement when probable cause ripened to impound and search his truck.

My last questions would be: "Did Harrell call himself by the same name that had been used to identify the last man seen with the victims? How was he dressed?"

Roberts: "Objection, Your Honor. Irrelevant."

The judge: "Step up here. Detective, stand over there." The lawyers would discuss the objection outside Gainey's earshot.

Like every other judge in every other courtroom in America, she presided from on high: a platform elevated to the point where a man of average height standing beneath it couldn't look at her without craning his neck. She strained and looked down at me. "Relevance, counsel?"

"Mr. Harrell said his name was Norman Harrell. That's relevant to what Detective Gainey knew at the time. And Detective Gainey knew that the person he was dealing with had changed clothing, which is relevant to his entire picture of the scene and what he was evaluating."

"How is that going to take the taint off the truck?"

"Well, Your Honor, what it's going to do is establish that at the time the truck was impounded there was probable cause to search it."

"What does his dress have to do with anything?"

"It's relevant to the probable cause determination, Your Honor, as to the vehicle—"

"You can confirm that he's Mr. Harrell. After that, we're finished with this. It's not necessary for the decision that I am now in the process of making."

I was being sent away. I turned to leave, then turned back: "It may not be, but it is necessary for the decision which might in fact be the *proper* decision."

If the small plastic jar of pens that sat on her desktop could have accommodated a thunderbolt, she would have hurled it at me. But her most lethal weapon was the authority she wielded, and she knew it. "Confirm the identification, counsel."

"Not the dress?"

"No."

The rest of the hearing was anticlimactic. We offered three P.G. County officers to show that the police had had probable cause to arrest Harrell for traffic offenses; two she heard from, one she dismissed. She'd heard enough. "You can't," she said, "start an operation, as in this case, a want for criminal conduct, and then because you can't substantiate the criminal conduct that you started out with, make up another set of criminal conduct. And that's what you're trying to do, make up this traffic matter."

"It's not being made up," I interjected. "It's not like I'm creating this out of whole cloth." But I was getting nowhere, and the hearing ended abruptly. I would get one last chance to argue my position the next day . . . for what it was worth.

For three days Norman Harrell had sat quietly at his table, taking in the proceedings like a man at the racetrack watching his long-shot pick take a lead into the stretch. Now, lumbering from the court-room, he grinned and nodded at the judge and broke his silence: "You have a nice evening, now, Your Honor."

"Good afternoon, sir," she answered.

OUTSIDE THE COURTROOM I saw Eric Gainey, slumped on a long bench with other officers. "Listen, man," he said, "I'm really sorry. I'm real sorry I fucked up this case."

I said, "You didn't fuck up anything. You guys did just what you should have done under the circumstances. You did a great job, and so did the cops in P.G. The judge is just flat-ass wrong—and we've got to make her change her mind." I thought, *Fat chance.*

I started down the hall, leaving the Hawkins family behind but then went back; it would be best for them to be able to adjust to the bad news gradually. I gathered them in our familiar anteroom. Two days before, it had served as an impromptu chapel; now it was once again a squalid way station littered with dated newspaper sections and dented Styrofoam cups. I started to give them all the ugly details but stopped; I couldn't shatter all at once whatever faith they'd developed in the judicial process. Instead, I said as little as I could without lying to them. I told them that we'd run into some trouble but we'd get past it, and if anyone wanted to, they could call me at the office; I'd be there very late.

Crossing the plaza outside the courthouse, I was relieved to see no sign of the press. My parents had enough to worry about without turning on their TV and hearing that their son was about to lose his best evidence in the most important case he'd ever tried.

"JUDGES WEAR the black robes," I was saying, "and they can do anything they want in the courtroom, but in the end they're just like everyone else. They might try to make it seem as if everything they do is based on some objective view of the law. But they're just like you and me, you know—they're ruled just as much by their hearts as by their heads. And the only way I'm going to be able to save this thing is to figure out . . ."

I had a captive audience in Detective Dean Combee. The lighted clock in his cruiser said it was nearing midnight, but I was just getting started. He'd just come off his shift and I'd just left my office, still wired from an evening spent combing through casebooks, scribbling on legal pads, and contemplating the question of the week. Why? Back then, my wife and I worked in the same building, our son was in a day-care center near the courthouse, and the three of us would commute together every morning. But that summer, on more nights that I care to remember, I'd send them home at the end of a workday, spend five or six more hours at my desk, and catch a ride home with Combee. I'd first heard about the murders from him, before I'd ever heard the name Norman Harrell, and in our regular nighttime travels we'd turned the case over again many times more.

This night, though, he kept changing the subject. The Harrell case wasn't on his mind as it was, obsessively, on mine. Instead, he was preoccupied by a murder scene he'd recently been summoned to, and a suspect who would remain at large for as long as it took for Combee to build a case against him; it seemed as if Harrell was old news to him. I thought, *This is why cops and prosecutors sometimes talk past each other.* Cops are on the front lines, and we're not; we have the luxury of looking to the long term and they don't. What they put together we have to keep together. They have to spring to action as soon as they hear that a body has dropped, and once on the scene they know that the killer might still be lurking in the shadows. We get called later, after time has cooled the body, and the killer's ardor too. They thrive in the niche of time that exists between the dead of night and the following day; that's when their cases are made or broken. Combee had lived with Norman Harrell in his head since the previous May, and he'll no doubt remember how Diane and Trina died until the day he dies himself. But that night Dean Combee thought about Norman Harrell like this: *He's off the streets for now, and another killer isn't.*

It was past midnight by the time Combee pulled into my driveway. In nine hours I'd be back in court. Sure, cops and prosecutors are different, but there'd been a lesson for me in our disjointed conversation: Do what's in front of you. Don't question the forces that buffet you about without deigning to explain. Do what you have to do today; tomorrow and the next day are imponderable. And who knows . . . By then, maybe something might turn up.

I watched Combee's car from my front walk as he drove away from my house. The hum of his engine was drowned out by the shrieks and whistles of crickets on the prowl. For someone, at least, the day was new and full of promise.

IT WAS TIME FOR final arguments on the defense motion to suppress.

Hawkins family members were, as usual, massed in attendance in the courtroom. They were joined by another group of interested people: MPD officers and homicide detectives. Word had spread that a judge was about to suppress essential evidence in a murder case based on a finding of illegal police action, and law enforcement had turned out to see what would happen.

In the law, the past is predominant: how other cases have been decided, how those cases are similar to or different from the present case. In the law, the past has a name; it's called precedent. There's also a hierarchy of influence among these past cases: Supreme Court decisions trump everything, followed by appellate court decisions, with trial courts at the bottom of the precedental totem pole. Trial court judges deciding legal issues studiously try to keep their rulings in line with appellate court precedent, because more than anything else they hate being reversed on appeal; in the genteel environment in which judges move, it's the closest thing possible to a public spanking. For a trial lawyer, the term "legal research" can be boiled down to one sentence: Find the most influential cases that involved facts similar to yours and were decided in a way that favors your side. The problem is, there are far fewer published cases than there are factual permutations in the world, so there's always room for interpretation and argument. In the Harrell case, I thought that the precedents were on my side. But had there ever been a case with facts precisely like mine? No, never.

The judge placed no restrictions on our arguments. I wasn't looking at a watch and had no sense of time; I believe I may have spoken for twenty minutes uninterrupted. This wouldn't be a long time to address a jury without stopping, but jurors aren't supposed to engage in conversation with a lawyer; one can't say, for example, "You lost me there, Counselor, start over." Judges in an oral argument routinely interject questions and comments; it's how they let the lawyers know what they're thinking. Not this judge, though, not on this day. I'd prepared for a dialogue and ended up delivering a monologue.

But once Roberts began speaking, human interaction commenced—a conversation between two people—and all I could do was sit back and watch as she and the judge finished each other's sentences and completed each other's thoughts. Then the discussion shifted to an appellate case I'd emphasized in my argument. On facts similar to those in the Harrell case, the court had allowed the government to use the challenged evidence; if Judge Queen agreed with my contention that the similarities were significant, it would give her support for ruling for our side. Roberts rolled through the facts in that case and said that it wasn't compelling precedent in this case. The judge raised her hand. "Why isn't it, counsel? Why isn't it?" It was a simple question, perhaps even rhetorical. But out of the thousands of words uttered in that courtroom on this subject during that week, these were the first that suggested that the judge acknowledged the existence of two points of view. The moment passed quickly, though. Roberts neatly parried the question, and the arguments soon ended. The judge invited us to submit legal briefs to her that night; she would give her ruling the next day.

When Roberts sat down, I recalled a moment the day before. Sitting at my table in the courtroom, waiting for the judge to take the bench after a break, I happened to overhear an exchange between her and another lawyer who was assisting her in the case. The lawyer had asked her what she thought the judge was going to do with the motion. Roberts hadn't even looked up from something she was reading. "It looks like she'll do," she replied, "whatever we want her to do."

"CAN YOU GIVE us your name, please, and spell your last name?"

"Deborah Courtney. C-O-U-R-T-N-E-Y."

"Just for the record, ma'am, you walked in today on a crutch or a cane. What is that a result of?"

"I've had arthroscopic surgery."

"And when did you have the surgery?"

"On Thursday of last week."

"Are you prepared to go forward here and testify? Is that okay?"

"Yes."

The judge had decided to use the balance of the day to hold a hearing on the government's motion to admit evidence of Harrell's threats against Diane Hawkins. Deborah Courtney was the government's first witness. Seeing her take the stand, I thought: *If the judge throws out our evidence tomorrow, this might be the closest we'll ever get to having our day in court.*

"Are you familiar," I asked, "and were you before May 26, 1993, with a man named Norman Harrell?"

"Yes."

"Is that individual in the courtroom today?"

"Yes, he is."

"Can you identify him for the record by where he is sitting and what he is wearing?"

Deborah shifted in her chair and winced. She looked right at Harrell for one, two, three seconds. A year before, she'd come to my office and broken open the case for us; now she was face-to-face with her former friendly antagonist.

"He's wearing a blue prison jumpsuit, white T-shirt, and has his finger across his mouth."

I looked over at Harrell. He took his hand away from his mouth. He wasn't smiling.

An hour later his scowl had deepened. Deborah had gone through her story: all of Harrell's talk about Jamaican-style killing, about child support, about Diane. Through it all, the judge was listening to this testimony with rapt attention. Earlier that day she'd reviewed our motion to admit into evidence at trial the disturbing photographs of the bodies of Diane and Katrina; copies of the pictures had been attached to our papers. I knew she knew how these victims had been killed.

Roberts rose to question the witness. An hour or so later she sat down, frustrated. Deborah Courtney was invulnerable to cross-examination. Teetering close to tears, she couldn't be badgered. Simple questions prompted rambling reminiscences about her friend Diane and the times they had shared together, and her feeling of loss was palpable. She treated Roberts as if she were an old friend, calling her "honey" and "hon." But she never looked at her. She directed all of her answers to Harrell. "Isn't that right, Danky?" she said at one point as she described how Diane and Harrell had met. And he dropped his head, and I thought I saw him blink twice.

After Deborah finished testifying I spoke with her in the back of the courtroom. "From where you were sitting," I said, "you could see better than I could. Were those tears in his eyes?"

"Sure they were," she said. "He knows what he did, and he knows that I know."

The hearing ended with testimony from Carlene Hawkins and Sharon Randle, two of Diane's nieces. Carlene testified about Harrell's statement, on the Sunday before the murders, about hurting Diane if she pressed charges for child support; Sharon testified about similar statements he made at Diane's house in the summer of 1992. Like Deborah Courtney's, their testimony not only incriminated the defendant, it also humanized the victims.

In the end, the answer that lingered longest in memory had nothing to do with the evidence against Norman Harrell, though it had everything to do with what the case was really all about. Sharon Randle had just taken the stand. I asked her what her name and age were, then asked if she had known someone named Diane Hawkins. She said yes. I asked, "What was your relationship with Diane Hawkins?" It was a preliminary question; it called for a simple answer such as "She was my husband's aunt." Never having testified before, she took the question literally and answered it as fully as she could:

"She was my aunt.

"She was my friend.

"She was my confidante.

"She was everything to me."

IT WAS MIDAFTERNOON the next day when Judge Evelyn Queen took the bench to announce her ruling on the defense motion to suppress statements and physical evidence.

"Taking up the motion. That is, the subject of whether or not the evidence in the defendant's truck was going to be inevitably discovered under the circumstances of this case. That is the government's position. The defense's position is that under *Wong Sun* and its progeny, that truck represents poisonous fruit which, because of the violation of illegally arresting Mr. Harrell, must be suppressed."

As she spoke I was scribbling her words on a legal pad, even though a court reporter was sitting right below her, keeping a record. I wanted to have something to do; I didn't want to be looking at her when she took the life out of my case.

"I initially posed the question, and the question is still the question before me. Whether or not Lieutenant Baker of the Prince George's County Police Department, when he flashed his light through that truck, was legally in a position to view the interior of that truck.

"This court is inextricably drawn to the decision that, yes, he was legally standing looking in the truck."

I kept writing, because I still didn't want to look up.

"Initially, the court was in possession of information that a broadcast called for P.G. County police to stop Mr. Harrell. Upon exploring what to do with the truck, the government has explained, or has produced evidence that shows, that at the time that the broadcast was initiated in the District of Columbia it was that a tan and brown truck and its driver, presumed to be Mr. Harrell, were being sought in connection with a double homicide. Meaning, he could have been a suspect and/or he could have been a material witness.

"P.G. County had a right to rely upon that when they stopped the truck. Stopping that truck in reliance on that radio broadcast, which gave them an articulable suspicion to make a *Terry* stop, they could take him out of the truck and hold him.

"At this point in time Lieutenant Baker, who Corporal Barnhardt testified discovered the blood, had a right, for his own safety, to view, review, and look at the interior of the truck. He was legally standing in a spot or position that permitted him to look inside the truck.

Once he is permitted to look inside the truck legally, there is no taint on the evidence.

"In addition, this court finds that it was inevitable that the truck was going to be looked into. Notwithstanding the illegal arrest, if when Detective Gainey had appeared on the scene he had said he is not under arrest—take the cuffs off of him, he is going to follow me in his truck down to D.C., or wherever—before Mr. Harrell could reenter, the police had the absolute right to look inside that truck for their own safety. It was inevitable, if they looked inside that truck, that they were going to see the bloodstains. The bloodstains could not be missed.

"Accordingly, the truck and its contents will not be suppressed."

WE HAD SURVIVED.

So, what had happened?

For the last four days this had been a police case, cut adrift from the deaths that had brought us all to the courtroom. To Judge Evelyn Queen, raised in the Washington of a different era, this was all about Prince George's County. Hearing about a black man lying face down in handcuffs may have raised the specter of the earlier unreformed and unrepentant cowboy force. Perhaps she looked at Michael Barnhardt and saw a stereotype—the militaristic white cop—and not the officer I'd come to know, a man brave enough to chase down a murder suspect in the middle of the night, sensitive enough to move him off a curb and out of sight so a television cameraman couldn't take his picture. Perhaps she looked at Norman Harrell and saw Terrence Johnson, the unlikely hero in another decade's melodrama over police brutality. It was only because of the fortuitous involvement of Deborah Courtney, Carlene Hawkins, and Sharon Randle that the focus had shifted back to where it should have been all along: to what Norman Harrell was charged with doing, and why the police officers in this case had had a reason to fear him.

That's the best explanation I'm able to come up with now, twelve years later. Maybe the real reason was more simple: maybe she'd never encountered the law on inevitable discovery and needed the week to master it. Maybe it was more personal: I'd come before her and failed to present to her the proof she'd wanted at the beginning of the hearing; later, she couldn't hear the message because she didn't favor the messenger. Maybe it was more strange: maybe she sympathized at first with Harrell because she'd looked into his eyes and discerned an innocence that others didn't see.

Whatever it was, in the immediate aftermath of the hearing I wasn't inclined to mull it over any further. All I knew was this: *Today, Norman Harrell is off the streets. And tomorrow, I'm going to trial.*

But I couldn't help thinking that Norman Harrell knew something, too. He knew that for four days he'd won someone over to his side. This woman had seen things his way for a while; hell, she might even come back around his way. Just wait until he had *twelve* people in a jury box to hear him say his piece. He knew a dude who'd gone to trial once and got himself a hung jury, then went again and got himself another one—the government ended up dropping the thing altogether. No sir, things didn't look so bad after all.

CHAPTER 10

I WAS ONLY FIFTEEN WHEN the Vietnam War ended, which means that I never went to battle for my country, which means that I have no right to use war as a metaphor for anything. But at least this can be said of murder trials, as it can't of football games or most other activities where military comparisons abound: They involve matters of life and death. And though the intensity of the courtroom can never approach that of the battlefield, there are still strategic and tactical similarities between the two endeavors. The government marches into court, the story of its case broken down and spread out among its witnesses and evidence. It has the burden of proving the defendant's guilt as to every detail of the charged crimes; it has an obligation to *advance*. Its means are by necessity conventional: amassing all its resources, then proceeding in straight lines in the open, abiding by standard rules of combat. So many elements need to converge in one place that before the effort is undertaken, the notion of victory can seem implausible. The defense, on the other hand, has no obligation to advance; it has no obligation at all. Instead, its mandate is to *destroy*—to assault the government's proof, to undermine it, to erode it, to blow it up, by whatever means—and it can conceal itself in the dense underbrush of a case and strike when and where it wants to. If you have a problem with these tactics, if you believe they're somehow underhanded, then think of the colonists lying in wait for the redcoats, and remember: We've never been a people inclined to make it too easy for established authority.

There's a phrase for the disorientation that befalls soldiers caught in the maelstrom of combat: the fog of war. I've never experienced the real thing, but I've known its pale imitation in my profession. Later, once the Harrell trial was over and the fog had dissipated, I'd be able to read the transcript of the proceedings—the dispatches from the front, as it were—and see it more clearly for what it was, and what it wasn't. I'd see it as not so much a struggle between "good" and "evil"—an especially facile phrase in this context—but as nothing more or less than an engagement of opposites. One side attacked on the other's home ground; one side pursued a strategy of attrition and the other, subversion; each side, in turn, made gains, made mistakes, took losses. At the end of every murder trial, no matter what else has happened, one man is left standing. He's the defendant, and he's either walking one way with the marshal to confinement or the other way with his family to freedom. And there is a moment in the conflict that sets the course of that man's personal history one way or the other. When you're living through it, when your days are accretions of thousands of moments, you can often barely distinguish one from the other. It's only later, when words on a page summon echoes from the past, that you can see where the almost inconceivable became the inevitable.

"GOVERNMENT, YOU MAY OPEN."

Sitting behind me were sixty family members and friends of the Hawkins family—and my wife, Patrice, who had wrangled a folding chair and was sitting in the courtroom aisle. Sitting to my right was a jury of twelve D.C. residents—ten blacks and two whites, seven women and five men—plus two alternates.

These jurors had survived—perhaps to their private consternation—a process of elimination, called "voir dire," that had taken three days to complete. More than a hundred people had been called to Judge Queen's courtroom and undergone pointed questioning by the judge and the attorneys. What have you heard about the case? Would the nature of the charges make you tilt against the defendant without ever listening to the evidence? Or toward the prosecution? How's your health? Would you have problems on your job if you had to take a few weeks away from it? Have you ever been charged with a crime? If so, do you think you were treated fairly by the government? If not, would you hold it against the prosecutor here? And, over and over again: Can you be fair? *Can you be fair?* The ones who said they couldn't were dropped quickly by the judge; most of those who equivocated soon followed. A group of fifty or so remained for the lawyers to choose from. We knew very little about them—age, home address, occupation—but we had to make unsparing assessments of their intellect, their morals, their judgment. There are a lot of theories about jury selection, some quite sophisticated. But the most honest come down to this: look into their eyes and listen to your gut. The government needs a unanimous jury to convict, so we look for consensus builders—though pro-establishment follower types are welcome to us. The defense needs only one stray juror to hang a case, so they look for independent thinkers—though antisocial eccentrics are fine with them.

Down to my last decision in the Harrell voir dire, looking at two rows of strangers and considering whether I could spend weeks in their company and then entrust my case to them, I'd done what I always do: blur my eyes to obscure individual features, look across the faces, and see if I note any oddities. Any slouchers? Any fidgeters? Hostile vibes? I'd paused at one woman, age forty-five, round-faced. She was smiling at me. She was smiling at *everyone*.

Given the circumstances, she seemed strangely jovial. She'd said she could be fair, said it eagerly—maybe too eagerly.

Now this woman sat as one of the twelve jurors, in the top row toward the right, her hands clenched in her lap, looking like someone who'd just answered the phone and heard the words "Are you sitting down?" She wasn't smiling.

"This is the story of a mother and a daughter," I said, "Diane Hawkins and Katrina Harris, who walked among us once on the earth as living and vibrant human beings. Until a cool night last May, when they were hunted down in their own home and cut open like they weren't even people. And during the course of this trial the government will show you convincingly and overwhelmingly that the man who is responsible for doing that, the man who plotted vengeance against Diane Hawkins and took her daughter, too, is none other than the man who sits before you, Norman Harrell." I turned around, pointed at him, and looked him in the eye. He didn't flinch, but just measured me with a stare as if he were sizing me up for a wall mounting.

"Now, how do we know Norman Harrell did this? How do we know that he committed these brutal murders? Well, first we know because he told people he was going to do it, and he told people he was going to do it exactly the way he did it. We know by the words that were uttered from his own mouth to witnesses, not even weeks before the murder, that he was going to kill Diane Hawkins if she took him to court for child support and he was going to kill her exactly the way she died. That's the first way we know that Norman Harrell did this, by words uttered from his own mouth.

"How else do we know Norman Harrell did this? Well, ladies and gentlemen, we know because the physical evidence in the case tells us that he did it, in the form of bloodstains found inside the defendant's vehicle no more than two hours after the murders were committed, bloodstains which have been conclusively and to a one-hundred-percent certainty established are *not* consistent with

Mr. Harrell's blood. Bloodstains which were *human* blood. Bloodstains which were consistent with the blood of the *victims* in this case."

I paused. I wanted my last words to linger a few moments in silence. In the communications business this is referred to pejoratively as "dead air." Broadcasters abhor it; for them, every second has to be filled, for fear that the audience will change stations. Trial lawyers too often follow the example, racing through their parts as if remote controls were being aimed at them. But trials are different from TV or radio shows. They require more commitment, more focus from the audience—the jury—and sometimes a little quiet is a good thing. Sometimes the mind and heart need time to absorb what the eye and the ear have taken in.

After a moment I continued.

"How else do we know Norman Harrell did this? Well, ladies and gentlemen, we know it because the bodies of Diane Hawkins and Katrina Harris will tell us, by the way that they were killed and the manner in which they died." This was my way of saying: Diane and Trina won't be here, but they'll be testifying against Norman nonetheless. "I don't like to have to go through this. But it's something you're going to have to know now because you'll see it in the trial. You'll hear evidence, ladies and gentlemen, that Norman Harrell was a hunter, that he was trained in the manner of draining and gutting an animal. And as you'll see, ladies and gentlemen, that's exactly the way Diane Hawkins and Katrina Harris died in this case. They died as if they were animals."

I scanned the faces of the jurors, but saw no visible reactions. They'd been told during voir dire to expect to hear gruesome evidence during the trial; maybe they'd already steeled themselves. Or maybe they were shell-shocked.

"How else will we know that Norman Harrell did these murders? We will know, ladies and gentlemen, because common sense will tell us that crimes such as this are not done for no reason." Judges always instruct juries that the government is only required to prove the defendant's guilt, not his motive: the who, what, where, and when of the crime, but not the why. Juries never listen to this. They *always* want to know why. "Crimes such as this are done by people who have an important reason, if only to themselves, to do something like this. And you will hear, ladies and gentlemen, that Norman Harrell was the only one who had a motive, a clear compelling motive to commit these crimes. Because not just two weeks before the murders, not just six months, not just a year, but for a long time, Norman Harrell had been telling people and had made his feelings clear about child support. To be blunt about it, he wasn't going to pay it. He didn't believe in it. He didn't think it was up to a man to have to pay it. He thought the man should just be able to take care of his child himself and that the courts shouldn't get in the way. And you'll find in this case that Mr. Harrell had a motive, a motive that he expressed and a motive, ladies and gentlemen, that had tragic consequences for the decedents in this case. Because you will also hear that *the very day after* these murders took place, Diane Hawkins and Norman Harrell were going to go to court for the first time on a child support matter that she'd brought against him."

I paused. The basic themes of the story had been established. Now it was time to add detail, starting from the night of the murders. I took the jury to the scene.

"Thirty-four sixty-one Eads Street Northeast is a two-story home with a basement. It's a row house and it sits at the very end of the street next to an alley. You'll hear a lot about that house, not just as a place where bricks were stacked and people got shelter. You'll hear about it as a place that was a meeting point for a whole family. It was a centrally located place and it was where people in the Hawkins family met and talked and socialized." In other words, ladies and gentlemen, it was a house just like your house, or your brother's house, or your grandma's house where the family goes on Thanksgiving. Every story has a place, and everybody has a story. If you hear my story and you think of the places in your story, then maybe you'll see yourself in my story too.

I described the people who had lived in the house on Eads Street—Diane, Katrina, Reco, Shante, Rock, and Kiki—then moved on to the events of the evening of May 25, 1993: Harrell arriving at the house for his unexpected late evening visit; Harrell acting nervous as he sat in the living room; Reco leaving Harrell behind in the house; Mike Harwood and then Reco finding the butchered bodies on the scene. I went through the broadcast lookout for Harrell and his Ford truck, then took the jury out to Prince George's County—to Karen Boulevard, where the police stopped Harrell's truck—then to the FBI, where the blood inside the truck was linked to the victims. The abstract words were rushing after human shapes and it was all coming alive in my mind's eye—everything I'd done on the case for more than a year, all the people I'd met, all the places I'd visited. I never use notes when I talk with a jury; eye contact is too important. But even if I'd been in the habit of relying on notes in an opening, I wouldn't have needed them in this one. It was all too ingrained, too personal. No one needs a cheat sheet to tell his life story, and this had become a chapter in mine.

I moved to the autopsies. As committed as I'd become to the memory of Diane Hawkins, I was capable of discussing her death with professional detachment, and proceeded to do so.

Then came the moment I'd dreaded for months: describing the autopsy of Katrina Harris. In grand jury session, in pretrial hearings, even in casual conversations with my wife about the case, I'd come to this point and, inevitably, have to stop. Diane's murder, savage though it was, could be viewed through a narrow lens as having had a purpose. Inexcusable, yes, but in my mind I could understand why, in the twisted perspective of Norman Harrell, he decided to kill Diane: He'd loved her, then he hated her, she was standing up to him and he couldn't take that, so in a few minutes of rage he did everything he could to destroy her in the only way he knew how. But why did he have to visit the same rage on Trina? If he felt he had to silence her because she saw what he did to her mother, a simple slitting of the throat, a pillow over the face, would have sufficed. So now I had to face the fact again: I still hadn't come to terms with her death.

I knew very little about her. Even to those closest to her she'd been an enigma: always watching and never joining, but smart, almost scary smart, and with a smile so sweet she didn't show it often, as if she knew it was a resource not to be carelessly depleted. In life, she was the quiet little girl who was going to show everyone; she was still water running deep, potential in repose, a blank slate awaiting inscription. Now she was just a symbol: of how things can go terribly wrong in an instant, of the helplessness of innocence in the face of evil and violence. I just knew this for sure: The heart that once beat inside this young girl's chest had animated her as she went about a simple, love-filled life, and the man who'd seen fit to rip it from her being was sitting calmly a few feet away from me.

I walked over to my table and picked up the autopsy report. After long seconds I continued, the words coming out quickly.

"You'll hear how Katrina Harris suffered from some twenty-seven stab wounds. You'll hear that some of those stab wounds were in the top of her skull. You'll hear about how, how Katrina Harris was stabbed with so great a force that a knife was broken off into her skull—a thirteen-year-old girl. You'll hear, finally, that two of the wounds in Katrina Harris's neck were separated only by a small strip of skin narrowed to one-half inch at the greatest diameter. In other words, Katrina Harris's head was left attached to its body by a piece of skin no more than one-half inch in diameter."

When I was a child and my family would get bad news, we would tend to congregate—if that's the word for a family of three—in our living room. The house would get so quiet that the only noise would be the low drone coming from the refrigerator a room away. I'd always thought it was as close to total, lonesome silence as I could ever be a part of, until this moment. There was no refrigerator drone to be heard in this room, no rumbling ventilation system, no human sound other than what was coming from me, in a voice that sounded hollow in my ear, as if it were somebody else's.

"And you'll hear, ladies and gentlemen, a term in the autopsy report which is not medical, where the writer resorted to common language. You will hear: 'The heart is absent.'

"The heart is still absent, ladies and gentlemen."

I stopped, then turned toward my table and returned the autopsy report to its place. I then talked about the significance of child support in the case, and Harrell's history of nonpayment; about his fiercely held opinions on the subject; about his threatening statements to Deborah Courtney and Carlene Hawkins and Sharon Randle about Diane; about the court hearing that went on while Diane was being autopsied. I talked about Harrell's hunting, and about the manual that set out the blueprint for the murders, described field-dressing hunted game—and bore the defendant's fingerprints.

I was giving the jurors as much detail as I could without losing them. Once we started putting on our case, things would get more confusing. The government can't present its witnesses in the same way a relay race is run, with each having a discrete responsibility and then handing off the testimonial baton to the next; the logistics of the operation don't allow for that. Instead, the first witness's account might spill over into the next one's, the third witness might take ill and have to be replaced at the last minute by the fourth, while the eighth asks to go fifth because she's been called out of town, and so on. In reality, a trial proceeds in the same way a movie is produced, with scenes shot out of sequence and the complete product only apparent after final editing. This was my only chance, before closing argument, to tell the jurors the story of my case in a logical, coherent narrative. It was also my only chance at making a good first impression. I needed to convey to this jury—picked from a citizenry with a shared history that made them skeptical about law enforcement—that I knew the facts cold, and that I was a fair man. Without using the words, I was saying: *Trust me. I've lived with this case for a year and I know it backward and forward. I won't lie to you, and I won't lead you astray.*

I'd been speaking now for at least forty minutes, moving slowly in front of the jury, keeping a respectable distance of about seven feet; I didn't feel I knew them well enough yet to get any closer. It was time to start thinking about winding down. But before I finished, I had to concede weaknesses in our case and try to turn them into strengths.

About the fact that there were no witnesses to the murders: "The very absence of eyewitnesses, we would submit, will substantiate Mr. Harrell's premeditation. Because you *will* hear witnesses testify about the way Mr. Harrell acted on the night of the murders. You *will* hear about his presence at Diane Hawkins's house to begin with. You *will* hear about the statements that he made to the witnesses who were leaving the house that night, asking them when they were going to get back, being very concerned with when they were going to get back. Because he knew at that point, the evidence will show, what he was going to do. There are no witnesses to this crime, ladies and gentlemen, because Norman Harrell didn't want there to be any witnesses to this crime. And the evidence will substantiate his premeditation and will show you that he planned and plotted this crime."

About the fact that Harrell had no blood on his clothing when the police first saw him: "That's another element that goes towards your finding of premeditation: Mr. Harrell had changed clothes. Of course there was no blood on his clothing. He was wearing different clothes at that point and he'd had two hours by that time to get rid of the clothing and anything else that tied him to the crime"—including the murder weapon. Juries always want to know where it is. If the prosecutor doesn't have the weapon, he'd better tell the jurors about it at the beginning of the case, and had better provide his own explanation. Otherwise, it takes on the talismanic significance of the mythical sword in the stone.

"What I have said here has been an opening statement, but what the evidence will show, by the witnesses' own mouths, is what you should take into account. Because, really, what the lawyers say here doesn't matter." I didn't say this at the beginning because I didn't want the jury to tune me out, but I had no problem saying it now, right before another lawyer would be rising to speak to them. "What matters is the *witnesses*. What matters is *their* testimony. What matters is the *evidence* that will come in through their testimony. And it will be based on those witnesses and that testimony and that evidence that we will ask you at the conclusion of this case to find this man, Norman Harrell, guilty beyond a reasonable doubt of the deaths of Diane Hawkins and Katrina Harris."

I sat down heavily. I glanced over to the jury box, trying to get a measure of my performance, but it was an island of inscrutability.

Roberts asked the judge for a ten-minute recess before she gave her opening. At least that was a good sign: She didn't want to follow me right away.

AFTER MONTHS OF WAITING, I'd finally be hearing how Norman Harrell was going to defend himself.

I knew that Roberts had closely monitored the Andre Brown trial in May, and that she'd long been searching for a connection between Brown's crew and the murders of Diane and Katrina. It's a classic defense strategy: attack the prosecution from two different directions and force it to prove not only why the defendant is guilty but why some other vile character isn't. The defense is called "guilt of another," and it's been tried often enough that it has generated a fair amount of case law in D.C. The main case as of 1994 was referred to, in legal jargon, as *Brown-Beale,* after the names of two defendants (the "Brown" being no relation to Andre). Under that case, the defense could point the finger at another possible suspect if it had hard evidence that "clearly linked" the suspect to the crime:

in other words, more than just a suspicion or hunch, more than just a possible motive. Based on my investigation, the only thing linking Andre Brown to these murders was bad karma in River Terrace. But I still didn't know if the defense had been able to come up with something more.

During a break, I saw Roberts in the hallway. Our exchange was clipped and businesslike. I asked, "Any *Brown-Beale* issues in your opening?" The case law required her to tell me and the judge before she mentioned this defense to the jury. She answered, "No, nothing to worry about." That, I thought, takes care of that.

A minute later she was striding into the well of the courtroom. All of the jurors were sitting back in their chairs; three or four were looking away. She walked directly up to the jury box, close enough to reach out and touch the jurors in the front row if she'd wanted to.

"Now, one might call it placing the cart before the horse. Ladies and gentlemen, it's classic, it's basic, it's elementary: You have to investigate a case before you can solve it. You don't, you can't, decide that a man is guilty and then build up a case against him. You have to investigate the case before you solve it. It's basic. It's *elementary.*" She punched out each word vigorously, and as she gestured with her hands, the jangling of her bracelets added emphasis. With her short-cropped hair and short-sleeved dress she cut a sleek and streamlined figure. The floor beneath her feet was carpeted, yet the efficiency with which she moved made her high heels sound as commanding as a general's boots.

"But, ladies and gentlemen, in this case you will learn that the government didn't do that. Someone pointed a finger at Norman Harrell and the government, rather than investigate that finger, rather than investigate why it was that these murders could have happened, rather than investigate the evidence surrounding how these murders happened, the government decided that it had solved the case."

Of course that's where she's going, I thought. Put the government on trial. Tell Norman, you keep your head down and don't make a sound and I'll make the whole case be about them, not you. No matter how much a prosecutor does to investigate a case, there's always something else he could have done—a witness who couldn't be found, a lead that couldn't be followed. Look for the gaps in the government's long lines of marshaled proof—create some if you have to—and make the jury think that the case is more about those empty spaces than anything else.

"Now, ladies and gentlemen, the government is wrong because the person or persons responsible for the deaths of Diane Hawkins and Katrina Harris are not on trial in this courtroom. The evidence will show that Norman Harrell is not guilty. What's this case all about? What's this case really all about? Well, I need to tell you, more importantly, something about what this trial is not going to be about. You see, during the course of this trial neither Mr. Harrell nor I are ever going to be about the business of trying to suggest to you that what happened to Diane Hawkins and Katrina Harris was anything less than a nightmare. We would not and we will not try to suggest to you that the murders in this case were not heinous. They were brutal murders. The issue in this case, ladies and gentlemen, is not whether or not those ladies were brutally murdered." I had to admit: She handled this well. Other defense attorneys might jump straight to the attack and neglect the human touch, but she didn't. Norman Harrell might have felt no sorrow about these deaths but Michele Roberts did, and the jury had needed to hear her say so.

"The issue in this case, what this trial is about, is whether or not Norman Harrell committed these offenses. That's the issue. And, ladies and gentlemen, after you have heard the evidence, after you have heard the evidence, the answer to that question will be a resounding *no*." This last word fairly exploded from her lips. A couple of jurors who had been staring at their laps looked up, as if startled by her vehemence.

She continued: "What's this case all about? Who is this case all about? Who is the person the government has suggested to you is a cold-blooded, *calculated* killer? Allow me to introduce you to Norman Roderick Harrell. Norman Harrell. He's not an old man, he's not a young man. Smack dab in the middle. He's forty-five years old. You will learn that he was born and raised, reared, lived in the Washington, D.C.–Maryland area all of his life. He's got a family here: sisters, brothers, cousins, aunts, nieces, nephews, a wife, sons. You will hear from people that know Mr. Harrell. They will tell you he worked hard all of his life trying to take care of himself and his family, and for the last ten years he worked for the same company, Yellow Freight Systems, hauling cargo as a truck driver. That's Norman Harrell. That's what the evidence will tell you about Norman Harrell."

In other words: he's just like you.

"And people who have known Norman Harrell will tell you he's an honest hardworking man, not the cold, calculated killer that the government is trying to suggest to you he is. That's who he is." My table was located next to the jury box, close enough to be able to sense restlessness, to hear sounds of satisfaction or discontent, without looking over. The jurors were completely still; a few had even leaned forward in their chairs.

"Why does the government say Mr. Harrell committed these offenses? They say child support, that Mr. Harrell hated child support, hated the notion of being financially responsible for his own son. That's what the government says. The evidence, ladies and gentlemen, will tell you quite the contrary. The evidence will tell you that Norman Harrell didn't reject his son, didn't reject financial responsibility for his son. Indeed, the evidence will show that Norman Harrell embraced his son. *Embraced him.*"

She briskly recounted the romantic history of Harrell and Diane, and described their baby. "Now it was unclear who the daddy was for a while, but not for long. Because as Mr. Harrell would come past the house and visit with the Hawkins family and look at little Rock—that's his nickname—he could see he looks like a Harrell, he talks like a Harrell, he cracks like a Harrell. *Yes, that's my son.* Ladies and gentlemen, contrary to the notion that the government has tried to suggest to you, he didn't reject financial responsibility for that boy. He *embraced* him. The evidence will show that Mr. Harrell would come past that house whenever he had a chance. He would bring Rock candy, toys, food, clothing. Rock would come to Mr. Harrell's house. Rock knew his cousins, his brothers, his aunts. Rock, unlike too many unfortunate members of this community, didn't suffer the indignity of not knowing who his daddy was. He *knew* who his daddy was. It was Norman Harrell. He didn't reject financial responsibility for that boy. He *embraced* it."

This was Michele Roberts's turf, her territory. Her diction was precise, her rhythm staccato, and her vernacular uniquely African American: "He cracks like a Harrell." "He knew who his daddy was." She could say things that I couldn't—witness her observation about fatherless children in the inner city—and say them in a way that I'd be well advised never to try to imitate. If I was able to connect with these jurors, it was because of the story I told: its pathos, for sure, but even more than that, all its assembled particulars, with all the attendant sweat and strain. She was connecting with them because of something completely different: the experiences they'd shared together without ever having met.

"Indeed you will learn—you will learn from some of the same witnesses that will try to convince you that Mr. Harrell hated child support—you will learn, and they will tell you—no, they will *admit* to you—that Mr. Harrell offered to do the most that any parent could do for their child. Not merely send checks every month. No, he offered to take custody of the boy: 'He could live with me.' Again not rejecting, not rejecting the notion of responsibility that the government suggested, but *embracing it*. And, ladies and gentlemen, you know where Rock was on May twenty-sixth? He was in Disney

World with some family friends and some school friends, and you know who paid for Rock to go to Disney World with his school friends? Norman Harrell, the same man the government says would kill at the notion of having to do anything financially for that boy. That's where Rock was, and his daddy paid for the school trip."

The words were plain and simple, and they were hitting their mark. Real eloquence is driven by poetry—the right words in their right order—and poetry is driven by rhythm. Shorter words can be delivered more rhythmically than longer ones—think "Four score and seven years ago" or "The only thing we have to fear is fear itself." It's a lesson many lawyers never learn. Roberts had learned the lesson—or maybe she'd been born knowing it.

She turned now to Deborah Courtney, a critical figure in our case, and dismissed her allegations with just one sentence: "This witness who'll suggest this nonsense about Jamaican killing—well, she says that Mr. Harrell would always talk about Jamaican killings in front of all these people, but mysteriously enough there will be no other person that heard that, in any way." But as she picked her points of attack, she wasn't above turning the government's resources against it: "This very same witness will tell you that about a month before the murders, she told Mr. Harrell a secret: 'Norman, I shouldn't be telling you this, Diane told me this in confidence, but she's dying of cancer.' Ladies and gentlemen, why in the world would Norman Harrell kill someone that he was told was dying?" Just about every juror was leaning forward now.

"And there's more. The government again says child support, the man hates child support, turned him into a raving killer. You know what Norman Harrell did to the first woman that dared do what the government says is the unthinkable? You see, you're going to learn there was a woman who dared, *dared* issue a child support action against Norman Harrell. You know what he did to that woman? *She's Mrs. Norman Harrell. He married her.*"

It was a risky strategy, contesting Harrell's hostility to child support. My evidence on this point was strong, and it had a paper trail going back eight years. But she made the argument with such élan that the facts almost didn't matter. Someone on this jury could end up discounting the support motive for no other reason than that Michele Roberts regarded it with disdain.

"How does the government say it happened? How does the government say that Mr. Harrell committed these offenses? They tell you over and over again about the cuttings. Well, ladies and gentlemen, what counsel didn't tell you is this. It's certainly true that within hours of the bodies being discovered, the police did have an encounter with Mr. Harrell. You know what they did, they searched that man from the top of his head to the bottom of his toes. Did they find anything which might have been used to commit these offenses? A knife? No. They searched that man's truck from here to there and they did it not once, not twice, but since these homicides, three times. That truck has remained in the custody of the police department. Three times they searched that truck from beginning to end. Did they find anything that may have been used in connection with these killings? No." I'd already covered this in my opening—discussing how Harrell had time to ditch any incriminating evidence before the police stopped him on the night of the murders—but she was on such a roll that I wondered if the jury remembered.

"Again, bear this in mind. Police have an encounter with Mr. Harrell just two hours after the bodies are discovered. And you will see some horrible pictures of the crime scene that show one very, very clear fact. Diane Hawkins at least did not go out without a fight. You're going to see overturned sofas, overturned tables, overturned chairs. When you see the crime scene you will know that whoever did this, those folks were covered with blood, ladies and gentlemen. Diane Hawkins fought whoever it was that ultimately ended her life. And again when the police saw Norman Harrell and examined his body, you know what they didn't see? *You know what they didn't see?* Not a single scratch. Not a single scratch or cut on his body."

This wasn't the first time I'd thought about this argument. Even days after I first started working on the case I'd wondered about it myself, and I'd spent a lot of time discussing it with the doctor who'd autopsied the bodies. I knew now how two smaller females could be overpowered by a man such as Norman Harrell without laying a hand on him, and I had a witness lined up to explain it to the jury. But I hadn't said anything about it in my opening. In trial you make choices, and with each choice you make you have to abandon options. I'd chosen to spend more time on the details of my case, moving as much of it into position as I could in the time I had available to me. But I'd given Roberts an opening—exposed a flank, one could say—and she'd exploited it. The image of an unscratched Norman Harrell would linger in the jurors' minds until I could get the doctor on the witness stand, halfway through my case.

She talked about how Harrell's fingerprints hadn't been found in the Eads Street house, how the bloody footprint found in Diane's kitchen hadn't matched any of Harrell's shoes or boots. "But we got some blood, Mr. Flynn tells you. Ladies and gentlemen, you would expect, after hearing that opening statement, to see a whole lot of blood, wouldn't you? Well, you're going to learn how much blood we're talking about. And this is what's critical. The evidence will show, and the government's own experts will tell you, that they haven't a *clue* how long the suspected blood may have been in this truck. They will tell you they haven't a clue if that blood has been there for a year, two years, or two minutes. And they will tell you some other significant things. They'll tell you, oh, no, we're not saying that that blood belongs to either of those two people. In fact, they'll tell you, the best we can say is that that blood has some characteristics, and that millions of other people share the same blood characteristics."

This is the job of the defense lawyer. If a prosecutor says, a DNA test eliminated 97 percent of the population, a defense lawyer says, I can work with what's left. Three percent of 240 million? Do the math—it's millions. Never mind that millions of people didn't know Norman Harrell, had never been inside his truck, had never touched the dashboard or the armrest or the cooler he carried with him, had never been in a position to leave their blood on anything belonging to him. Let the government make that argument. Meanwhile, take your shots and put them on the defensive. Set off enough incendiary devices, create enough diversions, kick up enough confusion, and the long, clean lines of the government's case will start to rupture. Meanwhile, stay hidden at all times and keep your head down. Don't tell the jury what you're going to prove; you don't have to prove anything. Don't say your client is going to testify; keep your options open. And for God's sake, don't give the government anything to aim at.

I put down my pen and sat back. *This is great stuff.* I looked over at Harrell. *Whatever you're paying her*, I thought, *it's not enough*.

"How will the evidence show Norman Harrell could have done this? There is *nothing* the physical evidence will show that helps you know who did this," she exclaimed, voice rising. "Somebody pointed a finger at Norman Harrell, and you're going to learn who pointed that finger at Norman Harrell, and you're going to learn why. You're going to learn that that finger was pointed at Norman Harrell by someone too frightened and too guilty to admit that there were reasons for someone else to want to harm him and his family."

Guilty? I was confused. I knew Reco felt guilty about leaving Diane and Trina behind with Harrell, but how did Roberts know that? And what did that have to do with anything, anyway? I stood and said, "Your Honor, may we approach?"

But the judge waved me off. "I will take it up later."

Roberts continued, "His name is Reco, Reco Hawkins, the son of Diane, about twenty-one years old, who associated with persons

involved in the distribution of drugs, whose friends just months before
these murders themselves committed a vicious, vicious murder."

I tried again, this time louder: "Your Honor, may we approach?"

Now the judge relented, telling the jury to talk quietly among
themselves while she had the lawyers come to the bench.

"Your Honor," I began, "I asked Ms. Roberts before opening statements, are we going to get into *Brown-Beale* issues, evidence of guilt
of another. This is something that I was specifically concerned about.
The defense has been after this theory now for several months. You've
already been apprised of everything the government has done to investigate this. There's now been a clear implication of evidence of
guilt of another, and it's not there, and this is not appropriate. This is
a clear *Brown-Beale* issue. It should have been hashed out ahead of
time. I strongly object to this opening statement continuing until
there's a proffer as to what exactly is going to come out. This has
tainted this jury."

The judge turned to Michele: "Counsel?"

"I told Mr. Flynn and I still maintain this is not a *Brown-Beale*
issue at all. This evidence is relevant to that witness's bias—Reco
Hawkins. And his giving, providing the information—"

"Hold it. Hold it," the judge said. "You're saying that one of Reco's
friends did this?"

"No, I'm not."

"Or an enemy of Reco's or an enemy of Reco's friends?"

"I'm happy to make a brief proffer right now, Your Honor. Reco
Hawkins's associates had committed an offense, had committed
actually two murders, had themselves been arrested and believed that
Reco was cooperating with the United States as a witness against
them. These murders took place at or about the time the grand jury
was examining the murder charge in that case, and Reco knew that
they were concerned that he was actually cooperating."

As it turned out, this was just an assumption. In those moments,
I saw that the defense didn't have anything that we didn't already

know about. All along, we were aware of three facts: that Reco Hawkins's mother and sister died by brutal violence; that Andre Brown's crew was capable of brutal violence, that Andre Brown's crew knew Reco Hawkins. We'd found no evidence of a fourth fact—that Andre Brown's crew killed Reco Hawkins's mother and sister, nor, for that matter, that any of them had even given Reco Hawkins a thought after they were arrested. It was now becoming clear that the defense didn't have anything more on this, either.

So Roberts was opting for another strategy: get the facts of the Andre Brown murders before the jury by confronting Reco with them. The law gives defense attorneys a wide berth in probing the possible bias of a government witness—letting an attorney, for example, accuse a police officer of fabricating testimony in retaliation for a brutality complaint filed against him in the past by the defendant. Roberts was no doubt relishing the chance to cross-examine Reco; it was easy to imagine what questions she might ask.

As of May 26, 1993, Mr. Hawkins, you'd heard that Andre Brown and his henchmen had killed a young man named Michael Graham, correct? And that they'd also killed a young woman named Robbin Lyons, right? You were an associate of Andre Brown, weren't you? As soon as you saw what had happened to your mother and sister, you thought of Andre Brown, didn't you? But you knew that if you told the police about Andre Brown's crew, your life could be in danger, am I correct? So instead, you gave them the name of my client, Norman Harrell—Norman Harrell, the patsy—didn't you? Didn't you?

And the beauty of the strategy was this: Once Reco answered "yes" to the first three questions, it wouldn't matter if he denied everything else. Let the government try to keep its case in order once the jury had heard about the abominable Andre Brown and his band of amoral flunkies.

Most judges, however, would see this as a subterfuge, an attempt to inject allegations into the trial that weren't based in fact and would only confound the jury. Defense lawyers are expected to try to cause confusion in a trial, but the law draws the line at uncontrolled chaos. Roberts should have brought the matter up ahead of time, before the jury came into the courtroom, so she could get a ruling in advance—and so I wouldn't be given the chance to interrupt her in the midst of a compelling argument. So why hadn't she? Probably because of the very same self-assurance that characterized the rest of her presentation: She was certain she could do this, and didn't give the matter much more thought. Great trial lawyers need to have great confidence, but confidence can get you in trouble sometimes.

"What you've done," Judge Queen now said to her, "is just gone a step too far. There was no problem when you said that known associates, known drug dealers may have done this. That's okay. But when you start going to specific associates, you have a problem. You've got to give me some proffer as to how specific associates of Reco Hawkins could have done this, since all those specific associates were in D.C. jail—Mr. Brown, Lloyd Johnson, Chauncey Turner, Harvey Newman." Luckily for me, the judge had presided over Andre Brown's trial in May and knew all the players.

"Your Honor," Roberts replied, "that's why I'm telling you this isn't a *Brown-Beale* problem. Because if I knew who committed the murders then I'd tell Mr. Flynn and get my client out."

"But you're suggesting specific individuals by saying that they're associates of Reco Hawkins who had just done two other vicious murders. That's where you went too far. You cannot get to specific people who allegedly committed two other murders in D.C. and Maryland. You can talk about Reco Hawkins's bias, you can go into his drug associations, you can say drug dealers are known to kill each other. But when you talked about specific people, specific incidents—that is, two vicious murders just months before—that's where you went too far."

We went back and forth for another fifteen minutes: Michele Roberts trying to move the judge, the judge holding fast, and me monitoring the judge's reaction for signs of slippage. At one point I looked over at the jury. They'd long since exhausted their repertoire of small talk with one another and were now shifting around uncomfortably, waiting for the trial to begin again. Finally, the judge sent us back to our tables and turned to the jury. "Ladies and gentlemen," she said, "counsel Ms. Roberts made reference to another vicious murder by associates of Reco Hawkins. The court has no evidence of a connection between any other homicides or persons in the River Terrace community and these homicides or this case. Counsel will now continue her argument. You are not to use that statement in your guidance of what's going to come into this case."

No more than a minute later Roberts had brought her argument to a close and sat down.

She'd made just one mistake: She'd raised her head when she hadn't needed to, and she'd taken a hit from an unexpected source. I couldn't count on that happening again.

CHAPTER 11

THIRTY AUTUMNS AGO I WAS a sophomore at Notre Dame. As was my usual practice, I'd procrastinated my way into trouble a week before midterm exams. I was as easily distracted as any nineteen-year-old, and my mind was uncomfortable at rest and prone to wander—still is, for that matter. In my dormitory, there was a chapel with a confessional in the back. Sometimes in the evenings I'd sneak into the priest's box and study there in quiet solitude. One night I stayed up very late reading Hemingway's *For Whom the Bell Tolls* from start to finish, trying to get ready for a test. One passage made such an impression that I wrote it down in a notebook, which I still have. In a rounded, meticulous hand I recorded the soldier-narrator's musings as he cleared his head before detonating a bridge:

> Turn off the thinking. You're a bridge-blower now. You're an instrument to do your duty. There are necessary orders that are no fault of yours and there is a bridge and that bridge can be the point on which the human race can turn. You have only one thing to do and you must do it.

The handwriting in the notebook is that of a boy, and it was a boy's challenge that I faced then: striving to hold on to a decent grade in an American Lit. course. Yet something about the passage struck a chord, and I preserved it for later times, when things might be tougher and I'd have to discipline myself to narrow my focus to the job at hand.

It was a lesson that would serve me in the Harrell trial. I had a discrete and specific mission from which I couldn't be diverted: to put on as many witnesses as I could each day, to have them ready to come into the courtroom in waves, so I could overwhelm the defense with the sheer quantity of the government's evidence. Nothing else in the present mattered, and the past and the future mattered least of all.

A LUNCH BREAK followed opening statements. We returned to court at 2:15. The judge generally broke for the day at around 4:30. I had thirty-eight witnesses to call in my case. This day, I had more than two hours to work with: enough time to put on at least three of them and seize the momentum in the trial.

For months I'd been playing around with my witness sequence: what prosecutors refer to as "order of call." In baseball it's called the batting order, and there's an art to putting one together. The ideal leadoff hitter bats for a high average and sets up other hitters in the order by getting on base often. In a trial, the first witness serves a similar function: to set the stage for everything to follow.

In the Harrell case, I needed as my first witness someone who could testify about what the crime scene looked like, so I could get the larger photographs and exhibits in front of the jury right away and give it a sense of place. This eliminated anyone who didn't go into the Eads Street house the first night. I needed someone experienced at testifying in court and able to relate a significant amount of basic information about the case with relative dispassion. This ruled out the civilians. I needed someone who had a global sense of the whole case from start to finish, someone who could convey, in words and attitude, the entire arc of the story—the evidence technicians wouldn't be able to do this.

The man who stepped first into the witness box fit all these criteria. Not coincidentally, he was the man who'd first alerted me to the murders of Diane Hawkins and Katrina Harris: Detective Dean Combee.

A week before, driving me home on the night before final arguments in the motions hearing, he'd been preoccupied with another murder case. Now, I was asking him to put himself back inside the house on Eads Street, next to Diane and Katrina, and it was all rushing back to him. In other hearings and trials in which I'd presented him as a witness, his tone had been assertive, his gaze level, his manner self-assured. This day, he was a different man. As he described the Eads Street scene in all its particulars, his stare remained fixed on a point on the floor ten feet or so in front of him. He never made eye contact with me, or with anyone else in the courtroom. His voice was so subdued that I could barely hear it, and the court reporter had to lean toward him so as not to miss a word.

A witness can't summarize his testimony for the benefit of the jury; he can't say, "Let me tell you what you should really be taking from this." Combee was a man without artifice or pretense; he would never have presumed to tell a jury what they should be thinking about anything. But every time he shifted heavily in his chair, every time his voice faded into a whisper, the message was being sent: *In this job, I thought I'd seen it all. But I've never seen anything like this, and I hope I never do again.*

As Combee walked slowly from the stand, I looked at the clock on the back wall of the courtroom. It was 2:45.

The second witness: Deborah Courtney. Detective Combee had spoken about seeing the mutilated victims with his own eyes, which still were fixed in a thousand-yard stare whenever he talked about the experience. While that testimony was still fresh in the jurors' minds, I would put Deborah on the stand to establish the link between Diane's fatal wounds and Harrell's statements about Jamaican-style killing. I had another reason for wanting to have her testify early: I knew that Roberts would have her investigators feverishly seeking ways to discredit her, since she knew how devastating this testimony could be. I wanted Deborah on and off the stand before this effort could possibly gain traction.

In direct examination, Deborah's testimony was more muted than it had been during the pre-trial hearing—she was clearly straining, having to rehash the same painful story—but it was still as moving as ever. Roberts's cross-examination was succinct: Lacking the means to attack, she wasn't going to give Deborah the chance to do any more damage to the defense.

I looked back at the clock after Deborah left the stand. It was 3:25. I had an hour more to work with, on the crucial first day of trial.

The third witness: Carlene Hawkins, with her account of Harrell's threats about Diane. By sandwiching Deborah Courtney between Combee and Carlene, I was able to create for Deborah what might be called a zone of corroboration. In a trial, every part of the story relates to every other part. The art of order of call comes down to one word: context. Surround your key witnesses with other consistent evidence so they're not perceived by the jury to be on their own, but rather part of a larger whole.

I looked at the clock after Carlene left the stand. It was 4:00, time enough for at least one more witness.

I planned to move to the events of May 25, and I thought my next three witnesses were lined up: Toi Cohen, Reco's friend who was with him that night and saw Harrell at the house, then the two officers who stopped Reco in the neighborhood and were the first to talk with him. I went outside the courtroom. No Cohen; she was running late. No officers; they'd stepped away. Only one witness was sitting in the anteroom, waiting for his turn to go on the stand: Reco, conservatively dressed per my instructions in a collared shirt and dress slacks.

Problem: I wasn't ready to put him on. I knew that one way or another Roberts was likely to go on the attack with him, to whatever extent the judge would allow. I needed to introduce Reco Hawkins to the jury in the right way: through the people who were with him that night and could describe his ordeal in human terms. When the jurors first saw Reco on the stand, I wanted them already to be viewing him as a sympathetic figure—a young man who'd found his mother and sister slaughtered, not as someone who might be remembered as a drug dealer with shaky friends.

Another problem: If Reco testified now, then Roberts might be able to start her cross-examination by closing time. Her questions—posed with a tone of authoritative insinuation—would linger with the jurors after they'd left the courthouse, and she'd still have overnight to think of more.

I had no other witness to call, and there was still a half hour of trial time remaining in the day. I approached the bench. "Your Honor," I said, "I could call another witness now, but I believe that witness will take a while and we wouldn't finish today—"

The judge replied, "You mean you want to break *now*?"

"Um, yes."

She looked at her watch theatrically.

There was a long pause.

Then: "That's fine. I have another matter I need to take care of, so we'll end right now."

I'm pretty sure that when I was reading *For Whom the Bell Tolls*, I must have come across a couple of sentences about good old dumb luck. Since I was nineteen and pretty much untouched by any other kind, I never thought to write them down.

———————

I HEARD A VOICE somewhere deep, deep in the back of my mind.

It was a man's voice, and it got louder with time. The voice was resonant and reassuring, but the sounds I heard made no sense; they weren't even words. I was in a place where people should have known me but they looked at me as if I were a stranger, and though I'd known some of them my whole life they were saying things I'd never heard them say before. All I knew was that something vile was about to happen, but I couldn't pull myself away. The resonant, reassuring voice might have belonged to someone who could make sense of things, maybe even lead me away from this wild conflagration of images, but I didn't want to hear it, I turned away from it, because I knew it was beckoning me to go somewhere I didn't want to go. Minutes went by and I heard the voice say numbers, then a distant place name that I recognized, then another. I heard music that I'd heard before and then I heard another voice, the lilting voice of a young woman. She was singing a song I'd heard before, somewhere. The song was . . . it was . . . about an auto insurance company. I felt myself stumbling through darkness and looking at garish orange numbers inside a lighted box. The numbers said 6:00. I pushed on the box and all the voices went away. I stared at the floor and for the first time I formed thoughts I could decipher.

The thoughts were something like this:

Officer Robinson recovered Trina's blood patch at her autopsy, but nobody's been able to contact him. I need to put him on soon, and if I don't find him, how am I going to get that into evidence?

The thoughts came from the left side of my brain—the practical, logical, anal-compulsive side—as it lurched from sleep. That side would carry me through the second day of trial—as it would every other day, for as long as I was putting on my case—until sunset, when it would finally start to flag.

———

DAY TWO.˙ Nine witnesses: Toi Cohen; the two officers who stopped Reco; the friend who was with Reco when he found the bodies; Reco himself; Detectives Whalen and Gainey, who drove with Reco the first night and took his statement; Mike Harwood, the first to go into the house; one of the evidence technicians who processed the crime scene. I'd never put on so many witnesses in a day. Each one had to be taken methodically through his testimony; in a case built on details, I couldn't leave anything out. But it was just as important to build momentum and set a pace, to give the jury—and the defense—the sense that my evidence was an inexorable, implacable force.

As every witness stood to leave the stand, I would say the same thing to myself. *Did I remember to bring out everything?*

Then: *How much time do I have? Who else is out there that I have to talk to? How much more do I have left to do?*

And finally: *Keep going, keep going, keep going.*

I WAS ABLE to move my witnesses and evidence into place so efficiently because outside the courtroom, the government had a second layer of organizational infrastructure: model police officers, a motivated family, and a dedicated and resourceful paralegal from my office. Inside the courtroom, though, there was no second layer; I commandeered the prosecutor's table by myself. This was how I liked it. At home, I was a committed family man; at work, I was still a confirmed bachelor. I didn't want to have to adjust my vision of a case to accommodate someone else's. I didn't want to have to explain to anyone why I'd called this witness and not that one, or to have to justify why I'd fought the judge on one adverse ruling and surrendered on another. And at the end of every day, I didn't want to have to clean up files that someone else had left strewn all over my table.

The table faced the judge; four feet or so behind my chair was a wooden barrier, about three feet high, that separated the trial participants from the audience. Between my chair and the barrier were eight stacked boxes filled with document folders. Two police officers used a large hand truck to haul them over to court in the morning and back to my office at night. Other officers were responsible for all the diagrams and photographs; a couple of the mounted displays were larger than the men who carried them.

The area behind my chair was cramped, and passage back and forth was difficult. At one point Roberts needed to get by. A bulky crate sat in her way; she asked me to move it. I tried to make a joke: "That box just contains all the evidence we've been hiding that exonerates your client." She didn't laugh. She just cocked an eyebrow and said, "I don't doubt it."

"Ms. Cohen, did you overhear any conversation between Mr. Harrell and Ms. Hawkins at that time?"

"No, I didn't."

Toi Cohen was testifying about seeing Harrell at the Eads Street house just a short time before the murders.

I continued: "What were you doing with the baby at that point?"

"Playing with her."

"Who was in the house at that time?"

"At that time, I believe Katrina had left. I think she went to the ice cream truck. So it was Reco, Diane, myself, the baby, and Mr. Harrell."

Trina went to an ice cream truck?

I went on: "How would you describe Ms. Hawkins's mood?"

"As we were talking, it was fine, and then when she found out that the defendant was in the house, she didn't talk much."

I'd spoken with Toi several times before; she'd never told me about Trina going out to an ice cream truck. She probably didn't think it was important, and as far as the evidence against Harrell was concerned, it wasn't. Most likely, it was hearsay—Trina had probably come back in the house and told Toi where she'd been—and anyway, it wasn't relevant to the charges against Harrell.

Toi finished her testimony, but even as I called my next witness the thought stuck with me: *An ice cream truck?*

I'd put Toi Cohen on the stand to convey hard information about Reco, Diane, and Harrell, not to impart a poignant anecdote about Trina. Now, much as I might have wanted to, I couldn't seize on this image and expand on it as a novelist would; I had to move on.

Over the months before a murder trial, a prosecutor throws everything that's in him into a case: consoling the victim's survivors, walking the witnesses through traumatic recollections, tapping into memories of tragedies in his own past to find common ground with the bereaved. By the eve of trial, he's had to pull some of himself back. His emotions have been blunted, and his focus has shifted; he's a tactician with a plan. Once in trial, he has to deal with many things at the same time: how he's asking his questions, why the juror next to him seems inattentive, how his witness is holding up, whether his next witness is going to be ready. He can't linger over anything that doesn't help him meet the cold, hard legal requirements he has to meet to prove his case.

But the rules of evidence place no restrictions on the imagination.

On a spring night ripening into summer, a thirteen-year-old girl sitting in her house hears a sound uniquely pitched to the ear of a child—the faraway clanging of the bell of a Good Humor truck coming tantalizingly closer on a nighttime run—and dashes from her house to answer the call. She stands, out of breath, with a couple of moist bills pressed in her palm, gazing at the splash of color on the side of the truck: Eskimo pies and strawberry cones, nutty buddies and chocolate éclairs, arrayed in so many rows and columns that she can barely take them all in.

It's an image too evanescent to be confined in a courtroom. But in a quiet moment at day's end, it would still endure.

The girl skips back to her house in her last hour on earth and peels a wrapper from a popsicle. She feels a last little surge of the thrill of Christmas.

AT THE BEGINNING of each day, and following every break, the jurors filed into the courtroom in a long line. Six of them assumed seats in the front row, eight in the back. Their names had been provided on a list I was given in voir dire, but I mentally referred to them only as numbers on a seating chart. One sat farthest from me on the front row and Six closest; Seven sat farthest from me on the back row and Fourteen closest. Throughout the trial, I'd sneak glances their way and try to monitor their demeanor. *Five looks like he's on my side; he's solid as a rock. What's going on with Fourteen? She's the one who smiled a lot during voir dire—I've got to watch her. Why isn't Three paying attention today? He looked like he was on my side yesterday. Did I just see Twelve staring at Harrell? She's unemployed . . . maybe she's got a grudge against the system, maybe she's going to tilt the defense's way? Make a note to focus on her when it comes time for closing argument.*

Once the trial ended, I'd probably never encounter any of these people again. But for as long as they were right next to me in the courtroom, I would track the moods and movements of each like an obsessed lover.

"NO FURTHER QUESTIONS, Mr. Hawkins," I said.

Reco rose slowly from the witness chair. The collared shirt and dress slacks he'd worn on Friday were gone; he'd come to court this day in jeans and a T-shirt with a psychedelic picture of a woman falling out of a skimpy dress. "I'm sorry, Mr. Flynn," he'd told me in the hall beforehand. "I didn't think I was going on today." It could have been worse; I'd once seen a defendant take the stand in a gun possession case wearing a tank top bearing a picture of . . . a gun. The jeans made Reco's legs look long and the shirt captured the cut of his chest. In a fair fight with Harrell he might have been able to exploit his youth and score some points—but of course there'd never be such a thing as a fair fight with Norman Harrell. After his testimony Reco walked right by the man, but they didn't look at each other.

On the stand, Reco had been deferential and self-effacing, comporting himself in a way that would have made his mother proud. When Roberts pressed him on cross-examination, he steadfastly kept an even tone. It was as if they were at the kitchen table, she trying to start an argument, while he just kept reading his newspaper.

As Reco walked out of the courtroom, I noticed a couple of jurors following him intently; their eyes seemed wet. Perhaps those jurors—and others, less demonstrative—had picked up on something in the young man that others had missed.

Reco's lifestyle had elements that were lamentable, even worthy of reprobation, but once you put those flaws in perspective you could begin to see him as—bear with me—a hero. By a serviceable definition of that word—someone who does something that's very hard to do under arduous circumstances and causes something great to happen—Reco Hawkins qualified.

In the early morning hours of May 26, 1993, stopped by the police in his neighborhood, he had choices. We always do. He knew who'd slaughtered his mother and sister. But he was agitated, even hysterical, and the survival instinct is a strong one. Somewhere in his head there had to have been this thought: *If I point the finger at Danky and the charges don't stick, I'm next in line—if he can do this to them, he can do it to me too.* Reco could have taken the easiest way out and retreated into silence. But he didn't.

And what if he'd acted on the impulse to seek his own vengeance—put the police off, let them leave River Terrace without a clue, rallied his friends into a posse? The law would have had to punish him eventually, but would any of us really have castigated him? It wouldn't have been hard for him to get his hands on some guns on the streets of D.C., and he knew the way to Harrell's house. You can see it in your mind, can't you? Harrell walks out his front door a couple of days later, thinking the coast is clear, then is riddled with bullets on his doorstep and falls bloody into his dirt patch of a garden. Just try to tell me there isn't some perverse satisfaction even in reading those words on the page. But Reco Hawkins didn't go down that road, and in all the times I spoke with him—in all the times I spoke with others who spoke with him—I never heard a word that suggested he regretted his choice. Reco helped the police and they caught Norman Harrell. Without Reco, they wouldn't have—or they would have caught him after he'd had time to wipe everything clean in his truck, and the case would have been that much weaker. And Reco kept on helping—he never ran, he came to court, and he never shirked a single hard question about his past.

Reco Hawkins did what the system tells people to do, and what too many people don't do—even when the stakes are less high than they were for him, and the emotions less raw, and the decisions less difficult.

DAY THREE. Eleven witnesses: two officers on the stop of Harrell in P.G. County, and Detective Herman Johnson on his later interview with him there; Deborah Courtney's son Tracy, who testified that while his mother and Rock were at Disney World he was never contacted by Harrell about their well-being (and thereby implicitly contradicted Harrell's assertion to the police that he'd gone to Diane's house on the night of the murders to try to find Tracy); Ron Branch, on Harrell's statement to him the next morning, admitting knowledge of that day's court hearing on Diane's claim; an MPD officer on the search of Harrell's truck and recovery of blood-stained items and two MPD detectives on the search of Harrell's house in D.C. and recovery of the hunter's manual and plastic gloves; two MPD officers on the recovery of evidence at the victims' autopsies, including blood samples from both and jewelry from Katrina's body; and FBI lab analyst Tim Feola on finding Harrell's fingerprints on the hunter's manual. The assembled narrative of these eleven witnesses carried Norman Harrell from D.C. to P.G. County and back, and took all the physical evidence from Harrell's house and truck, put it into police hands, and brought it into the courtroom.

The next day I would put eight more witnesses on the stand, for a total of twenty-eight in three days. All had given voluminous written statements to the police or testimony to the grand jury. Under the rules, I was required to give Roberts a copy of each witness's prior statements immediately before her cross-examination of that witness. As a courtesy, I was giving them to her a day or so in advance, but this was still a daunting amount of paperwork for her to absorb and master. As time went on, I noticed that her cross-examinations were getting shorter.

Something else happened as the days went by, as one by one the witnesses came forward and the trial took on its own momentum: Judge Queen, gradually but inevitably, faded from dominance. Her power to admit or bar a piece of evidence, to sustain or overrule an objection, to allow or forbid an argument wasn't diminished. But now, with the ultimate decision in the case being in the dominion of the jury, her authority was no longer unilateral. Her main interest in the case seemed to be to have it finished soon, and so I could placate her in small ways: having my evidence organized and my witnesses prepared, avoiding thorny issues that might unduly delay proceedings. Occasionally I faltered, and when I did, I felt her wrath. But as the trial took on the pace of a timeless ritual, she gradually became more and more of a detached—not to say benevolent—presence in the courtroom, and for me this was a good thing.

———

THE CLOCK ON the courtroom's back wall said that it was 12:45 P.M., time for a lunch break on day three. But I was a prosecutor in the middle of my case-in-chief, so for me that term was a misnomer: on this day, as on every other, I wouldn't eat lunch or take a break. Every day, the judge gave the jurors seventy-five minutes and they relished every second of it—as they should have, for why should they have been deprived of a respite from all the carnage and the melodrama? Later, as they filed in for the afternoon session, their murmured exchanges would speak of restaurants visited and excursions enjoyed. But I made my living off carnage and melodrama, so my time was spent much differently: five minutes discharging the morning's witnesses; an hour or so on preparing the afternoon's witnesses; five minutes getting caffeine to last the day from vending machines in the courthouse basement; five minutes at the end reaching out to family—a rushed call to my wife to check on my toddler son, whom I was seeing less and less of, and another to my parents, to check on my father's radiation treatments.

It's impossible to quantify time spent on nagging preoccupations and thoughts that intrude persistently on the business at hand. If I could, I'd probably find that during the Harrell trial, an ample amount of time was committed to self-flagellation over abandoning my other life, and a steady drumbeat of thoughts contemplating the unresolved question of every day: whether it's ever the right thing for a person to forsake the people closest to him so he can serve society at large.

Having fought that question to a draw, I would return to the courtroom for the afternoon session.

WILLIE HARRIS was a man who'd been left in limbo.

Since July 15, he'd come to court every day. Before trial, I'd put him on the government witness list, hoping I could find a role for him. The process of attaining a measure of peace of mind—which thus far had been denied him—might be kick-started if he could somehow contribute to the prosecution of his daughter's murderer. In other cases, I've reserved for the parent of a slain child a special part: identifying a photograph of their son or daughter in death to fulfill the government's obligation to identify the body of the decedent. But I'd sensed enough agony in the silences of my talks with Willie to know that it would have been inconceivable to put him in front of a roomful of people and ask him to look into the dead face of his daughter. Lacking any better idea, I had to put him on hold. In the meantime, he couldn't even be a spectator at the trial. By established court rule, any potential witness is prohibited from sitting in the courtroom and watching other witnesses testify. And so a few times each day, I'd look to the back of the courtroom while I was putting on my case and see Willie looking back at me through the doors' windows: on the outside, looking in.

During a break, I went into the hallway and found him. I recalled him mentioning that he gave Katrina some jewelry not long before she was killed. It had been his last gift to her. Now I held a pendant and necklace in front of him. Are these what you gave to her? Can you come in and identify them? The jewelry had been recovered from Trina during her autopsy and had special evidentiary significance. By being left behind on her body, the jewelry suggested that the killer wasn't a stranger bent on robbery, but rather someone with a personal grudge.

Willie looked closely at the jewelry. It would have been easy for him to say yes. Even if his memory was uncertain, it would have been easy for his mind to defer to his heart. A few more seconds passed. Finally: "You know I want to help you more than anything. But I'm just not sure. I have to be able to tell the truth, and I'm not sure."

I thanked him for being honest, and told him he could come into the courtroom to watch the rest of the trial—but only *after* the next witness testified.

———

THE NEXT WITNESS was Dr. Carol McMahon, to testify about the autopsies of Trina and her mother.

The doctor described Diane Hawkins's autopsy first. She detailed all of the wounds, then charted them on two diagrams. Some of the Hawkins family members in the courtroom were hearing the details for the first time. But not a sound came from the gallery behind me: no gasps, no cries, none of the stir that greets dramatic moments in courtroom movie scenes. The jurors were just as quiet, but their body language was voluble. They were hunched forward in their chairs, and several of the women and one of the men appeared moist-eyed. A young black female—One—drew her jacket up around her shoulders, though the courtroom was warm.

I asked the doctor about Diane's neck wound: What did it say about the mental state of the attacker?

"Looking at the entire picture and evaluating the wound with all of the bruises and blows to the face, as well as the chest wound, you're probably dealing with an enraged, a very angry individual. He doesn't necessarily have to be big and strong. But, of course, that helps. And the victim does not necessarily have to be weak. Any of us, when we're threatened, will put up a fight if we're able to, but if an assailant mounts one good surprise blow and then overwhelms us, then it's easy for him to continue on with other wounds. The key element is the element of surprise. So I will go out on a limb and say that this was done by someone who was enraged—yes."

In her opening statement, Michele Roberts had fired a shot: "When the police saw Norman Harrell and examined his body, you know what they didn't see? Not a single scratch or cut on his body."

This was my chance to fire back. "Doctor, what is a defensive wound?"

"A defensive wound is a wound that an individual sustains in an effort to defend himself or herself from an assailant. Usually these wounds are caused to the extremities, on the hands and the arms."

"How would you characterize the wounds to the arms of Diane Hawkins?"

"The wounds of the upper extremities—that is, of both fore-arms—those were certainly defensive wounds. In other words, the decedent was doing what she could to attempt to defend herself."

"Was there any indication of any wound on Ms. Hawkins that would have been incurred in the course of attacking her attacker?"

"There was no bruising of her hands. Her fingernails were short and clean with no broken edges, and apparently there were no residues found under them."

"There was no blood under the nails?"

"No."

"No tissue under the nails?"

"No."

"No hairs or fibers under the nails?"

"No."

Now I asked the doctor about Katrina. She described the girl's wounds: the knife wound in the skull, the gaping wound in the throat, the hole in the chest, and twenty-four other stab wounds. Halfway through, I glanced at the jury. Number One had twisted in her chair and brought her feet up underneath her.

"Doctor, can you draw from Katrina Harris's injuries a conclusion as to the strength of her attacker?"

"In this case, it's a little easier because we're dealing with a thirteen-year-old child. Probably any adult male would be stronger than a thirteen-year-old female child. So it didn't have to be a very strong man. But certainly the degree of mutilation, particularly in the chest, would suggest a strong individual."

"You stated earlier, as to Ms. Hawkins, that there was no indica-tion of any residue under her fingernails: no tissues, fibers, or hairs or any matter of that nature. Would your answer be the same as to Ms. Harris?"

"Her nails were clean and short with no broken edges, and her hands appeared very clean with the exception of small wounds on her left hand. So yes, I would draw the same conclusion as to Katrina Harris as I did with Diane."

"Are there any injuries on Ms. Harris, such as bruised knuckles or injuries of that nature, which would lead you to the conclusion that those injuries were suffered by Ms. Harris in the course of striking a blow against her attacker?"

"No. There were no bruises. There were basically no marks. I can't say what she did or was able to do, but I have no physical evidence that she struck her assailant or tried to strike her assailant, and only minimal evidence that she was able to defend herself or tried to defend herself."

I turned to the judge. "Nothing further, Your Honor."

Cross-examination was brief.

FROM AN EARLY AGE, we're taught to avoid stereotypical thinking: to view each person as an individual, to refrain from imposing pre-conceptions from the past on the ever-changing present. It's only when we get older that we learn that in the real world of complex interactions, where we're called upon constantly to act on limited information to try to predict the future, stereotypes and generaliza-tions are a part of daily life. When we can't take the time to learn everything about the person in front of us, it's human nature to be guided by the lessons of our history. A woman who's had a failed relationship with a younger man will superimpose his face over that of every one of her younger suitors. An employer who's been cheated by an ex-con employee will hold it against every other job applicant who has a criminal record. And a prosecutor and a defense lawyer will each assume the other is going to cut corners to achieve their ends, because they've both learned something the hard way: that they serve their cause poorly when they let down their guard.

There comes a point, though, in certain human interactions when the stereotypes and generalizations fall by the wayside, and we let ourselves believe in the good faith of the person standing in front of us.

The reconciliation between me and Michele Roberts began—as reconciliations often do—in the middle of an argument.

We were sitting in the anteroom during a trial break, squabbling about fingerprints. I'd told her that I could arrange to have a police expert witness to come testify about a crucial point in the defense case—that Harrell's prints weren't found on the murder scene—and now I was having to tell her that he'd become unavailable due to some other commitment. I was about to say something else but I never got the chance. She exploded, and for at least the next minute—it seemed like ten—I felt the full force of her rhetorical fury. "You can't do this to me," she said, standing over me and pacing. "I promised this jury that they'd hear from me about those finger-prints, and you told me as a courtesy that you'd have that witness here in court, because I don't have all the *contacts* that you do at that F-B-I, and now you're pulling the rug out from under me," and so on.

Finally, I couldn't take any more. I stood up. "Look, I don't know what kind of treatment you've gotten from other prosecutors in the past. I don't know how much you've been jacked around or treated unfairly or ambushed or however you want to put it. But I don't play that way. I'm not going to let you hang out to dry on this. It's an issue you're entitled to raise, and I'll see that you can raise it. I'll *stipulate* that Harrell's prints weren't in that house; you won't even need a witness."

I wasn't being magnanimous in offering this, and in no way should I be congratulated for it; it was, self-evidently, the only fair thing to do.

She sat down and didn't say anything. Her shoulders eased, and she slumped a bit in her chair. She started to say something but didn't, and then she started to smile but didn't really do that, either. She just said, "I appreciate that." But for the first time in all of our encounters, the admirable but intimidating righteousness, the fearsome self-assertiveness was gone, and she was another lawyer just like me, thrown into a morass and trying to do her best with it.

By the time we had that exchange, she'd already transcended in my mind the stereotype of a defense lawyer: a true believer who'd stoop to anything to get her client off. She'd been haughty with me at times, even dismissive, but she'd always been honest—that's all it takes. And I'd like to think that that exchange, brief as it was, tipped the scale in my favor, and I finally transcended in her mind the stereotype of a prosecutor: overzealous, willing to run roughshod over everyone to get a conviction.

I'll at least say this: From then on, I don't think she ever again thought that I had even an iota of evidence, let alone a box full of it, that would exonerate her client.

"THEY SEARCHED that man's truck from here to there," Michele Roberts had said in her opening. "Did they find anything that may have been used in connection with these killings? No." For some months, I would have agreed with that statement. Then I met with Bob Spaulding about the blood patterns in the house, and called in Dean Combee so we could sit down with Sharon Randle, and not long after all that I knew the truth. I knew that an object found in Harrell's truck had come directly from the murder scene. It was an object that Michele, her assistant, and the defense investigators had seen and touched during pretrial discovery, but no one on the defense team would have known its significance except one: the defendant himself. And I could be sure he hadn't told anyone.

"Can you state your name for the record, please?"

"Sharon Randle."

"Tell us about what your relationship was with Diane Hawkins."

"She was my aunt by marriage and a good friend."

"How often would you say that you saw Ms. Hawkins over the last several years before she died?"

"I saw her very often."

"How often in the last six months before Diane Hawkins was killed did you help her with the cleaning around the house?"

"Within the last six months, I guess maybe every other weekend. She really just cleaned . . . She really base cleaned like on weekends, so I would say every other weekend."

"Now, when you say 'base cleaned,' what do you mean by that?"

"I mean base cleaning where you scrub the baseboards of the walls and, you know, mop and scrub the floors and all of that."

"Would you be the one out of the family who would be helping her with that when she did that?"

"Yes."

"What about other members of the family? Did they help her clean as much as you did?"

"No, they didn't."

"Were you over at Diane Hawkins's house the day that she died, earlier that day?"

"Yes, at about one o'clock."

"How long were you there that day?"

"I guess that we were there for maybe half an hour or forty-five minutes."

"Did you have an opportunity to go through the various parts of her house?"

"Yes."

"Did you have an opportunity to go down into the basement area that's off the kitchen?"

"I didn't go down, but I went toward the stairs because I was trying to get to Kiki so that she wouldn't go down the steps—that's the baby, Diane's daughter. We always tried to keep the basement door closed, because there were steps there and she could fall down the steps. So Diane was upstairs and went towards the kitchen and then Diane yelled downstairs and said, 'Sharon, make sure that the basement door is shut.' And when I saw Kiki going towards the kitchen, that's when I went back there and saw that door was opened. So, I pulled little Kiki on into the living room and I shut the basement door."

"Did you notice anything that was right inside of the door at the time that you were pulling Kiki away from going down the steps?"

"Yes."

"What was that? How would you describe it?"

"There was a red cooler there, on the top steps."

"I will be showing you what's been marked as government exhibit number eight." Behind my table was the red-and-white cooler that the police had found upended on the front passenger floorboard of Harrell's truck. Until a few months before, I'd assumed it had belonged to him. Now I knew better. I picked the cooler up gently, with both hands, and slowly carried it to the witness stand. "Can you tell us," I asked Sharon Randle, "if you recognize this object?"

"Yes."

"Can you tell us what that is?"

"It's a cooler."

"Is that the same cooler that you saw inside of the basement steps on the date that Diane Hawkins died?"

"Yes, sir."

"Had you ever used this cooler before that day?"

"Yes. I'm not sure how many times, but a lot of times."

"What sort of things would you use the cooler for?"

"We used to sit out in Diane's yard and drink beer—keep the beer in it, or sodas. Or we might take it to the park or something like that."

We called two other witnesses to corroborate Sharon Randle's testimony: Diane's sisters, Barbara Harwood and Ruby Marbley.

When the police unsealed the Eads Street house in September 1993, following the visit of the bloodstain-pattern expert, these two women had reentered it to clean it and remove the belongings of Diane's family. Both were certain: The red-and-white cooler described by Sharon Randle was no longer in the basement at that time. Though they wouldn't have known this at the time, the cooler had been sitting in a police evidence bin for about four months.

Government exhibit number 8: a plastic cooler, one of millions mass-marketed, a mundane household object. But this one had once held something precious, so it was as sacred as a chalice. It also held something else: the answer to so many questions.

Now it all made sense.

Norman Harrell came into the kitchen with dripping heart in hand, looking for a container. He reached into the cabinet and a drop of Trina's heart blood fell on the counter. Maybe the door to the basement was open, maybe he nudged it open. He found Diane Hawkins's cooler, and he used it to carry her daughter's heart from her house.

The cooler was Diane's all along—it was the missing piece of the puzzle. Why didn't I mention it in my opening statement? Because I didn't really have to, and I wanted to see how the trial played out before I showed my hand. Besides: Norman Harrell had seized on the element of surprise in subduing his victims. Can anyone begrudge me for wanting to turn the tables on him at his trial?

IT WAS LATE, and I'd set my mind on striking out for home. I shut my office door and locked behind it all the words of my witnesses and all the images of my victims. But if I thought I could leave the trial behind me, I was mistaken. I should have known: it would track me down and sneak into my house and make itself at home in my head for the rest of the night.

If the mornings and afternoons belonged to the left side of the brain, then the night belonged to the right: imaginative and creative, sure, but maddeningly undisciplined and prone to fall victim to whimsical diversions.

Nighttime was when I'd find myself scrambling around for a scrap of paper, a napkin, even one of those little cards that tumble in threes from magazines, just so I could memorialize a line of questions, a strategic gambit, or a turn of phrase—only to wake up the next morning and watch an idea that glowed incandescently in the dark fade into nothing in the light of day.

But nighttime was also when I'd find myself stumbling from half-sleep and calling my own number at work and leaving myself a ten-minute message that laid out an entire argument that I would deliver, word for word, to a jury just days later.

ON THE FIFTH full day of trial, the government put on the last witness and admitted the last exhibit in its case-in-chief. The traditional phrase that marks this occasion is: "The prosecution rests." The phrase is succinct, but it doesn't come close to capturing the mood of the moment. Someday, in some trial, I might have the nerve to stand up in court and use a phrase that does: "The prosecution can finally get some rest."

CHAPTER 12

Y OU'RE A DEFENSE ATTORNEY and you represent people
charged with murder. Years ago, you got into this line of work
because it's all you ever wanted to do, from the time you first started
thinking about doing anything. Not because of the money—God
knows there's not much of it to be found in taking on the cause of
accused indigents. And not because of any renown it would bring
you—not when the one question you'd hear more than any other,
from family, friends, and even strangers at cocktail parties, would be
"How do you live with yourself, representing those people?" No, you
did it because at some point in the distant past, something in the
way the government used its power made you want to line yourself
up on the other side, the side of the downtrodden and vilified—you
were just contrary enough to want to make sure that all that authority wasn't misused, to make sure that every time the government
pointed its long finger of condemnation at somebody, it would be
challenged to prove it was right.

So now you're in a trial, seated next to a man charged with double
homicide. From this position you've watched a prosecutor struggling
over six days to build his case. Rushing, harried, into court each

morning, sweating from toting fat briefcases of papers through the summer torpor. Grimly assembling each day's witnesses in the hallway and then shuttling them back and forth all day like a tour guide with a busload of schoolchildren. Asking each witness what seemed like a thousand questions just to win small, incremental victories. You've had the luxury of sitting back and choosing from an array of targets, taking refuge in the strategy of counterattack, and by the time the government rests its case, you're thinking that you've scored enough hits that you stand a fighting chance at a hung jury, maybe even acquittal.

So what would make you put on a case yourself? The defense certainly doesn't have to. The government has the burden of establishing the defendant's guilt; under the law, the defendant has no obligation to do anything, and in every criminal trial in the U.S. the judge instructs the jurors that they're not to hold it against the defendant if he decides to sit back and see if the government can prove its case. So why would you take the risk of calling your own witnesses and give the prosecutor the chance to make up lost ground? Why engage your adversary like that when you don't need to?

Because the decision isn't yours to make. Because you're not the one whose life is on the line; your client is. You can talk to him, you can try to persuade him, you can tell him over and over to leave well enough alone, to let you do your job, to follow your advice. But he's the one who's had to sit there and watch all these people he used to know accuse him of something that . . . Well, hell, you both know he did it, but he's still had to listen to it all. Everything you know about him tells you he's not going to sit there and take it, not this stubborn behemoth who thinks of himself as the type of guy who sees what he wants and goes out and gets it. So you put a case together for him. But you tell him: We don't have anything to prove, so we're not going to try to fight back against everything all those people said. And if he wants to get up there at the end and try to save his own skin, there's nothing you can do to stop him.

If you're the prosecutor, you're sitting there after you've rested your case and all that's going through your mind is, *It could have been better.* You're thinking a lot more about what went wrong than what went right, and you're thinking about how you never really connected with two or three of the jurors, and how you never really had one of those moments that you look for, a moment that comes out of nowhere and turns a trial your way. And then you hear the defense attorney say, "The defense calls its first witness," and you just say three words to yourself: *Thank you, Jesus.*

A DIGRESSION ON qualified truths, outright lies, and innocent mistakes, and why the differences matter.

This is what is known as "an admission with an explanation":

> And the Lord God called unto Adam and said unto him, Where art thou? . . . Had thou eaten of the tree, whereof I commended thee that thou shouldst not eat? And the man said, the woman whom Thou gavest to be with me, she gave me of the tree, and I did eat. (Genesis 2:9–12)

This is history's first recorded lie, promptly impeached by forensic evidence:

> And the Lord said unto Cain, Where is Abel thy brother? And he said, I know not; am I my brother's keeper? And the Lord said, What hast thou done? The voice of thy brother's blood cries unto me from the ground. (Genesis 4:9–10)

And this is what is known as a "mistake in perception":

> And Jacob came unto his father and said, My father, and he said, Here am I, who art thou, my son? And Jacob said unto his father,

I am Esau, thy first born . . . And Jacob went near unto Isaac his father; and he felt him, and said, Thy voice is Jacob's voice, but the hands are the hands of Esau. And he discerned him not, because his hands were hairy, as his brother Esau's hands, so he blessed him. (Genesis 27:15–23)

Cross-examination: It's mankind's oldest quest, distilled to its essence. It's the grand drama of the search for truth, reduced to a one-act play. In its purest form, it's hearing a story you haven't heard, told by a person you've never met, and within a matter of moments conceiving a strategy to expose all its weaknesses. And more than anything else, it requires the ability to distinguish intuitively between human deception and human error, and to act accordingly.

The defense would call nine witnesses. Most would target discrete parts of the government's case. The defense strategy: get in, get out. My job would be to probe their accounts, to neutralize them— or, if the opportunity presented itself, to bring them around to my side.

FIRST TO THE STAND: the Maryland state official in charge of the program that administered hunting tests and issued hunting licenses.

His testimony: that his records showed that Norman Harrell Junior—the defendant's older son—had taken a written hunting examination and obtained a license in 1985.

The subtext: that the hunter's manual found in the defendant's bedroom—which contained a practice examination, with answers filled in—belonged not to the defendant but his son, and that the son, and not the father, was the serious hunter in the family.

The first question a lawyer should ask himself, before rising to cross-examine: is the witness lying? If not, has his testimony been shaded to fit the other side's needs? Next: How many questions do I absolutely have to ask? Did the witness say anything that hurts my case? If he didn't, then the cardinal rule of trial practice applies: less is more.

As for this witness: He wasn't lying, and he had no interest in the outcome of this case. Still, his testimony had to be clarified—as briefly as possible.

On cross-examination: Only license applicants born after 1977 were required to take the test. Anyone who had obtained a license before that year could maintain the license forever without taking the state examination. The fact that Norman Harrell, the defendant, wasn't registered in the Maryland records didn't mean that the man had no license—in fact, it could mean that he was a longtime license holder who'd been grandfathered in under the state's regulations.

Why, I thought, put this witness on the stand when Norman Junior could come in himself and testify about being a hunter, taking the test, owning the book? Then I looked through my notes: Norman Junior wasn't on the defense witness list. As it turned out, he was nowhere near the courthouse.

NEXT: Harrell's former labor representative and coworker at Yellow Freight. He came to court in knock-around clothing, his manner aggressive and stubborn, his hair resentfully unkempt.

His testimony: that in his personal opinion, the defendant was a "very truthful man," and that he had a reputation in the community as an "up-front, tell-it-like-it-is type guy, just like I am." *Well, there it is*, I thought. *There was only one way that Norman Harrell's supposed reputation for honesty was relevant, and that would be if he testified.* The law doesn't allow a defendant to offer character evidence on the subject of his truthfulness unless that trait is actually going to be at issue in the trial. I was going to see Norman on the stand. All those notes that I'd started taking fourteen months before, preparing for that very event, would finally come in handy.

Was this witness lying? No, at least not yet. He was offering his personal opinion, nothing more. But he still had to be challenged. Character witnesses can make or break a case for a defendant. The great defense lawyer Edward Bennett Williams once won an acquittal for a disgraced politician by surrounding him with civil rights leaders whose testimony carried great weight with an all-black jury. On the other hand, if a character witness goes too far in endorsing a defendant's honor, he can open doors that the defense would rather keep closed.

And so it was with this witness. Full of himself, exhilarated by the experience of being the cynosure of all eyes on a public stage, he made a gratuitous offering: In all the years he'd worked with Harrell at Yellow Freight, "he was never disciplined for any reason whatsoever."

"Well, sir, are you aware that Harrell received a warning letter from Yellow Freight supervisors on June 12, 1992, for failing to follow company policies? And another on June 16, 1992? And three others, on November 1, November 30, and December 1, 1989? Sir, do those letters affect his opinion of whether Norman Harrell was a reliable worker and a truthful person?"

"No, sir, because I disagree with those letters."

"Do you disagree with them in your capacity as a union representative?"

"No, I disagree with them as a human being who knows the English language. They are blatant falsehoods."

"Were you there for any of those incidents?"

"No."

The fact that Harrell was an indolent, insubordinate employee didn't make him a double murderer. But it wouldn't make the jury feel any better about him either. And the funny thing was, none of this would have come out if this witness had been smart enough just to keep his mouth shut.

"Sir, do you know that Mr. Harrell has been charged with two counts of first-degree murder?"

"Yes, sir, I do."

"And the nature of those charges has not affected your opinion of him as a truthful individual?".

"That's correct."

"Could you tell us what would affect your opinion as to whether he was a truthful individual?"

"If he lied to me as his union representative."

I remembered old Jim Ballard and the other truckers, all keeping safe their brother's secrets. What was it with these Teamsters? To them, Norman Harrell was a union man and nothing else mattered. This was just another dispute they were having with the bosses.

As the witness barreled out of the courtroom, he gave Norman a wink, blissfully oblivious to the damage he was leaving in his wake.

NEXT: an African-American gentleman in his seventies, outfitted impeccably in a dark suit and tightly knotted necktie. As he walked slightly stooped to the witness stand, nodding and smiling at the jurors as he passed them, I thought to myself: *This man could say that the sun rises in the west and I could no sooner attack him as a liar in front of this jury than I could slap the court reporter in the well of the courtroom.*

His testimony: He'd been Harrell's friend for forty years, had hunted with him about twenty times, and had never known him to hunt big game or to skin any animal.

Was he lying? Of course not. Besides, I suspected Michele didn't particularly care about what came out of his mouth. She just wanted the jury to see that this wonderfully dignified fellow, with creases in his face that spoke of decades of hard contact with everything life could try to wear a man down with, still believed in Norman Harrell enough to come to court for him, dressed as if for church.

On cross-examination: three main questions. "You're Norman Harrell's friend, correct?"

"Yes."

"You don't know how many times he hunted with other people, do you?"

"No."

"You don't know what he did when he hunted with those other people, do you?"

"No."

"Thank you, nothing further."

NEXT: two witnesses, also friends of the defendant, who claimed that they'd seen him early on the evening of the murders dressed in blue overalls—the same outfit he was wearing when he was stopped later in P.G. County.

Could this testimony damage our case? Definitely. If the jury believed Reco Hawkins was right in saying that Harrell had been wearing a long-sleeved blue work uniform—not overalls—at Diane's house, then he had to have changed clothes between the murders and the stop. But if the jury believed these witnesses, it would reopen the question of why Harrell had no blood on his clothes when the police stopped him.

Were these witnesses lying? Maybe not, but they were certainly mistaken.

Cross-examination: The first witness had to admit that she couldn't say for sure when she'd seen Harrell wearing the blue overalls—whether it was on the night before he was stopped by the police, the night before he was actually arrested for the murders, or some other night. The second witness had a different problem: Until he'd been contacted by the defense, many months after the night he was describing, he'd given no thought to how Norman Harrell had been dressed at the time. By contrast, Reco Hawkins had given the police a clothing description for Harrell just hours after he'd left him at Diane's house.

NEXT FOR THE DEFENSE: Reco Hawkins, soon to be followed by his sister Shante.

As Reco entered the courtroom, several jurors swiveled in their chairs to watch him: what's he doing on Norman's side? They didn't know yet what I knew. Months before, after Sharon Randle had identified the red-and-white cooler as belonging to Diane Hawkins, I'd shown the cooler to Reco and Shante and neither had recognized it. After Sharon had testified, I'd informed Michele of this and invited her to call Reco and Shante in her case.

The defense was in a box. They couldn't leave the issue alone. But the only way to attack Sharon Randle's testimony would be to call their own witnesses to say that before the murders the bloodstained cooler had actually belonged to Harrell, not Diane—an assertion that was only marginally less incriminating than the alternative. It was ironic, to say the least, that two of the defense witnesses would be Reco and Shante. Another dilemma: If Michele called either as a witness, it might help her to undermine Randle's testimony, but it would destroy the last vestige of any argument that the Hawkins family was biased against Harrell and would twist the truth to hurt him.

Michele's questions were brief. She ended by showing Reco the cooler: "Do you remember seeing this in your house?"

"No," he said.

Cross-examination: "Mr. Hawkins, before your mother and sister died, how often did you personally get involved in cleaning up around the house?"

"Not too much. Just basically my room and stuff."

"Your room was upstairs, correct?"

"Yes."

"And how about your sister Shante? How much was she involved in cleaning up?"

"Not too much either."

"Would you say that you and Shante cleaned up around the house about the same amount of time?"

"Yes."

"Now, during that time and prior to May 25, 1993, did you know someone named Sharon Randle to come by the house?"

"Yes."

"And isn't it fair to say that Ms. Randle helped your mother clean up more around the house than you did?"

"Yes."

"And isn't it also fair to say that she helped out around the house more, for example, than your sister Shante did?"

"Yes."

"Now, during that time, your mother wasn't feeling as well as she was prior to the months leading up to her murder, was she?"

"No, she wasn't."

"And so she needed more help around the house cleaning and doing things that she used to be able to do by herself, am I right?"

"Yes."

"And that's because she was sick, correct?"

"Yes."

"Now, who would you say helped your mother out the most cleaning: you, Shante, or Sharon Randle?"

"Sharon the last couple of months. It would be Sharon."

Harrell watched Reco walk out. If he felt at all sheepish about enlisting in his cause the son of the woman he'd murdered, he didn't show it. As for Reco, he didn't give Harrell the satisfaction of receiving even a glance from him, and any unease this experience had caused him remained concealed behind the mask of a face he presented to the world.

––––––––––

THE NEXT WITNESS took the stand for the defense.

"Ma'am," said Michele Roberts, "in a loud and clear voice so that every member of the jury can hear you, would you state your full name for the record, please."

"Gale Belinda Harrell."

"And how old are you, ma'am?"

"Thirty-five."

Here she was: the former Gale Tolson, the former plaintiff in the case of *Tolson v. Harrell*, the current wife of Harrell. Early in our investigation she'd avoided cooperating with us, claiming a marital privilege. I was now seeing her for the first time: the recluse emerging, presumably, to carry her husband's banner. She was an attractive, light-skinned black woman with a full figure. As she walked past me, I noticed she was wearing stockings. I had a sudden image of what today's dawn had brought for her: the task of rousing herself to dress up and come testify at her husband's murder trial. And another thought: *Oh, if I could only have heard whatever telephone conversation passed between the jail and her house last night.*

Michele took her through background questions: how she knew the defendant, how many children she had, where she was living as of the night of the murders (with her mother) and why (she was recovering from surgery and couldn't handle the steps at the house she shared with Harrell). Her answers were clipped, addressing only what was asked, without elaboration. I was getting the sense that she wasn't about to take any risks here. On and off the stand, she was thinking, the quicker the better. And something else: She had no edge, none of the simmering righteous rage of a woman who believed her husband to be the victim of trumped-up charges. She gave off the air of a woman joylessly performing a marital duty.

"I would like to direct your attention," Michele said, "to the date of the incident and ask you, 'Were you still living at your mother's house?' "

"Yes, I was."

"Did you have occasion on that day to see your husband, Norman?"

"Yes, I did."

"And approximately, if you know, what time did you see Norman?"

"He came by about five thirty or six."

"When you saw Norman, your husband, on that day at about five thirty or so, what was he wearing?"

"Blue work pants and a shirt."

"Now, how long can you recall, Mrs. Harrell, that Norman stayed at the house?"

"He stayed until about seven thirty, seven forty-five."

"And you didn't go with him, I take it?"

"No, I didn't."

"Mrs. Harrell, what kind of vehicle did you and your husband own back in 1993?"

"Norman had a truck that was like a camper type. He had a black van, and he had a Trans Am that was nonfunctional and just stayed in the driveway."

"Mrs. Harrell, I'm showing you an exhibit, and I'd like to ask you if you recognize it." She held up the red-and-white cooler.

"Yes, I do."

"What do you recognize this exhibit to be, ma'am?"

"That's a cooler that Norman used to keep in his truck."

"Finally, Mrs. Harrell, just a couple of questions. You say that you and Norman have a seven-year-old son named Torey?"

"Yes."

"When Torey was born, were you and Mr. Harrell married?"

"No, we weren't."

"Did there come a time after Torey was born that you filed a paternity action in connection with Torey's birth and Mr. Harrell?"

"Yes, I did."

"Do you recall what year that was?"

"Nineteen eighty-seven."

"Could you tell the ladies and gentlemen of the jury when it was that you and Norman Harrell married? Was it before or after you filed the paternity action?"

"It was after."

"That's all I have," Michele concluded.

The judge looked at me. "Cross."

I took a moment to appraise Gale Harrell. Did she even look over at Harrell, even share a private smile with him? Not that I ever saw.

WHAT CAN YOU MAKE of a woman like this?

What is it that first draws her to a man like Norman Harrell?

What is it that keeps her by his side, after all the rancor and the litigation and the unpleasantness?

How far is she willing to defend him?

And finally: What does it take to coax the whole truth from her? Or does it come out on its own if you just have the patience to stand back and give it time to gather itself and throw its shoulders back and come forward with dignity?

"GOOD AFTERNOON, MA'AM."

"Hi."

"Ma'am, you filed the action that you were just asked about in 1987, correct?"

"Correct."

"And that related to Torey, who was the child that you and Mr. Harrell had in common?"

"Correct."

"And at that time you filed for that action, you and Mr. Harrell weren't married, right?"

"Correct."

"You were working at that time?"

"Correct."

"And you filed that action because you sought financial support for Torey?"

"Yes."

"Now, there came a time in 1988, did there not, that the court ordered Mr. Harrell to pay two hundred dollars a month to you, correct?"

"Correct."

"And it was your understanding, was it not, that he was to pay that money to you and that you were to use that money for the support of Torey, correct?"

"Yes."

"Now, there came a period of time when you didn't receive any money, correct?"

"Yes."

"And that period of time lasted for some four years, correct?"

"I don't know if it was four years or not."

"Well, do you recall appearing at a court proceeding in 1991 when Mr. Harrell was found in contempt of court for not paying?"

"Yes."

"And do you recall at that time that he owed you some five thousand eight hundred and sixty dollars in child support, correct?"

"Yes."

There's a cadence to an effective cross: questions being asked in such a way as to induce short responses, one after another, as if the witness is being lulled into agreeing with everything the questioner is saying.

"Do you recall that order being in May of 1991?"

"I don't know the month."

"Would it refresh your recollection if you were to look at the records in this case? Have you ever had a chance to look at the records?"

"Yes, I have."

I took the records to the witness stand. I'd wanted to get them into her hands as early as possible in the questioning. I didn't know yet whether she'd be trying to buck on me; I wanted her to see the printed pages that didn't give her room to maneuver.

"Mrs. Harrell, if you could take a look at this, you see that it indicates that on May 29 of 1991, Mr. Harrell was found in contempt of court, correct?"

"Correct."

"For failure to pay the five thousand eight hundred and sixty dollars in child support which was owing as of 1991, correct?"

"Yes."

"Now, at that point it was your understanding, was it not, that Mr. Harrell once again was under a court order to pay you child support for Torey to make up that five thousand eight hundred and sixty dollars?"

"Correct."

"And in fact, he didn't do that right away, did he?"

"No, he didn't."

"In fact, you had to go back to court to get more relief from the judge, isn't that correct?"

"Yes, we did."

"And at a certain point, the judge ordered that Mr. Harrell's wages be attached. Do you know what I mean by that?"

"Yes, I do."

"And what that means is that you were going to get money from the state after Mr. Harrell's wages were docked so as to pay the money to the state first. In other words, Mr. Harrell's wages would be attached, an amount would be deducted, and it would go to the state, and then the state would pay you?"

"Correct."

"Now, at this point you were still interested in pursuing this action against Mr. Harrell, is that correct?"

"Yes, I was."

"And your interest was in getting that five thousand eight hundred and sixty dollars that was owing to you, correct?"

"Yes, it was."

"Did you have any conversation with Mr. Harrell during that time period from 1987 to 1991, when Mr. Harrell was found in contempt of court for not paying you?"

"We had conversations, but it was not about the money."

"If you'll think back, are you *sure* there wasn't a time during those four years when you ever once called Mr. Harrell on the phone or encountered him in person and said, *I want my money. The court said you have to pay it. I want it.* Did you ever say that?"

Michele Roberts rose. "Your Honor, may we approach?"

As we were converging in front of the judge, I glanced over at Michele; she looked distracted. I'd been in her position before in a trial: squirming in my chair as I watched the other lawyer take my witness through a line of questions that I sensed would hurt my case; knowing that I had to break things up for at least a minute, if for no other reason than to disrupt my adversary's rhythm; using the few seconds it took to navigate between my table and the judge's bench to formulate a strategy to cut off the whole inquiry.

At the bench, Michele stated her objection. She said the questions were irrelevant to the main issues in the trial.

I explained to the judge where I was going.

The judge overruled the objection.

I returned to my table and began again with Gale Tolson Harrell: "Ma'am, I believe that I asked you: Between 1987 and 1991, when you weren't getting money from Mr. Harrell and when you in fact had a court order that he should pay you each month, what kind of conversations did you have with him?"

"I didn't have any conversations with him because I felt as though it was in the court's hands."

This was the way it was going to be: She'd take two steps toward me, then one back.

"Now, in between 1988 and 1991, when the contempt order was issued, you hadn't seen a dime, had you, from Mr. Harrell?"

"That's true."

"And so it went to court. And were you in court when Mr. Harrell was found in contempt?"

"Yes, I was."

"And isn't it true that Mr. Harrell told the judge that the judge should just put him in jail because he wasn't going to pay child support, no way, nohow?"

"To that effect, yes."

"And so the judge took him up on that and put him in jail?"

"Yes."

"And he got out only because he agreed to pay money under a court order, correct?"

"Correct."

"And it still took some time for him to do that, and even as of later on that year he still hadn't, correct?"

"To the best of my knowledge, that's true."

"And during this time it's safe to say also that you all weren't getting along very well, correct?"

She hesitated. "We had a cordial relationship."

I was going to have to back up and go at this a different way.

"How would you define *cordial*?"

"We would see one another in passing. Norman was a friend of one of my relatives."

"Well, are you saying that your relationship was such that each of you would go to the other's house?"

"No."

I picked up a document from my desk, so she'd see I had it in hand. "In fact, ma'am, isn't it true that in a letter you wrote to the court on December 2, 1991, you included this sentence: 'Our relationship has not been one where I visit his house under any circumstances'?"

No hesitation: "That's true."

That was her whole answer: "That's true." Not "That's true, but I was overreacting," or "That's true, but let me explain." Whatever Norman Harrell had thought she was going to say about all this—whatever it was that had made him press his lawyer to call her to the stand on his behalf—she was having none of it.

"Now, I think we covered this, but I just want to ask you again. There came a point in early 1992 when Mr. Harrell's wages started getting attached, correct?"

"Yes."

"And at that point you started seeing money each month because the state of Maryland had intervened?"

"Correct."

"Now at that point, you didn't drop the child support action against him, did you?"

"No, I did not."

"In fact, you wanted to press on because you were finally seeing some money, correct?"

"Correct."

"And so you kept the child support action going all the way through 1992. And in fact, only in August of last year did you ever drop it, correct?"

"Correct."

"Now, you and he got married in September of 1992?"

"Correct."

"And at that point, did you begin living with Mr. Harrell at 4615 A Street?"

"Yes, I did."

"Your mother was still living over at 2070 Addison Road in District Heights, correct?"

"Yes."

"And that was the address that you had listed in the very first paper that you filed in your support, was it not?"

"Yes."

"And it's the address where you continued to receive payments from the state of Maryland once they'd started garnishing or attaching Mr. Harrell's wages, correct?"

"Yes."

"Now, September of 1992, at that point you were married and you were living with Mr. Harrell and with his sister and with Torey at 4615 A Street?"

"Yes."

"And from September of 1992 all the way up to the time of the incident in this case, you continued to live at 4615 A Street up until the time that you had your operation, correct?"

"Yes."

"Now, Mr. Harrell continued to live there too, correct?"

"Yes."

"Now, you didn't drop the child support matter, though, did you?"

"No, I didn't."

"You kept that child support action going from September of 1992 all the way *past* the time of your operation in May of 1993, correct?"

"Correct."

There are times when you're in trial and everything slows down and it's as if you're outside yourself, watching yourself in action. No less an authority on the law than Eddie Felson, the hungry pool shark in the classic movie *The Hustler*, described the same sort of sensation: "When you're right and you know you're right, all of a sudden it's like you've got oil in your arm and the cue has nerves in it—it's a wooden stick but it's got nerves in it—and you feel the roll of the balls and you don't even have to look, you just know." For a trial lawyer these occasions are rare and precious; you might only have two or three such experiences over the course of entire career. Athletes know this feeling, and actors do too, or so I've read; I think it's unique to those vocations where two of the most absorbing human activities—performing and competing—are combined. I just know from my father's lamentations about the drudgeries of his job that he never knew the feeling that I was having right then, and I'd have given all my money just to have been able to buy it for him.

"Ms. Harrell, you kept that child support action going, even though you and Mr. Harrell were now living together and your son was living with you, right?"

"Yes."

"And you never contacted the state of Maryland to tell them that your address changed, did you?"

"I sent them a letter telling them that we had gotten married."

"Well, did you say in that letter, because of the fact that you and Mr. Harrell had gotten married and you were now going to be living together with the child, 'I want to have the charge dropped'?"

"I did send a letter but I don't recall the date of it."

She hadn't answered the question. I looked closely at her; the expression on her face said, just keep doing what you're doing. You're getting there.

"Okay. Well, you ended up sending a letter in August of 1993, correct?"

"I don't know what the date of it was. Do you have a copy?" She knew the date. She knew when she'd sent the letter, and she knew why.

"Ma'am, I'm showing you an exhibit and I'll ask, do you recognize it?"

"Yes, I do."

"Is that the letter that you're referring to that you sent to the Office of Child Support Enforcement for Prince George's County, indicating that you wanted the child support charges to be dropped in your case against Mr. Norman Harrell?"

"Yes, it is."

"Now, that's the *only* letter you sent to them in regard to dropping the child support charges, correct?"

"Yes, it is."

"Now by this time, by the time you wrote this letter—*in August of 1993*—it had been almost a full year since you and Mr. Harrell had gotten married, correct?"

"Yes."

"And on this letter you listed your address the same as you had all the way through the other correspondence with that office—as 2070 Addison Road, Apartment No. 2, District Heights, Maryland?"

"Correct."

"Now, from September of 1992 all the way up until August of 1993, you were still receiving, at your other address, a check that had been taken out of Mr. Harrell's salary, correct? Even though you were all living together at 4615 A Street with the child that that money was going over to Addison Road to support?"

"Correct."

"Now did you and Mr. Harrell ever have any conversation about the fact that between September of 1992, when you got married, and August of 1993, his money was going over to his *mother-in-law's* house when you were actually living over on A Street supporting the child?"

A few seconds went by. "We had talked about it."

"He was angry about it, right?"

"He was . . . *concerned*."

"And when you say Mr. Harrell was *concerned*, how many times would you say you had conversations about it?"

"Maybe four."

This was either a simple mistake or an intentional underestimation. When asked to calculate the number of occasions when they've experienced a regular occurrence—say, encountering a casual friend in the neighborhood—the first instinct of most people is to come in

on the low side. But once time has been broken down into manageable intervals for them—"Isn't it true that you generally see him
about three times a month, so it would be fair to say that just last year
you probably saw him about forty times?"—a more accurate estimate
emerges.

"Well, would it be unreasonable to assume that the subject could
have come up, say, *once a month*? Every time Mr. Harrell opened up
his pay envelope and saw that more money had been taken out and
sent over to his mother-in-law's address?"

"It was not that frequent." She wasn't going along with me yet.

"And is it safe to say when you say he was *concerned* about this,
wouldn't another phrase be that he was upset or angry about it and
he wanted you to do something about it?"

"I don't know if he was angry. He was concerned, as I said,
because we talked about it."

It was tempting to ask how he expressed his concern: whether his
chosen form of communication had been the menacing threat, the
hand to the throat, or the backhand slap to the face. But I was never
going to get that out of her. A pattern had developed: If I had a
document in my hand, a written record on a particular issue, she
wouldn't lie about it, nor would she embellish it or try to explain
it away. But to the extent there was still a private side to her life
with Norman Harrell she would try to maintain it, if only just to
preserve a point she could make in her defense when he inevitably
confronted her later about her testimony.

I walked back to my table and flipped through some papers, even
though I knew what my next question would be. I wanted to give the
jury a chance to think: of course Harrell was upset when Diane
Hawkins filed her own claim against him. He was already getting
his wages garnished and the money was going over to his mother-in-
law's house. Then Diane came along, wanting a piece of what was
left. It was the sort of predicament that could send a certain sort of
man over the edge.

"Now, you became aware in May of 1993 that your husband had been arrested and charged with the murders in this case, correct?"

"Yes."

"When did you become aware of the fact that it would be the government's theory in this case that Mr. Harrell murdered Diane Hawkins because she was taking him to court for child support?"

"I never knew that that was the reason for the arrest, that it was because of child support." For the first time during her testimony she looked away from me, then back.

"Well, you were having conversations with Mr. Harrell about the case between late May and August of 1993, correct?"

"Yes."

I couldn't ask her about these conversations; they were marital communications, and under D.C. law a spouse is barred from testifying about them. But I knew that she knew more than she was saying; she just needed some cover. I thought back to June 1993.

Two weeks after Harrell was arrested he had a preliminary hearing, when his lawyer had a chance to cross-examine a government witness about the case. I didn't know Gale Harrell then, and I couldn't recall now if the woman before me had been in court for the hearing.

Ah, what the hell, I thought, *go for it. She seems like the type who'd show up for something like that.*

"Did you attend the preliminary hearing in this case, ma'am?"

"Yes, I did."

"And don't you recall at the preliminary hearing the detective sitting in the seat up there and taking the oath and indicating that at the time that Diane Hawkins was killed she had a child support action pending against Mr. Harrell? Do you recall that?"

"Yes, I do."

"So October of 1992 had gone by, and November and December and January and February and March and April. All of those months had gone by, and you had not dropped the action?"

"Correct."

"May of 1993, Mr. Harrell is charged with this murder, and you attend a preliminary hearing. You see a detective take the witness stand and say that Mr. Harrell had a child support action brought by another woman as to another child, and they were supposed to go to the court the next day after the murder, right? You knew that, right?"

"From his testimony, yes."

"And it was only then, after you heard about that, that in August of 1993 you finally dropped the charges?"

"That's true." She settled in her chair.

In a flickering instant, I thought, *She's glad the truth is out.*

Gale Harrell had confirmed in person the tale told by the dry historical record. Surely she knew her husband had killed those people. She knew it so well that the knowledge frightened her, and she acted on her fear and dropped her own case.

"Now, as to the Ford truck," I asked, "he was the only one in your family that drove that truck on a regular basis, is that fair to say?"

"Yes."

"And it's even fair to say he was somewhat protective of it. He didn't let anybody get into that truck, did he? He didn't lend it out a lot, correct?"

"Not to my knowledge, he didn't."

"He drove it on a regular basis and drove it himself, right?"

"Correct."

"And you can't give the jury a reason why there would have been blood inside that truck in the early morning hours of May 26, 1993, could you?"

"*I sure can't.*"

I LEFT THE COURTHOUSE that night in a rush. If I got on the highway early enough, I could beat rush-hour traffic, make the half-hour trip to my parents' house, visit for a while, and then get back into town for a few more hours of work.

My father came to the door to greet me, leaning heavily against me as he never had before. Walking to his place on the downstairs sofa next to my mom, he had to hold on to objects to keep from falling. For the next twenty minutes or so, while my mother and I talked about how he was doing, he stared to one side at a mindless television drama of the sort he'd never before had patience with. Mom told me later why he seemed so transfixed by the program: He couldn't move his head without becoming dizzy.

During our conversation, she kept consulting a green spiral ledger she was holding on her lap. I'd seen it before. Inside were her copious handwritten notes on my dad's situation, meticulously memorializing everything from medical diagnoses and recommended courses of treatment to emergency contact numbers and directions to doctor's offices. On the coffee table in front of my father sat a sizable stack of index cards. These, too, I'd seen before. They contained all of his own notes and lists on the same subject, including a comprehensive, relentlessly detailed accounting of his blood pressure and pulse readings as he'd registered them himself on a device at the local drugstore.

This was my parents' way of chasing down the answers to the mystery they were living: to write everything down. I'd also been keeping notes, of all the conversations I'd had with my dad's doctors, so I knew the impulse well; I still do. Faced with something you can't control or explain, you convert as much of it as you can into straight lines of letters on a page and it becomes more real, less ephemeral; you can make more sense of it, maybe even achieve some mastery over it.

I left my parents a short time later. My father had hobbled upstairs to join my mother in seeing me off, and as I drove away from their house to return to an office full of paper, I turned to see them standing together, backlit, in the doorway of their home.

———

IT WAS NEARING noon on the seventh day of trial. Michele Roberts moved to the podium. "Norman Harrell," she said simply.

Harrell got up from his seat and lumbered through the well of the courtroom to the witness stand. He was dressed for battle in a dark gray suit, provided daily by his sister, that he changed into every morning so the jury wouldn't know he was being held in jail during his trial and somehow prejudge him. He walked with the heavy grace of a power forward. His shoulders were slumped, but not from the weight of conscience; he looked calm, unruffled, about what was about to happen. Months before, I'd had the wild idea that I'd be able to break him on cross; people who knew him well had convinced me that he'd be done in by the weakness at his core. Looking at him now, I knew this wasn't going to happen.

The previous May, the police had started taking away from him all the things that were closest to him—his truck, first, then his liberty, and that meant he'd lost his job. His oldest boy hadn't come to court for him, he hadn't seen his younger boy in months, and just now a DA had even tried to peel his wife away from him. He'd always known it would all come down to him, anyway.

I looked over at the jury members. About half had turned away from him; the other half were looking down. Only one of them watched Harrell as he settled into the witness chair—Twelve, the forty-five-year-old woman on the back row whose sunny visage and unremitting pleasantness had persevered through days of gruesome and disturbing testimony.

Michele began with the basics: age, place of birth, family, schools, jobs. She took him back through his life, trying to humanize him for the jury. Some of what he was saying about his past was new to me, but I wasn't taking notes. I knew what I wanted to cover on cross, and I could remember what I needed. It was more important to listen to Harrell's voice, to watch his face and frame as he answered these early questions. Would his inflections change later when the questions got tougher? If he was sitting forward now while being asked where he went to school, would he signal defensiveness later, when the questions got tougher, by sitting back in his chair? I learned a lesson once from Detective Tony Duvall, who masterfully interviewed hundreds of suspects over a thirty-year career: "I never ask a motherfucker about the crime for at least an hour." It's in the early moments of a defendant's testimony, when his guard is down, that you get the truest picture of him.

Michele asked about Diane Hawkins: how Harrell had met her, what their relationship had been like. Then: "Did you have any occasion to meet any of Diane Hawkins's family and friends?"

Harrell began nodding before the question was even finished. "Yes I did."

"For example, Deborah Courtney—did you have any occasion to meet Ms. Courtney during the times you were friends with Ms. Hawkins?"

"Yes, I did."

"And how would you describe your relationship with Ms. Courtney?"

"It wasn't friends. You know, some casual, you know, if we see each other, we would speak or something like that."

"And Carlene Hawkins—how would you describe your relationship with Carlene Hawkins?"

"It was more like a friendly relationship."

"Do you recall Sharon Randle? Do you recall meeting her?"

"Yes, I do. We did not have no relationship. It was just a hi-and-bye thing."

"Where would you see her?"

"Over at Diane's house."

He wouldn't say anything bad about any of them. His message to the jury was: See what a reasonable guy I am? Deborah, Carlene, and Sharon all came in and testified against me, and I'm still not angry with them. Why would anybody think I got so steamed up at Diane that I wanted to kill her? Then again, he wasn't explaining why these women would come into court and try to frame him for two murders.

"Now, let's talk about Rock. Who is Rock?"

"Rock is her youngest son, Rasheen, the one that is by me."

"How is it that you learned that Rock was your son?"

"Well, a few years ago she took Willie Harris to court for child support for Rasheen, and the test came back negative."

"Well, let me ask you this: Was there a time when you decided that Rasheen was your son?"

"Yes, I did."

"And putting aside this other matter, was there anything about Rock's appearance that led you to conclude that he was probably your son?"

"Yes. A lot of his features." Harrell turned to look at the jury. "He has hands like me, ladies and gentlemen. And he has feet like me. He's kind of built like me, and plus he has a head like mine."

At the mention of his big head, Harrell tilted it toward the jury as if it were a trophy. A young woman in the front row of the box—one of the jurors who'd looked down when Harrell took the stand—shook her head. But then she smiled . . . until she caught me watching her and looked down again.

"Now, did you ever advise Rock that you were his father?"

"Yes, I did."

"Did you ever do anything special with Rock?"

"Like, I would go over there, and I would take him to the store, buy his clothes, shoes, buy him something to eat if he called me and told me he was hungry. And I would go over there and take him to McDonald's or a carry-out or somewhere and get him something to eat."

"And you would take him places, and were there times when other children would be a part of those trips?"

"Yes."

"Mr. Harrell, did you give Diane money for Rock?"

"No, ma'am. I felt I was doing, you know, my part of the job."

Michele asked him about the statements attributed to him by Deborah Courtney, Carlene Hawkins, and Sharon Randle. He denied making any of them: denied telling Deborah he would kill Diane Jamaican style, denied telling Carlene he would hurt Diane if she took him to court, denied threatening Diane in front of Sharon. For good measure, he denied knowing what Jamaican-style killing was and denied knowing any Jamaicans. If he'd been asked, he'd have denied ever hearing of Jamaica. Throughout all these answers he kept the same expression, maintained the same tone, held the same posture as when he'd given his name and age at the beginning of his testimony.

"Now, let me ask you this, Mr. Harrell. What is your view of child support?"

"I'm not happy with it, you know, as far as them garnishing my check or anything. I'm not happy with it."

"Again, generally speaking, what is your view of supporting your children?"

"That's *one hundred percent* support." Harrell punctuated his answer with a smile and a nod. His words rattled around in my head: Where have I heard something like that before? Of course: O. J. Simpson, being arraigned on national television in his own double murder case just two months before, vowing that he was "one hundred percent innocent."

"Now, let's talk again about this paternity action that was filed back in 1987 in Prince George's County. Why were you held in contempt?"

"Because I would not pay the full amount, what they wanted me to pay."

"What was the amount that you were under court order to pay?"

"Two hundred dollars a month."

"And how much were you paying?"

"A hundred and fifty."

This was a blatant lie, contradicted by seven years of official court documents. Had Michele planned to elicit perjury from her client? No, I'll never believe that. Possibly, she hadn't looked closely enough at the court records; for months before trial, we'd inundated her with hundreds of documents, photographs, and diagrams to review. Everyone involved in the case had found it, at one point or another, too big to be able to wrap our arms completely around it. But it's far more likely that Harrell simply went off on his own: No one was going to make him follow any plan if he didn't want to. Maybe he thought he was on a roll and could say anything and get away with it. Maybe he thought he could slip this by me and I wouldn't notice. Most likely, the truth was simply of no consequence to him, so he naturally assumed it was of no consequence to anyone else.

Michelle's questioning continued.

"And you were ultimately held in contempt?"

"Yes, ma'am."

"And they garnished your salary, right?"

"Yes."

"Now the person who filed that petition was whom?"

"My wife."

"Was she your wife when she filed it?"

"No, she wasn't."

"Did you marry her at some point after she filed it?"

"Yes, it was a few years later."

Michele asked now about hunting, and Harrell explained how he'd been a sportsman for twenty years but tracked only small game, never deer; how his son had gotten the hunter's manual some years before, in order to take a state examination; how Harrell had touched some pages in the book while helping him prepare for the test.

"Mr. Harrell, did you ever cut or skin an animal?"

"No, ma'am. I didn't want to cut. I felt kind of squeamish like, you know, I couldn't go in that part." He looked over at the jury and made a face.

Michele asked him about the red-and-white cooler; Harrell said he'd used it to carry his lunch to work and routinely kept it in his truck.

"Now, how long, Mr. Harrell, had you owned that truck?"

"Ever since 1986."

"And from 1986 until May of 1993, were you the only person that ever got in the truck?"

"No, ma'am."

"Can you tell us if you know of any persons who might have left any amount of blood in your truck?"

"Yes, my oldest son, Norman, Rasheen, myself."

"Let's start with you. What do you recall might have occurred between 1986 and 1993 which would have resulted in your leaving some portion of blood in the truck?"

"When I work on my vehicle, sometimes I might cut my hand or scratch it, and a couple of times I have cut myself at work and I have bled in it."

"What about your son Norman?"

"We were working on his car one day changing the brakes and he cut his hand, and when we got in the truck to go to the auto parts place together and get some more parts, that's when he got in my truck when his hand was still bleeding."

"And what about Rock?"

"Rasheen, he was in there with my son Michael's son, Diontee. They got to fighting in the truck one day."

"Do you know what portion of the truck they were fighting in?"

"In the front of the truck, the front seat."

"And did you actually see any blood on Rock?"

"No, I didn't. No, wait a minute. Yes, I did. Rock had cut his hand. My mistake. Rock had cut his hand."

It was as if Harrell felt himself under fire and scooped up his son to use as a shield. The best way for us to prove this was a lie would be to compare Rock's blood sample to the samples from the truck. Harrell knew this. He was daring us to stick a needle into his son's arm and draw his blood.

"Now, Mr. Harrell, let's talk about May 25 of 1993 and let me ask you straight up. Did you kill Diane Hawkins?"

"No, ma'am."

"Did you kill Katrina Harris?"

"No, ma'am."

Juries are sometimes unduly swayed by the force of a defendant's denial: the vehemence of his voice, the seeming authenticity of his outrage, when he says the words "I didn't do it." This can work both ways. I never approach jurors after a trial is over—I'd rather go on in blissful ignorance, believing every verdict is based solely on the merits of the prosecution's case—but once I was cornered in the courthouse corridor by a group looking to unburden themselves of anecdotes about the experience. One said, "You know what really convinced all of us he was guilty?"

"What," I said, holding my breath.

"The fact he never said that he was innocent."

Well, I thought, *he did say he was ten miles away from the scene of the shooting when it happened; maybe he thought that was enough.* Ironically, it's the easiest lie for a defendant to tell; he's been practicing it for months in every conversation he's had with his family, his friends, his lawyer. As denials go, Harrell's was a good one, and everyone in the jury box was now staring at him.

Michele took Harrell back to the Sunday before the murders, and he again denied telling Carlene he would hurt Diane over the child support case. He talked about the trip arrangements, how he'd been told he could only contact Rock through Deborah Courtney's son Tracy. Then Michele moved to the next Tuesday: how he went to work in the morning, then went to his mother-in-law's house to see his wife and son Torey, then went over to Deborah's house to see Tracy. In P.G. County, Harrell told the detectives that he'd wanted to find out whether Tracy had heard from Deborah about how Rock was doing and had only gone by Diane's house when he was unable to locate Tracy. Now he was sticking to that story, claiming that his visit had nothing to do with the child support hearing the next day; he said he'd never received any notice of the hearing.

Michele asked him how he was dressed when he made his rounds that Tuesday night. "Ma'am," he answered, "blue denim jean coveralls, a blue shirt, and brown loafers."

"Mr. Harrell, were you wearing socks that day?"

"When I was at work, I wore socks, but when I got off, I took them off."

"Why?"

"Well, my feet perspire a lot, and I don't like to have them on because sometimes, even though I put foot powder down there, sometimes they still have an odor at times." He looked down and shook his head. It was his way of saying, *Shucks, folks, I'm being straight up with you about my feet; you've got to believe me about these killings.*

"Was May 25, 1993, the first time that you walked over to Diane's house instead of driving?"

"No, ma'am."

"Why did you walk?"

"Well, I like to walk. I'm trying to lose some weight."

"How long a walk is it from your place to Diane Hawkins's house?"

"Anywhere from twenty minutes to thirty minutes."

"When you got to the Hawkins's home, was anybody home?"

"There was Reco, Diane, Kiki, and Reco's girlfriend, Toi."

"How did you get in the house?"

"Reco opened the door for me."

"Why did you go by the Hawkins's home?"

"Looking for Tracy."

"When you came into the home, where were you principally located, Mr. Harrell?"

"In the chair in the front living room."

"And what were you doing?"

"Sitting there looking at TV. First I was talking to Reco, and then he went upstairs to take a shower. Just sitting there looking at TV."

"Did you see Diane that evening?"

"She came downstairs later on. We spoke."

"Did she stay downstairs for any length of time?"

"No, she went either in the dining room or kitchen area, and then she came back and went straight upstairs."

"Did Katrina ever come into the house?"

"She came in later. She sat down there for about maybe three minutes, and then she went on upstairs."

"By the way, Mr. Harrell, Katrina Harris. Tell the ladies and gentlemen of the jury what kind of relationship you had with Katrina Harris."

"Me and Katrina got along good. She was something like a daughter I have never had because all I had was boys." Nothing about the tense exchanges, the petty slights, the mutual resentments, and nothing, of course, about how she died.

If Norman Harrell were a computer, he could have been wired in such a way that operations in one part of his circuitry could proceed completely independently of the operations of another part. But he was a human being—from all appearances, at least—which would have made me believe that his brain was then being flooded with images of the girl's final moments: how wide her eyes were when he first saw her staring at him from the steps, how she shrieked and turned to run and made him leave what he was doing to chase her down, the noise she made when he clutched her around the waist in the bedroom, and how she kept screaming and screaming while he kept stabbing her until finally she wasn't screaming anymore. No. His eyes were unblinking, his voice was even, and his face revealed no sign that his mind's eye was preoccupied by visions of a slaughter. If any of those images remained in his system, they were tucked safely away in a file he never looked at.

"Now, after Katrina came in the house, did anyone else leave the house?"

"Reco and his girlfriend, Toi, left."

"And after Reco and Toi left, did they ever return?"

"Reco returned."

"How long did he remain after he came back that second time?"

"He didn't stay there long. He gave me a soda. He took something upstairs to his mother, and I don't know if he took something to Katrina. And then he came back and went in the kitchen, and it sounded like the refrigerator opened and shut, and then he came in and we talked. And he said he was leaving, and I said I'm getting ready to leave too."

"And did Reco leave?"

"Yes, he did."

It's funny how things work out over the course of a trial. For all the controversy about Reco Hawkins, for all the allegations about how he'd set up an innocent man to protect his own murderous drug-dealing friends, his story about that night had been corroborated down to the last detail by none other than Norman Harrell.

"How long after Reco left did you leave, Mr. Harrell?"

"About a couple of minutes. I walked back over to East Capitol Street, where my truck was at."

"And did you go home?"

"No, I didn't. No one was home. My sister didn't get off of work until late and my wife and son were over at my mother-in-law's and I wasn't sleepy and so I decided to go for a ride until I got a little sleepy and I'd come back home."

Harrell described his route of travel: East Capitol Street to Central Avenue to Route 202 to White House Road to Richie Forestville Road to Walker Mill Road. He said that he then became aware that a police car was behind him; he denied turning off his truck lights to elude the police. Michele asked him about his interview with the detectives at the P.G. County station.

"Do you recall that at some point, Detective Stanton said words to the effect of, sometimes women can do things that drive you crazy, blah, blah, blah, and that you put your head down and wept? Do you recall that testimony?"

"I remember that testimony, but it wasn't exactly the way it happened. See, he was telling me that women, you know, have a tendency of pushing that right button, and I was sitting there looking at him and listening to him. And then Detective Johnson showed me some pictures of Diane and Katrina, how they were killed, and that's when I started crying. I never put my head down. I just started wiping tears from my eyes. That was it."

It was a convincing performance, except for one thing. Johnson and Stanton didn't have any photographs with them when they interviewed him.

VIEWED FROM ABOVE—from twenty or thirty feet, or from whatever you want to call the great wherever—the courtroom resembled a rough circle.

The curved judge's bench and the curved witness stand, positioned at what might be called the top of the circle, joined the curved lawyers' tables on the left and the curved jury area on the right, with an open space at the bottom of the circle, between the prosecutor's table and the jury area.

This open space faced the witness. It led to the aisle between the audience seats, which led to the doors in the back of the courtroom.

A few seconds after Norman Harrell finished his last answer, I rose and moved into this space: the space between him and the doors to the outside world.

Another circle was now unbroken.

"Sir, you testified here about a child support case that was brought against you in 1987 by Gale Tolson, your current wife, correct?"

"Yes, sir."

I'd been trained to fight the impulse to attack a hostile witness too quickly on cross. It was better to start by getting admissions from him—to use him to help shore up my own case—when he was still prone to be agreeable, before things turned nasty. But Harrell had lied during his direct testimony so brazenly, so *refutably*, that the lie had to be exploited immediately.

"Sir, in that case you were ordered to pay two hundred dollars a month child support, correct?"

"Yes, sir."

"Now there came a time in 1991, did there not, when you were found in contempt of court as to that matter, correct?"

"Yes, sir."

"And you have testified here under oath that the reason why you were found in contempt of court is because you weren't able to pay the *entire* amount, correct?"

"Yes, sir."

"And you have testified under oath to this jury that you were paying one hundred and fifty dollars a month when, in fact, the court wanted you to pay two hundred dollars a month, correct?"

"That's right. Yes, sir."

"Now is it not true that in May of 1991 you were, in fact, found guilty of contempt of court for a failure to pay some *five thousand eight hundred and sixty dollars* in child support?"

"Yes, it is."

"Okay. So, September of 1988 to September 1989, you're supposed to pay two hundred dollars a month, correct?"

"Yes, sir."

I went to the easel and started marking numbers on a blank sheet of poster-sized paper, large enough for Harrell and the jury to see them. "So, if we put two hundred dollars a month times twelve, that's twenty-four hundred dollars in the first year, correct?"

"That's right."

"Okay. Now, the second year, 1989 to 1990, it's two hundred dollars again, correct?"

"Yes, sir."

"Times twelve months, correct?"

"Yes, sir."

"Another twenty-four hundred dollars. And so that's forty-eight hundred dollars, correct?"

"Yes, sir."

Either he didn't know where I was going with this, or he didn't care. I might as well have been reciting a nursery rhyme to him: *Humpty Dumpty sat on a wall, correct, sir?*

"Now, Mr. Harrell, between September 1990 and May 1991, we have October, November, December, January, February, March, April, and May, correct? Eight months at two hundred dollars a month, correct?"

"Yes, sir."

"And correct me if I'm getting any of this wrong, but that's sixteen hundred dollars more, correct?"

"Yes, sir."

"So, as of May 1991, you, in fact, should have paid a total of sixty-four hundred dollars in child support, correct?"

"That is correct."

"Now, your testimony to this jury was that, in fact, during that entire time you were paying a hundred and fifty dollars a month to the petitioner in that action, Gale Tolson, correct?"

"Well, most of the time I was. I ain't going to sit up here and tell a lie it was every month."

"Well, in that case, why was it that the court found you in contempt of court in May of 1991 for failure to pay *five thousand eight hundred and sixty dollars* in child support?"

"Because I was not paying it all."

"Well, in fact, during that entire time period, you had only paid some seven hundred and forty dollars in child support, correct?"

"Yes, sir."

"So in other words, what you said to this jury under oath—that you had, in fact, paid one hundred and fifty dollars a month from 1988 through 1991—was not true, correct?"

"If that's what you want to call it, sir."

"Well, what do you call it, sir? You said under oath you were paying a hundred fifty dollars."

"Not every month. I was not paying it every month. I might have missed, what you call it, but it wasn't every month. Let me rephrase it. I was not paying it every month."

"Did you not testify under oath before this jury that the reason why you were found in contempt of court was that you were only paying a hundred fifty dollars a month in child support, as opposed to two hundred dollars? *Isn't that what you testified to under oath?*"

"Yes, I did."

"And that's *false*, correct?"

"Yes, it is."

It was a startling admission for a witness to have to make in front of a jury: that he'd lied about something he'd just told them under oath. But Harrell conceded the point readily. Maybe if you don't recognize the truth you can't regret being caught in a lie.

Still, he must have realized that he'd hurt his cause. From that point on, he changed tactics, contesting every issue. Maybe he thought, *That was all too complicated for anyone to even pay attention to it, but now I might as well just dig in.*

———

I MOVED TO the blood in Harrell's truck. He'd claimed that in three separate incidents he and two of his sons had all injured themselves inside the vehicle.

"Mr. Harrell, tell us about those incidents again, if you could, and be as specific as possible about when you recall them happening."

"Now I can't remember the exact date, the exact month, but I can tell you, you know, it was warm outside."

"You named several of them. Can you go through them one by one?"

"Okay. Norman Junior, we were working on his car changing brakes and trying to put the muffler back up there where it's sup-posed to be. He cut his hand on the brake job, and we had to go up to Capitol Heights Auto Parts to get some more parts, some wire hanger for the muffler, and that's when his blood could have gotten in my truck, because he was bleeding."

"How long was that before the murders happened?"

"It was some time in May, or right before May. I can't exactly tell you the exact week. Like I told you, I could not tell you the exact week and the time, but I know it was on Saturday. That's all I can tell you."

"So, it was some time in May of the year that Diane Hawkins died?"

"Yes, it was."

"And would you say it was a week, two weeks, or three weeks before that incident happened?"

"Maybe a week or so before then."

"I think you also described an incident where Rasheen, your son, had spilled some blood in the truck. How did that happen?"

"Yes. Him and Diontee got to fighting in there, about a week before that. It was on a Sunday."

"Sunday before—"

"It was before the trip."

"Before the incident with Norman Junior?"

"No, it all happened on the same weekend around the same time."

"Are these the only times that you can recall, in the whole time that you've had that truck, that anyone cut themselves inside it?"

"That's all I can recall off the top of my head."

"How long have you had the truck?"

"Ever since 1986."

"So it's your testimony here that in all the eight years that you had the truck, the only two times you can remember when someone cut themselves or bled in the truck just happened to be in the same month when Diane Hawkins was killed?"

"I don't keep records. As far as I know, my brother, he cut his hand in there about almost a year before that. I was helping him move. Well, he was doing the moving. I was standing around, so-called supervising. I helped him a little bit." Based on his work file at Yellow Freight, this was probably his most honest answer.

"Mr. Harrell, that was about a year before?"

"Almost."

"And when your son Rasheen cut himself, where did he cut himself?"

"On his hand. It wasn't that bad. Like a little scrape, like I said."

"So you don't even know whether or not it bled?"

"Yes, it went through the skin."

"And I believe you also testified on direct examination that you injured yourself?"

"Yes, sir."

"When did that take place in relation to when Diane Hawkins and Katrina Harris were killed?"

"About a week before that."

Now four people, including Harrell, had injured themselves and bled inside his truck in the year before the murders, and three in just the month before.

"Is there any other person who would have been in a position to bleed inside your truck from the time you got it in 1986 until May of 1993, that you can recall?"

"There could have been numerous people that could have got in there bleeding. You know, I don't pay attention to everyone that gets in there."

When Detectives Gainey and Whalen interviewed Harrell in P.G. County, they specifically asked him if he could think of any reason why there would have been blood in his truck, and he said no. We couldn't bring this statement out in our case-in-chief because of the judge's ruling before trial that this part of the interview had violated Harrell's Miranda rights. But Harrell was coming close to opening this issue up again. I just had to press him some more.

"Now, Mr. Harrell, let's just look at the incidents within a month of when Diane Hawkins and Katrina Harris were killed. Those, I assume, were all fresh in your mind the night you got stopped by the Prince George's County police, were they not?"

"No, sir."

"Well, let me put it this way. They're fresh enough in your mind today that you're able to tell this jury that you're pretty sure that all three of those incidents happened within a month of your being stopped by the Prince George's County police, correct? Today you're pretty sure?"

"I'm pretty sure."

I entered the space between us and walked slowly toward him. "It's been now fifteen some months since those incidents took place, correct?"

"I would say sixteen months or a little better."

"And at the time you were interviewed by the Metropolitan Police and the Prince George's County police, at that point it had only been three or four weeks, correct?"

"Yes."

"So your memory of those events would have been better at the time you were interviewed by the Metropolitan Police Department than it is now, since you were closer in time to those incidents then, is that fair to say?"

I turned my back on him before he even gave an answer.

"Yes."

"Now do you recall being interviewed by a Detective Gainey and a Detective Whalen within a matter of hours after you left the house at 3461 Eads Street, Northeast, in the early morning hours of May 26, 1993?"

"Yes, sir."

"And that was three to four weeks from the time that all of these incidents happened where people bled inside your truck?"

"Yes, sir."

"And do you recall being asked specifically by Detective Dan Whalen of the Metropolitan Police Department whether there was any reason whatsoever for there to be blood inside your truck?"

"No, he did not ask me that."

I was still walking away from him, and I felt myself do a small stutter step that I immediately hoped no one else noticed.

"And so, Mr. Harrell, you also deny that at any time you said to him, 'No, sir, there is no reason whatsoever for blood to be inside my truck'?"

"Like I said, he never asked me."

"And so you deny you ever said that?"

"That's right."

Harrell had just put into play his statement to Whalen about the blood. Under Supreme Court case law, once he took the stand and contradicted the statement, it could be brought out against him, regardless of whether the police violated his Miranda rights in obtaining it. Those rights, according to the law, can't be used by a defendant as a shield to allow him to commit perjury later at his trial.

Outside the courtroom, Detective Whalen sat waiting, ready to take the stand when the time came.

THE JUDGE ORDERED a ten-minute recess. I went into the corridor and bumped into a friend of mine from the office. "It's going well," he said. A pause. Then, with a smile: "You're getting a little cocky in there." After a second, I knew what he was referring to—the disdainful turning of the back, the calling out of questions over the shoulder, the step. As a prosecutor, I walk a fine line. I know that I'm at the center of my cases—that if the jury doesn't believe me, doesn't trust me, they probably won't convict—but if I ever make it seem that I think it's all about me, then they'll turn on me. I asked him if he had any other suggestions. "Yeah. This guy is a monster. Go after him as hard as you can and keep him on the stand for as long as you can. The jury will end up hating him more and more." *That'll be fine,* I thought, *as long as a couple of them don't end up hating me, too.*

"MR. HARRELL, you've testified here that the reason why you reacted emotionally when you were being interviewed by Detective Herman Johnson and Detective Dwayne Stanton was that he had shown you photographs of the decedents in this case, correct?"

"Yes, sir."

"Now, describe those for us, please."

"They were like, I can't say if it was a Polaroid camera, or like an instamatic, but they develop within a minute or so after they come out of the camera. They were them kind of pictures."

"And what was shown in the pictures?"

"They were showing Diane and Katrina and how they were murdered."

"How many photographs were there?"

"I didn't count them all. I'll be honest, I looked at about two or three and I pushed them away from me because I didn't want to see any more."

"So it's your testimony that they had a stack of photographs, basically?"

"A *nice*-size little stack."

It was a phrase—"a nice-size little stack"—that you might apply to playing cards or pancakes, but not those photographs. Johnson and Stanton hadn't shown them to Harrell—Stanton was outside the courtroom and could set the record straight—but Michele surely had, in the course of preparing him for trial. She'd first looked at those photographs months before, outside my office; they'd moved her to tears. I had to think that at some point afterward, she'd told someone—a colleague, a trusted friend—about them. I doubted whether words like "nice" and "little" had ever found their way into her descriptions.

In BASEBALL, a pitcher sequences his fastball, curveball, and change-up so as to keep the hitter always off balance, to make sure he never feels comfortable. A cross-examiner arranges his topics in the same way. Never, ever let a witness get a foothold in the box.

I decided to jump to the route Harrell took after the murders.

"Sir, it's your testimony that after walking to get your truck, you decided to drive around, because you had things on your mind?"

"Yes, sir."

"And I believe that is what you told the police too, that you had things on your mind, correct?"

"No, I just told them—it's the same thing. Yes, you can say it was things on my mind."

"Now, Detective Johnson and Detective Stanton—the folks that you say showed those pictures to you—they asked you what things you were talking about, didn't they?"

"Yes, they did."

"What did you tell them you had on your mind?"

"I said there wasn't nobody home." He stopped. "It was lonesome in there and I couldn't sleep."

He was trying very hard to seem vulnerable. But the word "lonesome" didn't sit easily on the lips of a forty-five-year-old man charged with double murder.

"What time approximately had you left Diane Hawkins's house?"

"It was after eleven o'clock because the news was on. The weather had come on."

"So the weather had just come on when you left the house, supposedly, correct?"

I deliberately used the word "supposedly." I didn't want my questions to convey the sense that I was believing what he was saying.

"Yes, sir."

"Which would make it, what would you say, eleven twenty?"

"Between eleven twenty and eleven thirty. Like I said, it was closer to eleven thirty."

"And then you walked over to where your truck was on East Capitol Street, right?"

"Yes, sir."

"How long did it take you to walk over to East Capitol Street?"

"Well, I did not have my watch on. My watch was in the truck."

"Is it safe to say it was about a thirty-minute walk, at the outside, from where you were on Eads Street over to where your truck was?"

"Yes, because I was taking my time walking."

"So that puts it close to twelve o'clock when you went over to where your truck is, roughly?"

"Somewhere along there."

"You go down Central Avenue to—up toward 202, correct?"

"Yes, sir."

"What made you decide to go out that way? It was just a drive?"

"Just a drive, that's all."

"Now, you got down to 202 and you took a right on 202, then I believe you said you went to White House Road and took another right?"

"Yes, sir."

"And then to Richie Marlboro, up to Richie Road, and shortly thereafter you got stopped by the police, correct?"

"Yes, sir."

By force of habit, I was slowly pacing back and forth. In some courthouses, there's a standing rule that lawyers have to remain seated at all times during trial. That rule alone would be enough to drive me out of the profession.

"Now, as a truck driver, you carry a lot of loads in the area?"

"Yes, sir."

"And, in fact, you've even carried loads into that very area around there, right?"

"Yes, sir."

"So you were familiar with the area where you were driving?"

"Yes, sir."

"Now, you recall the same interview I have already asked you about, when Detective Johnson and Detective Stanton were talking to you?"

"Yes."

"In the early morning hours of May 26, after you were stopped, do you remember Detective Stanton asked you where you'd gone, and you told the detective that you were lost, that you didn't know where you were?"

"No, sir, I did not."

"So, you deny having said that to Detective Stanton?"

"I couldn't be lost. I know the area. And I did not tell Officer Stanton I got lost."

"Sir, you're familiar with the area of Route 202 and White House Road?"

"Yes, sir."

"Can you tell us what is right there at the intersection of Route 202 and Addison Road?"

I'd made a mistake; I'd meant to say "White House Road."

"Isn't there," I continued, "a county landfill right there?"

"Not at Addison Road."

"I'm sorry," I said, "Route 202 and White House Road."

Then it hit me. I stopped pacing and turned on him. He'd shown himself.

"You *know* the landfill I'm talking about, don't you, because you were able to correct me when I got it wrong. Isn't that true?"

"Yes I do, but the landfill isn't there. That's the gate to go in there. That's the gate, but the landfill is miles off."

"So you know where the landfill is, and you also know where that gate is?"

"Yes, I do, but the landfill is not there. That's the gate, to go in there. That's the gate, but the landfill is miles off."

"So you know where the landfill is, and you also know where the gate is right at White House, correct?"

"You don't go in that gate."

"Which gate do you go in?"

"It's another gate you go in."

"You can't go in that gate?"

"You're not supposed to."

"Well, you're not supposed to, but after six o'clock on a weeknight like May 26, the gate is locked, correct?"

"I never paid any attention to it." He was backpedaling. "I know it's shut, but I don't know if it's locked."

"So you can tell us exactly where the gate is and you can tell us about the fact you're not supposed to go in there and you can tell us that the gate is closed, but you're telling us you never checked it and you don't know whether it was locked or not?"

"I had no reason to go up and check it."

I glanced over at Michele. Her eyes were fixed on a spot on the carpet in front of the jury box. Norman was on his own.

"So since you know that area well, as you continue back down

White House Road, you hit Richie Marlboro and you hit Richie Road, correct?"

"Yes, sir."

"And you know Richie Road?"

"I know Richie Road."

"You go up and down there all the time?"

"I know it pretty good."

"You know at Richie Road and Walker Mill Road, there's a gas station with a car wash attached to it?"

"That car wash wasn't there last year."

"How do you know which one I'm talking about?"

"You said Richie Road and Walker Mill Road. There was a High's store. The gas station is up a little farther."

An audible sound came from the jury box. I wanted to look over, to make eye contact with whoever it was who'd made the sound, so I could lock in with them: *You and I know where this is going. Just make sure it's not forgotten once you and the others go to the back to decide this case.* But I couldn't let my eyes stray from Harrell's.

"Okay, but it's on the route you were taking down White House Road up Richie Marlboro to the intersection of Walker Mill and Richie?"

"No, sir."

"Isn't it on the right-hand side?"

"It's on Richie Road and Richie Marlboro Road, not White House Road."

"You know the one I'm talking about?"

"I'm guessing the one you're talking about, but that's the only gas station in that area."

"Is that, in fact, a twenty-four-hour car wash?"

"I've never been in that gas station before. I couldn't answer you on that."

"Well, you were able to tell us what intersection it was at, weren't you?"

"Yes, sir."

"And you don't know for sure whether or not there is a car wash attached there?"

"No, sir."

"You heard the testimony that at the time the police officers saw you and stopped you, they saw water dripping out of your truck, correct? Did you hear that testimony?"

"That was only out of one officer, one officer. Yeah, I remember he said it."

"Isn't it a fact that you had just washed your truck?"

"No, sir."

I knew he'd say no. Ordinarily, I wouldn't ask a question that I knew would prompt a denial from a defendant; that's his lawyer's job. But I needed to in this case, so everyone on the jury would see why all this was important.

"Mr. Harrell, you hadn't washed your truck at all that night?"

"I had not went up in the gas station."

"Well, anywhere?"

"No, sir. There's no car wash around in that area. The only car wash they had was up on Marlboro Pike and Addison Road. There's none down there."

"That's a twenty-four-hour car wash too?"

"Yes, it is."

"In fact, there are a number of car washes in, say, a five-mile radius around where they stopped you?"

"Some, but not all night."

He knew the area. He knew where the car washes were. I wasn't going to get any more out of him than that.

I WHEELED INTO COURT a large reinforced-cardboard box on a hand truck. It contained all the knives the police had found in Norman Harrell's house.

"Sir, you testified yesterday that when you would go hunting, you wouldn't skin or gut any animals, correct?"

"That is correct."

"And you said that was because it made you squeamish?"

"Yes, sir."

"Now when you would go out then, what would you tend to take with you when you went hunting, since you were not going to be, by your testimony, skinning or gutting any animals?"

"A shotgun."

"And anything else?"

"And bullets."

"And you wouldn't need to take any knives with you because somebody else was going to skin and gut these animals, because it made you squeamish?"

"That is correct, sir."

"And as of May 26 of 1993, Norman Junior wasn't living in your house, correct?"

"No, sir, he was not."

"And the only thing that he had at your house that belonged to him were clothing and a hunter's manual and a certificate, correct?"

"Yes, sir."

"Isn't it a fact, though, that when the police went into your house to execute a search warrant they found a number of knives, including some hunting knives, inside your house?"

"Can you show me the knives? Like I say, I can't say whether they are hunting knives."

"Sir, I'm holding up what has been marked as a government exhibit." It was a knife with a hooked blade that was at least four inches long, and the handle added four more inches.

I could have walked up to him, stood next to him, held it up for him, and asked if he'd seen it before. If a trial were purely a contest of machismo, that's what I would have done: show the jury, the judge, and Norman Harrell himself that I wasn't afraid of him, that he was in my territory and I would dominate him here. It wouldn't have even been a particularly risky move; a U.S. marshal was stationed vigilantly within ten feet of Harrell and would have jumped him if he so much as reached out in my direction. I could have gone home at the end of the day and gloried in the memory of standing face to face with a murderer and holding my ground. And a few days later, I'd have had the chance to subject my masculinity to a more genuine test, as I contemplated the prospect of a just-acquitted, just-freed Harrell showing up on my doorstep. If this jury got the notion that I was willing to put a knife anywhere near Norman Harrell in this courtroom—or even that I was willing to walk within ten feet of him without trepidation—then all the words that all my witnesses had uttered would have been for naught, and the image of Harrell's essential docility would have been all that lingered.

I once watched the government's case in a murder trial disintegrate when a diminutive female prosecutor invited the diminutive but deadly male defendant to come off the stand and look at exhibits, then proceeded to dialogue with him for fifteen minutes just a few feet in front of twelve jurors who had to be thinking to themselves: *Why would anyone be afraid of this kid?*

Knowing all this, I stood a half-courtroom away from Harrell and held up the knife between thumb and forefinger as if I'd never held one before. It didn't even bother me that the jury might see that my hand was shaking just a little bit.

"Can you tell us," I asked him, "whether that's a hunting knife?"

"I did not use it as a hunting knife."

"Is it a hunting knife?"

"No, sir."

"What do you call it?"

"I call it a knife."

"It's just a knife?"

"I did not use it for hunting."

"What did you use it for?"

"I did not use it for anything."

"Well, it was in your house, correct?"

"Yes, sir."

"And you went out and bought it, correct?"

"No, sir."

"How did you get it?"

"A friend of mine gave it to me."

"You took it?"

"I accepted it."

"And it's your testimony you didn't use it for anything?"

"No, sir."

"But it just ended up in your house, and you didn't throw it away, right?"

"No, sir."

"But it's your testimony that you never used this for anything?"

"That is correct."

"But you admit that it was yours, correct?"

"Yes, I do."

I produced one knife after another from the evidence box, and we did the same back-and-forth about each of them. With each knife came more explanations: He used this one to cut metal parts on his truck, that one to cut hoses, and no, he didn't use a single hunting knife for the one thing it was meant to be used for. Then he started backing away from saying the knives were even his.

"Mr. Harrell, have you ever seen this item?"

"I believe so."

"Okay. This knife was in your house, correct?"

"I think so."

"And it's yours?"

"It's possible."

"Well, who else could this knife belong to, if it was in your house?"

"I don't know. If you went there, you could have put it in there."

"*If I went in your house, I could have put it there?*"

"Yes, sir."

It was the only time he ever let it slip: It was personal for him too. We'd been facing each other for hours on end with only occasional interruptions—from Michele and the judge, the people on the fringes. We were together, he and I, the distanced sibling and the only child, but something that fired our loner's souls—that moved him to pit himself against nature's forces in the wild, that moved me to solitary achievement in the world of enclaves and structures—had been horribly miswired in him. And the sad thing was, I don't think he ever knew it.

IT WAS TIME to bring this cross to an end. I had to get Norman Harrell back to facts he couldn't deny. I had to take him back to Eads Street.

"You don't deny that you came over to Diane Hawkins's house that night, do you?"

"No, sir."

"And you don't deny that the whole time you were there, there was no trouble, correct?"

"No, sir."

"No sign of any intruder, correct?"

"No, sir."

It was only a slight variation of the last question. *Drag this out*, I was telling myself. *Get him into your flow, and don't make your points too quickly or you'll get ahead of the jury.*

"No sign of anybody coming in to do anybody any harm, correct?"

"Well, I will tell you like this. I didn't know what was going on out back or on the side of the house. As far as the living room where I was sitting at, I can only testify to what was in the living room."

Harrell wasn't in the flow.

"Okay, Mr. Harrell. When you left the house, you didn't see any signs outside that anything was going on that would cause any trouble to anybody, did you?"

"I wasn't looking."

"Well, did you feel as if you were in any danger when you walked out of there?"

"No, I didn't."

"You walked at a nice leisurely pace right down that street, didn't you?"

"Yes, sir."

"And I assume that if you'd thought that there was any sign of trouble whatsoever in that house, by other intruders coming in, or people coming in to do harm to the people inside, you'd have high-tailed it out of there, wouldn't you, or you would have called the police?"

"I would have called the police if I had seen something going on."

"Exactly. You didn't see anything, correct?"

"No, sir."

All that, just to get him back to where he'd been before.

"And earlier, when you'd been inside the house, once Reco left, that left you there, correct?"

"Yes, sir."

My last question: "And you were the last adult in the presence of Diane Hawkins and Katrina Harris that night with their two-year-old inside of 3461 Eads Street, Northeast, is that correct?"

"Thinking back, really I will be honest, I couldn't tell you because I did not know if anyone was in the basement or anyone in the other rooms upstairs."

Again, I had to back up and circle around.

"Were there any signs that anyone else was in the house, sir?"

"Like I told you, I can only testify to what I saw in the living room."

"Did you hear any noises in any other part of the house that would have told you that anyone else was in there?"

"I wasn't listening."

"Did you hear, whether or not you were listening, did you hear any signs in the house that made you think that someone else was inside that house other than the people I named?"

"No, sir."

"And when you left, the only people still in the house were Diane Hawkins, Katrina Harris, and Kiki, is that correct?"

"Like I told you, I couldn't testify. I don't know who was in the kitchen or down in the basement."

"As far as you can testify under oath today, can you name anyone else who was in the house, dead or alive, other than Diane Hawkins, Katrina Harris, or the two-year-old, Kiki, when you left that house? *Can you tell us under oath any other names of any other people?*"

"Not to my knowledge. I couldn't tell you, sir."

Sometimes the fiercest struggles are fought over the smallest patches of ground.

IN A CRIMINAL CASE, the prosecution has the burden of proving a defendant guilty "beyond a reasonable doubt." Despite the best efforts of judges to define it for them, jurors can have their own ideas as to what exactly a reasonable doubt is. To some it means: "I didn't see it with my own eyes, so hell, yes, I have a doubt." To others it means: "I'm not completely sure the guy did this, but he probably did something else in the past and this is the first time they caught him, so yeah, I've got no doubts." Most jurors, though, interpret it in a way that's roughly congruent with what the law intended, and they appropriately scrutinize the government's case for weaknesses and wield their skepticism aggressively. D.C. jurors are famously independent-minded—a survey once revealed that there are more hung juries in the nation's capital than anywhere else in the nation—and so it can be quite a challenge for a prosecutor to cajole twelve individuals with different life experiences to coalesce around a judgment as unequivocal as a guilty verdict. With all that responsibility come but two benefits: Since we have the burden of proof, we get to put on a rebuttal case after the defense case, and we get to give a rebuttal argument after the defense's closing argument.

In this case, I called six rebuttal witnesses to the stand in less than two hours, all for the purpose of countering the defense on specific matters it had raised during its case. Two witnesses directly contradicted Harrell on claims that he'd made during his own testimony: Detective Whalen, testifying that when he and Gainey interviewed Norman Harrell in P.G. County, Harrell had stated that he knew of no reason why blood would have been in his truck; and Detective Stanton, testifying that when he and Johnson interviewed Harrell, they showed him no photographs of the victims or the crime scene. Other witnesses made minor points on subjects I wanted to be able to talk about in my closing argument, or to deprive Michele of the chance to talk about in hers.

For purposes of constructing a rebuttal case, Harrell's testimony had certainly provided a surplus of targets. If I'd had the time and the inclination, I probably could have brought somebody in from somewhere to call him out on virtually every sentence that came past his lips. But I could tell the jury was getting tired; they'd sat, passively for the most part, through the testimony of almost fifty witnesses in barely a week. During that time the prosecutor and the defense had been telling competing stories—"two victims dehumanized by a hunter" versus "innocent man wrongfully charged"—and each of the witnesses had had their own narrative, too. It was about time for the jurors to take over from us, to write the ending to the big story that was this trial.

But there was one matter I couldn't let go unresolved: Harrell's testimony about all the people who'd shed blood in his Ford truck before the police recovered it as evidence. Doing nothing about this wasn't an option. In quiet intervals during the trial I would imagine the jury in its deliberations, and after Harrell testified, I conjured up one voice of obstinacy: "The man said all those folks bled in his truck and the DA didn't do anything about it? I don't know about you but that's plenty reason for me to doubt." But I couldn't very well draw blood from all of Harrell's hypothetical sources and compare the samples to the evidence samples, not at this late date. It would require at least a week's recess, and I wanted to get this case to the jury soon.

Fortunately, I had a witness I could call on the subject. The case had really been about him from the very beginning. And if there was anything to the notion of karma—if history is truly circular and if everything that goes around really does come around—he would undermine Norman Harrell far more convincingly than anything that could be summoned from mere physical science.

"The government calls Rasheen Hawkins."

Down the aisle strutted an eleven-year-old boy. When I'd first met him, he'd told me his hero was Michael Jordan, and he appeared this day dressed in a North Carolina powder-blue sweatsuit. Rock was big for his age and he'd inherited his father's long face. As he loped up the steps to the witness stand I found myself wondering what other traits Norman Harrell had passed on to him. Then the boy faced me squarely and I saw his mother's broad nose and guileless features; he calmly folded his hands in front of him and stared at me levelly, and I caught a glimpse of his mother's nerve. Of course: Half of Rock had come from Diane and all the other Hawkinses going all the way back to Sary in Roanoke Rapids.

I thought, *This boy's going to turn out just fine.*

"In a loud and clear voice, could you tell us your full name?"

"Rasheen Hawkins."

"Do you go by a nickname, Rasheen?"

"Yes, Rock."

"Rasheen, I'd like to ask you some questions about the time before your mom died, okay? First, how old are you?"

"Eleven."

"Do you go to school?"

"Yes."

"You're not in school right now, right?"

"No."

"When you go back to school, what grade will you be in?"

"Fifth."

"Rasheen, in all the time that you can remember, can you recall ever getting into a fight with somebody either at school or outside of school?"

"At school. My old school, though."

"You say the old school. What old school was that?"

"River Terrace."

"And do you recall who it was that you got into a fight with?"

"A boy named Duran."

"Was that the only time that you can remember where you got into a fight with someone where you got hurt?"

"Yes."

"Can you recall how long ago that was? What grade were you in at River Terrace?"

"I think third or fourth grade."

"Was there ever a time that you can recall getting into a fight with a boy named Diontee?"

"No."

"Do you know any boys named Diontee?"

"No."

"Was there ever a time that you ever got into a fight with anybody inside of the vehicle of someone that you know by the name of Danky?"

"No."

"Is the person that you know by Danky in court today?"

"Yes."

"Can you point to where he's seated?"

Since coming in the courtroom, Rock hadn't looked at Harrell. Now he pointed at him.

"Now let me ask you about the time that you had the fight and you got hurt. Can you tell us exactly how you got hurt?"

"I was just fighting him, and I don't know how I got hurt, but I got a knot."

"And do you recall whether or not you bled at all from that knot?"

"A little bit."

"That day after you got into the fight and you had the knot and you bled a little bit, can you recall whether or not you ever went anywhere near Danky's truck?"

"No."

"Do you know the truck I'm talking about?"

"Yes."

"Can you describe it for us?"

"It's a pickup truck and it's brown and it has like a shed on the back and I think it had like a tan—I think it's got tan on it. I can't remember no more."

"Well, now, in all of life as far back as you can remember, were you ever inside that pickup truck at a time when you were bleeding from any kind of a cut?"

"No."

A few minutes later, Rasheen Hawkins walked out of the court-room, his shoulders drawn back proudly. They looked just sturdy enough to carry a family's legacy.

I TOOK A LONG PAUSE and paced for a few precious seconds in front of the jurors.

I was speaking to them for the last time.

The end of trial was near at hand. I'd given my main closing argument, and Michele had followed with hers. Now I had one last chance to address this small group of people whom I'd constantly observed and silently measured for the last two weeks. I was just a few feet away from them. I now felt comfortable enough with them to come closer than ever before, and I was looking each of them in the eye, one by one, trying to glean some hint of recognition, agreement—even empathy.

I knew my time was slipping away. Judge Queen had placed a one-hour limit on each side's argument—one hour to summarize almost two weeks of testimony, to put it all in a larger context and inspire twelve strangers to join together in a decision that they'd remember for the rest of their lives—and I'd had to divide my allotment in two, between main closing and rebuttal. My main argument had been comprehensive but rushed. Sitting down, I'd thought, *I could have talked to them for an hour just about the blood evidence— how the police found it, what the science said about it, and how it all pointed back to Norman Harrell—and still barely scratched the surface.* The first few minutes of my rebuttal argument had been a point-by-point refutation of Michele's main contentions, but had lacked a larger theme. Now, I knew the judge sitting behind me must be leaning forward, waiting for the moment when she could silence me. *There's so much to say and so little time*, I thought. *How should I end?*

I couldn't talk about everything I'd learned about Diane Hawkins and Katrina Harris, exalting them as noble characters in a tragic narrative. That discussion had its place, but not in a courtroom. The judge would rightly view it as tangential to the guilt or innocence of the man charged with killing them, and besides, it would have taken hours, not minutes, to do it the right way. I couldn't give the jury any final answers as to why Norman Harrell had seen fit to do what he'd done; the root causes of his malevolence would always remain beyond my understanding.

Standing before that jury, I wasn't a psychologist or a novelist. I was a prosecutor, as I'll always be.

Why did I choose this line of work? What have I been talking to the Hawkins family about over all these months?

Where are people supposed to turn for justice?

I knew how I was going to end.

I took one step closer to the jury box:

"Defense counsel has said that you should keep in mind the rights that Mr. Harrell has as a defendant before you. And I ask you to do that. In fact, I implore you to do it, just as Ms. Roberts implores you to do it.

"Mr. Harrell in this case has gotten due process under the law, in a way Diane Hawkins didn't.

"Diane Hawkins tried to invoke the system and Norman Harrell tried to keep her from invoking that system.

"Katrina Harris could not come in here because Norman Harrell made sure she could not come in here.

"You have taken an oath, and I'm sure you'll uphold that oath. That oath includes maintaining the presumption of innocence throughout this whole trial.

"But there comes a time when the presumption drops. And that presumption drops when you all get together and you look at the body of evidence here, and you look Norman Harrell squarely in the eye, and you say: *You're going to submit to the force of this system, and you're going to submit to the law, and you're going to submit to a judgment that says to you that we're finding you guilty beyond a reasonable doubt of the crimes that you've been charged with.*"

I heard Judge Queen behind me say, "Counsel, your time is up."

It didn't matter. I had nothing more to say.

ON THURSDAY MORNING, August 11, 1994, the judge instructed the members of the jury on the law that applied to the charges in the

case, and advised them on how they should go about their deliberations. At 11:35 A.M., they walked from the courtroom to a smaller
room nearby. The case was now in their hands.

Colleagues of mine who'd seen parts of the trial and knew the
facts of the case were optimistic about the final outcome. But I'd
seen too many good cases go bad to let my hopes be raised too high.

FIVE HOURS LATER, the jury members returned to the courtroom.
We'd heard nothing from them all day. The judge discharged them
for the day and told them to return at 9:30 the next morning and not
to discuss the case with anyone in the meantime.

Rumors were circulating among the courtroom clerks and marshals
about the course of the deliberations. I heard one that was heartening:
that when a custodian went into the room to clean up after the jury
left, he saw the government's photographs and diagrams posted on all
four walls. It suggested that the jury was going through the evidence
methodically and taking its obligations seriously.

I heard another rumor that was less heartening: that loud voices
were heard coming from the jury room—the commotion of a heated
argument.

OUTSIDE THE COURTROOM was a throng of Hawkins family
members, sitting and standing in the hallway. Earlier, I'd told them
that they didn't need to wait around, I'd call them as soon as I
learned of the verdict. But the group, which included Reco and his
sister Shante, had decided to stay; none of them wanted to miss
anything. I now told them they could go home for the evening: "Get
some rest, you all deserve it." Ellen Neblett stepped forward and
handed me a manila envelope. "When you get back to your desk,"
she said, "open this up, dear."

Back in my office, I closed my door, opened the envelope, and found a stack of greeting cards—at least fifteen of them, maybe twenty. The one on top bore the words "With Thanks From All of Us." On the inside pages was a verse: "We can't begin to tell you / All the things this ought to say / But there's a world of meaning / In the thanks it brings your way." All the remaining space was taken up with the signatures of Hawkins family members. I tried to count the names, but they were too squeezed together and I had to stop at about fifty. They included everyone who'd testified in the trial, just about everyone who'd been interviewed in the investigation, and even distant cousins who'd come to town for the trial and whom I'd only briefly met. The other cards were signed by smaller combinations from among the large group: one from Diane's brothers and sisters; one from Mike Harwood; two from Mike's parents (one quoting Isaiah: "Then shall His light break forth like the dawn, and His healing shall spring speedily"); one from Diane's children; one from Willie Harris; two from Ellen Neblett (one noting in passing, "So now the case is in God's hands"); and so on. There was a letter from Diane's son Tyrone, who'd been in jail since before the murders. There was even a card from Kiki; at the bottom, three words were neatly penned: "I'm three now!" The words appeared to have been written by an adult, but I wouldn't say for certain; I'd learned not to underestimate this little girl's capabilities.

Many of the family members had added their own inscriptions to the cards. Some were eloquent ("I greatly appreciate everything you and your staff have done in this matter, and I only hope that my family and I can get on with our lives the way I know my mother would have wanted it"). Some were awkwardly phrased, occasionally ungrammatical ("Mr. Flynn, it so good to know, that you all care"). All were suffused with a heartbreaking sincerity.

This is how the Hawkins family had spent its time while it kept its vigil outside the courtroom, waiting for a jury verdict that surely they all knew could end up compounding their pain. And yet their message to me wasn't one of fear or despair. It was, whatever happens from now on, we'll always know one thing. We weren't forgotten.

I SPENT FRIDAY in my office, packing up all the Harrell file boxes to ship to storage. If I couldn't put the case to rest just yet, at least I could start clearing floor space between my desk and my door.

At noon I got a call from Judge Queen's clerk: "Come on over. We have a note from the jury."

"Is it just a note," I asked her, "or is it an *important* note?" It was my way of trying to get her to tell me if it was a verdict. The judge had an idiosyncratic rule: she didn't want the lawyers to know the contents of a jury note until they actually were in the courtroom. But the clerk didn't bite; maybe she didn't catch the urgency in my voice. All she said was, "You need to come over."

WALKING DOWN the courthouse hallway, I saw the Hawkins group ahead of me. Several looked up at me expectantly. I told them that I didn't know if it was a verdict or not.

It wasn't. It was a note: "We are unable to reach a unanimous verdict."

The jury was hung.

I'd had a few trials end this way before—not many, but enough for me to know what I faced if I had to do this one all over again. Some evidence would be lost before the next trial, because it's impossible for even the most conscientious police officer to carry huge boxes filled with hundreds of objects between different buildings, periodically emptying them and then refilling them, without being victimized by the law of averages. Some witnesses wouldn't show up, because other matters in their lives would have to take precedence—health problems, sick children, bosses threatening termination over too many job absences. Other witnesses would show up, but tell their stories in a way that would be just different enough from the way they'd told them before that a sharp defense lawyer would have room to convince a jury that they were trying to stretch the truth.

I can deal with all that, I thought. *Something will turn up.* In the months that would pass before the next trial, I might even be able to make the case stronger—take another look at all the evidence and see if I'd missed something the first time around; go back to old Jim Ballard and see if he'd had a change of heart; find some other confidant that Harrell had confessed to in an unguarded moment. What I couldn't deal with was the notion of walking to the back of the courtroom, rounding up all the Hawkins family members, and putting them back in that little room to break the news. No matter how I phrased whatever I said, it would come out like this: *You know how hard the last fifteen months have been? Well, it's nowhere near over yet.*

The judge asked Michele and me what we wanted her to do next. The options were: do nothing; give the jury what's called an "anti-deadlock instruction," which would be a plea from the judge to the warring factions to find common ground; or declare a mistrial, send the jury home, and set a date for the next trial. I suggested doing nothing and sending the jury back to continue deliberations. It was too early for the heavy-handed anti-deadlock instruction, which is generally only given as a last-ditch effort to avoid a mistrial. The jury had had the case for less than eight hours; with more time, maybe they could reach a consensus. To my surprise, Michele agreed with me. I guessed she didn't want to do this whole thing again any more than I did.

I saw the Hawkinses outside the courtroom. The look on their faces said, are we going to have to go through this one more time? "Keep the faith," I told them. "The day is young."

Then I went back to my office and started unpacking all the boxes I'd packed up earlier.

AT 3:40 P.M. on Friday, the jury sent out another note: "We need a break." The judge called us to court and told us she was going to send them all home. The twelve walked in and took their seats in the box; most of them looked tired. When the judge said, "I understand you haven't reached a verdict," one rolled her eyes and a couple of others exchanged looks. Only one appeared to be as fresh as she was on the first morning we saw her in court: Fourteen, my forty-five-year-old friend in the back row. She was smiling beatifically and scaring the daylights out of me. *He's got her on his side*, I thought. Jurors are never all that happy about the prospect of sending a man away, but if they think he's innocent and they're angling to set him free, they can get downright giddy about it.

I VISITED MY PARENTS that night. Two days before, my father had felt too weak to attend closing arguments in the trial, but now he was doing markedly better; the radiation treatments seemed to be working. His balance had improved, his limp was less pronounced, and he could actually turn his head to follow a conversation without having the room go upside down. He was starting to take short walks to build up his strength. Earlier that day, Mom had driven him to the local high school track and he'd managed to make a complete lap without stumbling. "Tomorrow," he vowed to me, "I'm going to try for two."

The next day I returned to their house, unannounced; this time I brought Connor. It was a bright, mild day and the air was light and dry, as if April had suddenly dropped into the middle of August: a good day to take my father and my son to the track.

Twenty-five or so years before, my Cub Scout troop had chosen this as the site of a sports excursion and my dad had been a chaperone. The scouts raced each other in pairs, then the parents had their own competition. I could still recall my father's time to the tenth of a second—6.6 for fifty yards—an impressive showing for a forty-five-year old man wearing old tennis shoes and a torn gray work shirt with a tattered edge that flapped in the breeze. This day, my father was again wearing old tennis shoes and yet another in a long line of gray work outfits; my son, his first pair of blue jeans and his second pair of big boy's shoes.

The three of us did a lap together, then I dropped back to watch as my father and my son went on in lockstep. Connor had started walking the previous November, on schedule at eleven months, and he was now heedless of risk, bounding from place to place with reckless impulsiveness. About twenty-five yards in front of me, he ran ahead as my father faltered. I started to go over to them but Dad quickly regained his step and Connor, suddenly aware he was out in the lead by himself, slowed. I hung back as they walked farther and farther away from me, until they were all the way across the track: my son running ahead in spurts and then lingering, my father plodding unsteadily but unflaggingly, determined to keep pace with his grandson. They finished the circuit together, once again in lockstep.

At the end, Dad said, "Well, I made it," and smiled ruefully. Connor giggled and then babbled for a couple of seconds. Walking, he'd mastered. Talking was still in his future, along with just about everything else my dad already knew about.

MONDAY MORNING the jury began deliberations again at 9:30 A.M. Around lunchtime I called the courtroom and asked the clerk if she still heard loud voices coming from the jury room. "No," she said, "it's been real quiet back there."

THE CALL FROM the clerk came at 2:45 P.M.

"Come on over!" she said.

"How *important* is it that I come over?" I asked.

This time, she seemed to catch on: "You better get yourself over here as soon as you can."

I called Patrice in her office and told her that I wasn't sure, but I thought the jury had a verdict. She said she'd walk over to court with me. We didn't talk much as we made the five-minute trip; any prolonged conversation would have been forced.

The Hawkins contingent wasn't in the corridor outside the courtroom. Something—a tip? gut instinct?—had drawn them inside. The judge and jury weren't in the room yet, but the marshals and clerks were, moving about with newfound purpose.

Michele walked in a couple of minutes later. For the next little while, our relationship would turn chilly once again. Like fighters on either side of the referee after a boxing match, awaiting the final decision, we wouldn't acknowledge each other.

Judge Queen took the bench and turned to a marshal. "Bring the defendant out," she barked. Behind me I could hear the courtroom door opening and closing, opening and closing as spectators entered. I knew without looking back that the gallery was filling up. The word had spread quickly, just as it had that there'd been trouble at Diane's house on that May night fifteen months before.

Harrell was brought to the courtroom and looked toward the back—either to the Hawkins family or the door, I couldn't tell which—then to the judge. "Good afternoon, Your Honor," he said, nodding at her a couple of times, his usual mirthless smile in place.

The clerk rose from her chair: "Calling the matter of *United States v. Norman Harrell*, docket number F5480-93." The judge: "At two forty this afternoon I received a note indicating that the jury had reached a verdict in this case. I will bring in the jury now."

I took out my case file and wrote: "Verdict after fourteen and a half hours of deliberation" and then left a blank space for "G" or "NG." What a difference one letter would make.

The clerk walked around to the door next to the witness stand and disappeared behind it. Five, ten seconds went by.

My eye fell upon a telephone on my table. Suddenly I had a thought: My parents were probably at home. I could take the phone, bend over behind my chair, call them, and put the phone back on the desk; they'd be able to hear the verdict as if they were right there. I heard footfall and rustling on the other side of the courtroom door; the jury was lining up. *Will anyone notice? The judge is looking away, talking to her clerk. If I'm going to do it, I've got to do it now.* I picked up the phone and reached for the buttons. Then the door opened and the jury started to walk in. I hung up the phone.

Filing in and taking their seats, none of the jury members looked at Norman Harrell; none of them looked at me.

The judge said, "Will the foreperson please rise."

Juror Five stood. He was a thirty-four-year-old black male who worked for the D.C. public schools. He'd been attentive and grim-faced throughout the trial. He'd carried himself with an air of authority. He was a natural foreperson, if there was such a thing. He was holding a folded legal-size piece of paper in his hand: the verdict form.

"Sir, has the jury reached a unanimous verdict in this case?"

"Yes we have, Your Honor."

He unfolded the paper, looked down at it, then looked up at the judge. His hands were shaking slightly. Without thinking, I lifted my left hand and glanced down at it: It was still. Then I saw the moist palm print it had left on the table.

"Mr. Foreperson, on the charge of first-degree premeditated murder while armed, as to the death of Diane Hawkins, how does the jury find the defendant, Norman Harrell, guilty or not guilty?"

Behind me, someone took a deep breath.

The foreperson looked down at the paper again, then looked up. "Guilty."

"Mr. Foreperson, on the charge of first-degree premeditated murder while armed, as to the death of Katrina Harris, how does the jury find the defendant, guilty or not guilty?"

"Guilty."

I looked down at my case file and scribbled in the blank space, "G/G." The second "G" came out looking more like a "Q." There was dead silence in the room. Then I heard the judge say, "Does either side request a poll?"

I rose: "I do not."

Michele: "We request a poll, Your Honor."

One by one, the jurors were asked if they agreed with the verdicts as stated by the foreperson. They each answered yes firmly and un-hesitatingly. My friend in the back row looked as pleasant as ever. It was impossible to tell which ones had been holding out for acquittal. Whoever they were, they were now true believers in our cause.

The judge gave a speech to the jurors, thanking them for their service, but I didn't listen. I'd heard this ritualistic expression of gratitude before, and besides, I was preoccupied with trying to catch the eye of someone in the courtroom. He kept looking down. Finally he looked up and our eyes locked for several seconds. Then Norman Harrell looked away.

When the judge excused the jury and left the bench, I walked over to Michele. "You did a great job," I said, and I meant it. Sometimes life isn't so mysterious after all; in the end, we'd just had too much to work with. I turned and went to Patrice and hugged her; she had tears in her eyes. The gallery was spilling into the corridor. I wanted to speak with the family but had an errand to do first. I walked to a pay telephone and called my parents; there was no answer. Of course, I thought, they're at the track and my father is taking his walk; he's going for three laps. I was leaving a message about the verdict when Patrice came up: "Are you coming? The family is outside waiting for you." I finished my message and followed her through the main exit, into the plaza in front of the courthouse.

As soon as I got outside, a crowd engulfed me; all I could see around me was a revolving blur of beaming faces. It was a panorama of spontaneous joy, long awaited and long delayed. Hawkins family members who'd been in the courtroom were jumping up and down and crying and hugging each other and me, and cars were discharging more revelers at curbside. As each of the latecomers arrived— Mike Harwood, his brothers, a couple of Diane's nieces—they dove into the middle of our group and the celebration began again. I saw Willie Harris lingering around the fringes and I almost didn't recognize him: he was grinning broadly for the first time since I'd met him. Off to the side, I saw Elaine Hawkins, younger sister of Diane, lifting little Kiki high over her head, putting her down, then lifting her up again. The child was laughing as Elaine was saying something to her, over and over. It was only when the din subsided briefly that the words could be heard: "Your mama's smiling now, honey, your mama's smiling now."

Throughout the trial, I'd kept waiting for that spontaneous moment that would turn the case my way. When the moment finally came, it belonged to my very last witness, eleven-year-old Rock. I looked around for him now but didn't see him. I hoped he was off someplace doing what young boys should be doing on a summer day. It would have been fitting if he could have been with us—but probably best for him that he wasn't.

I heard a voice say, "We're forming now," then I felt someone touch my shoulder. I took a hand on my left side and another on my right, and watched a circle of people start to take shape—small at first, but then expanding, as the first in the ring backpedaled to make room for the others. There was a buzz of talk in the group but it gradually faded away, until silence fell on the courthouse plaza. Across from me stood Wesley Hawkins, the onetime orphan who was now the unofficial leader of the prayers of his adoptive family. A few seconds passed and then he intoned, in a halting voice, "Dear God, we wish to thank you for our mother, Magdeline Hawkins. We wish she was here, but we know she's with you, and she's at peace."

"Amen."

"Thank you, God, for letting all the remaining members of our family be together today."

"Amen."

"And thank you, God, for showing us your justice and your mercy in this case against Mr. Harrell."

"Amen."

I had my back to the courthouse, so I couldn't see what others could: Michele Roberts, standing under the overhang of the building. She was smoking a cigarette and looking at the prayer circle. I'm told that there was just a hint of a smile on her face.

EPILOGUE

THE CEMETERY where Dad is buried isn't far from where I grew up. My parents had had a place reserved in the same plot as my grandparents, just over the D.C. line in Maryland, but the day after my father died I convinced my mother to arrange for a place closer to her house so she could visit more often. The next day, she and I picked the spot for the grave: on a hill overlooking a lake, because my father loved the water, and next to an elaborate sundial sculpture, because he loved machines and gadgets. As it turns out, we needn't have gone to the trouble of changing locations. She hasn't been to the cemetery in ten years, and I rarely go. We don't talk about it, but I think I speak for both of us in saying that there's no comfort for us there.

He died on a Saturday night in December, less than four months after the Harrell trial ended. The cancer had spread from his brain to his spine and he spent his last week on his back in a nursing home, paralyzed from the waist down. Three days before he died, he told me he was looking forward to getting rehabilitation and learning how to walk again so he could go back home. To the very end, he fought. The last morning, I got a call that he'd been taken to the emergency room; he'd had a seizure of some sort. When I first saw him at the hospital, he was sitting up on a gurney and he looked exhausted.

"Dad," I said, "just put your head back, get some rest."

"You're trying to get me to give up," he said. It was the last thing he ever said to me.

Enough time has gone by now that he's no longer always with me. I think of him most often when I'm near the woods in back of my house. One day in his last week, I walked to the tree line; it was twilight, and a wan winter sun was surrendering to the horizon. I was wearing a Brooklyn Dodgers hat that I'd given him for Father's Day one year; somehow, it had ended up with me again in the last month or so. I took it off and fingered the edge, distracted. Hanging on to it were five or six of his white hairs, uprooted no doubt by his chemotherapy. After a moment I gently plucked them off and placed them into the soil next to some viny undergrowth that had fought off the cold and was still dense and green. Walking away, I thought I felt a light breeze kick up.

Now you know why I don't go to the cemetery. I don't need to.

ABOUT AN HOUR after my father died, Mom and I walked to my car in the hospital parking lot. Earlier it had rained, but now the night was incongruously clear and the sky was dotted with light. As we neared the car, she suddenly looked up and said, "Which star are you, Larry? Which star are you?"

So how does one adjust to the idea that one's partner in life is now just a speck in the heavens? In my mother's case the answer was, with difficulty. In the wake of my father's death she descended again into severe depression. Two years later, showing the resilient spirit that attracted my father to her almost a half-century before, she fought her way out of it. Undeniably, the disease changed her. As she'd be the first to concede, it pulled her more into herself and deprived her of some of her confidence and a bit of her pugnacity. But surviving the experience also left her with an afterglow that's almost beatific, an exemplary grace that enables her to approach life's vicissitudes with rueful, even cheerful, acceptance. She continues to live, in relative good health, with a keen mind and a bountiful memory, in the house of my youth.

THE WINTER AFTER the Harrell trial, I made a pilgrimage to another forest: the one off White House Road. When I was last there, I was looking for a little girl's heart. It was surely long gone by now, having had to find its own peace among the elements. But there were other things—stained clothes, some boots, a knife or two—and that's what brought me back. That, and the persistent need to know everything.

Summer's lush foliage was gone, and the sun was free to shine benevolently on the vulnerable forest floor. I stood at roadside and scanned a half-mile of bristly underbrush through the depleted trees, then beat a gentle path through brambles softened by the frost, under bony limbs holding pine cones that were huddled close together as if to ward off the chill.

You shouldn't expect any late surprises here. I didn't find anything that day, and I never went back. The woods remained as unknowable as the man who moved through them once in a midnight frenzy. But someday, maybe in some other winter, a passerby will stumble over something. If enough time has gone by and the woods have endured enough hard winters, the blood on the clothes will look like dirt and the blood on the knife will look like rust, and the passerby will go on his untroubled way.

Sometimes it's best not to know everything.

FOR TEN YEARS after the trial, Norman Harrell continued to mount various appellate challenges to his convictions. Michele

Roberts represented him on none of these; her last contact with his case was in 1994. Through the years since, she's continued to maintain a thriving legal practice. Every year or so, a newspaper or magazine will compile a list of the best private attorneys in Washington, D.C. Her name is always at or near the top—no mean feat in a town with thousands of lawyers—and it always gives me a bit of a thrill to see it. We don't have frequent contact, but when we happen to meet, we greet each other like old friends who went through a tough time together and don't really want to talk about it.

Most of the detectives and many of the officers who worked on the Harrell case have retired—prematurely, in my opinion, since they still have a lot to contribute, but they deserve every minute of the peace they're now enjoying. Notably, two remain on the force: Dan Whalen and Dean Combee, still working on the homicide squad, still doggedly tracking the city's killers.

NORMAN HARRELL'S last appeal was decided against him in August 2004. He has no further legal options. He's currently serving a mandatory minimum sentence of sixty years to life imprisonment. Under the law, he has to serve at least the sixty before he's eligible for parole.

He remains unrepentant, still denying his guilt as vociferously as he did when he testified at his trial. I know this because I saw him again in the summer of 2006.

On a steamy July evening, almost twelve years to the day after the Harrell trial began, Dan Whalen and I set out on a long drive to the federal facility in Allenwood, Pennsylvania. Since 1995, it had been home to our defendant. I'd told prison officials that I was a prosecutor on a temporary leave of absence from my job, that I had a continuing personal interest in the case of one of their inmates, and that I'd be joined by a homicide detective who had a continuing law-enforcement interest in the same case. I'd left out a few facts that would have been too hard to explain. That I was writing a book, for one. That when I first started it, I visited a cemetery, seeking benediction. That nearing the end of it, I needed to visit this jail, seeking resolution.

At the prison, we were led by a guard into a common area, about half the size of an elementary school gymnasium, filled with small desks surrounded by chairs. Here was where inmates met with visiting families and friends. It was early in the morning and the room was empty, but the prison officials had still given us the privacy of an office on the side for our own visitation.

Harrell walked into the office with a folder in his hand. Advancing toward me, he said, "Oh *yeah*, I remember you," and emitted something like a chuckle. He appeared no different than he had at his trial: still massive but no heavier, his hair and mustache still dark.

He'd been told in advance that we were coming and had agreed to meet with us. But once it became apparent that we weren't there to say that the whole thing was a big mistake and we had a court order for his release—once he realized that we were there to see if he was now inclined, after all these years, to come to terms with what he did—he stormed out.

During our brief time together, he unburdened himself of years of pent-up grievances: how all the witnesses had lied about him, how his lawyer had let him down, how the judge had been out to get him. "Why," he complained, "didn't she let me get into the trial that when the police stopped me that night, I had a gun in my truck?"

"Sure," I said, "you had a loaded pistol in your truck—the police found it later. Michele never asked to get it in because there's no way in a million years it would have helped you. It would only have hurt you—made you look more violent, made the jury—"

"Let me cut you off," he said, rising to stand over me. "Those two people got all cut up. I had a gun in my truck; why didn't I just shoot 'em?"

His parting line was: "This interview's over, mofo." Then he walked from the office, and his mood changed in a flash. Smiling again, he called out to the guard: "If you don't mind, sir, can you just take me back to my cell?"

Following him out of the office, I said to him: "Someday, Mr. Harrell, you're going to want to make your peace with all this."

Over his shoulder, he claimed the last word: "The man upstairs knows I didn't do this."

I'd looked at my watch when he came in, and now I looked at it again: we were with him for exactly twenty minutes.

Alone in the visiting area, Dan and I looked at each other. We'd spent five hours on the road the night before, taken two rooms in a cheap motel off the interstate, and now had five more hours on the road ahead of us—all for a burst of invective. After a moment, he said exactly what I was thinking: "It was worth it."

Why? Because with Harrell's every word, each of his gestures, his very presence, he'd reminded us of why we'd given so much of ourselves a decade before just so we could put him in a place like this, for good. Because a homicide detective and a prosecutor always gain something valuable from sitting across from a Norman Harrell, even if for a short time, since every insight we glean ends up being applied to cases we'll have in the future. And because Dan and I both knew that a long time before, we'd taken on the task of pursuing the truth, and that given the chance to get more answers to our questions, we couldn't pull off the trail. If nothing else, we knew we'd been faithful to the chase.

As we were escorted from the prison, Dan turned to the guard and said, "I guess I'll be back here when I'm seventy and he's eighty." The night before, on the long ride to Allenwood, he'd confided in me his plan for the not-too-distant future, when he'll be facing his last days in the police department: "I want to go around the country," he'd said, "to all the jails where all the worst dudes from my cases are being held, and sit them down one by one, and talk to them about why they did it."

If he ends up having that talk with Harrell, I hope I'll be there with him.

THE FAMILY AND FRIENDS of Diane and Katrina have gone on with their lives, though the events of May 25, 1993, have continued to reverberate.

The family elders—Diane's brothers and sisters, the ones who steered their children away from retribution on the night the bodies were found—are aging or passing on, in the natural course of things. Willie Harris has persevered, finding a niche for himself as Rock's surrogate father. Deborah Courtney has been able to remain, fortunately, Deborah Courtney: unconstrained, resolute, indomitable.

Other, younger, members of the family—some of whom saw more of the ever-vivacious Diane than her older siblings did—have suffered in numbers that seem disproportionate. Several have died premature deaths from various illnesses, including Wesley Hawkins, the stalwart leader of every prayer circle. A few have been plagued by adversities that can be easily traced to the murders. Mike Harwood is a case in point. In May 1993 he was working two jobs. After discovering Trina's body, he was forever changed, his nights sleepless and ridden with nightmares. Mike often told me that he had a sense that when he entered Diane's house Harrell was still there, and only escaped after he left; he wondered why Harrell had spared him. Not long after the trial was over, his nightmares spilled into daylight and became delusions. He stopped working. Seeking solace, he started using drugs, then was arrested and incarcerated. While in jail, he developed a heart problem and underwent surgery; when he was released he wasn't the same. He died of a heart attack in December 2004, at age thirty-nine.

Everyone makes choices, and Mike—or a shadow of Mike—made his. But looking at the long chain of events that led, as if by foreordination, to his end, it's hard not to conclude that Norman Harrell was as responsible for it as if he'd taken the knife to Mike that very night.

The torment of Mike Harwood was unique: Something in his being was let loose by a vision and he never got control of it again. For whatever reason, others in the family have been able to go through their ordeal and come out on the other side. Diane's children, for example, have managed to find their way, albeit in fits and starts. In the first several years after the trial, Reco ran into more trouble with the law, as did his older brother, Tyrone. Now, though, they're both working and raising children; their sister Shante is raising a family, too. Rock, who will always be eleven in my mind, is now a twenty-three-year-old man, and soon to be a father himself. Kiki, now fifteen, was a family mystery for a time, living outside their orbit. Some years before, custody of Kiki had been transferred away from the Hawkins family, and none of its members had contact with her for several years. Now, though, she has rejoined Diane's sister Ellen, and is reported to be well adjusted and a good student.

All in all, the members of this family have been able to find comfort in each other and in their faith, and have enjoyed numerous successes through the years: graduations, job promotions, the small daily delights of raising new generations of Hawkinses. More than anything that human hands could build, these successes stand as memorials to the ones no longer here.

Now, most of the members of that family are to me what Diane and Trina are to them: unseen presences, lovingly recalled. I haven't had much contact with the family since that August day when we clasped hands in the courthouse plaza. Several were of great help to me when I was writing this book: Mike Harwood and his parents, Carlene Hawkins, and Reco all come to mind. As for most of the rest, I decided not to bother them; they'd already given enough of themselves. Here and there I'll have chance meetings with one or the other, and I often see one of Diane's goddaughters; she's a paralegal in my office. But the plans that we all made to get together regularly, in festive circumstances, haven't been fulfilled.

While I wish it were otherwise, it's entirely understandable—healthy, even—that it turned out this way. Prosecutors of murder cases learn early on that our place in the lives of the decedents' survivors is transient, by necessity. Our faces, our names, everything about us is a reminder to them of the worst time in their lives, no matter how well our cases might resolve themselves.

In search of an analogy, I reach back to my own childhood and recall the day of the funeral of my uncle and cousin, killed together in a plane crash. My grandfather had died the year before; we used the same funeral director. At the end of the ceremony he approached my mother to console her; fumbling and at a loss for words, he finally said, "I hope I get to see you all again." She smiled at him sweetly and said, "We never want to see you again for as long as we live." To the typical survivors of a victim of homicide, it would be no easier to sit down to dinner with the prosecutor of their loved one's murderer than to socialize with the mortician who prepared the body for burial.

So it has been with the Hawkins family. Life is a precarious thing, and we walk through it unsteadily. Day by day, more than we want to acknowledge, we're held upright by the bonds that tie us to the people closest to us. When one of those bonds is violently severed, we need to reach to others to lift us up and pull us along for a while; for the Hawkins family, I happened to be there. Once they regained their footing, it was time for me to hand them off to others—to each other—and to say bravo and Godspeed.

And what did they give me in return? Just this: As much as I was pulling them, they were pulling me. At a time when I was anguished, they let me witness the power of their faith and the model of their perseverance. In the years since, I've had, as we all do, turbulent interludes, and I've drawn strength from the examples and experiences of those very turbulent times. But even more lasting was something else they gave me: By offering me the chance to extend myself outside my circumscribed existence—one bounded by the limits of my self-reliant inclinations—they changed me in ways that I've only come to appreciate with the passage of years.

The Harrell case was one of the last that I tried by myself. Gradually, I brought others into my endeavors: junior prosecutors, usually, what you might call professional younger siblings. I learned that an unkempt trial desk is the price one pays for the pleasures of partnership. I committed myself to finding ways to connect my work as a prosecutor with the daily lives of the people in the community I serve. I started seeking out opportunities to mentor, to teach, to counsel, and I spent six years of my career serving as something I'd sworn I'd never be: a manager guiding young careers, the ultimate big brother.

None of these things happened quickly. The deepest changes in one's life begin unconsciously and are built incrementally. But they happened, and looking back, it's easy to see when and why they started.

Am I a better husband, a better father than I would have been had I never met anyone named Hawkins? That's hard to say. I'd like to think that, left to rely on my instincts and the inspiration of my parents, I'd still have been a reliable source of affection and strength for my family. But I do know this: Any time you've been privileged to be made a part of something strong that's been forged by others, it stands to reason that you'll redouble your efforts to forge something strong of your own.

All of this, then, was one family's gift to another.

It's tempting to say that the story ends here. In a world full of ambiguity, it's human nature to strive for finality—that's why we keep score in our games, assign grades to our students, render judgments in our trials. But life itself—the messy business of muddling through, of getting past school and earning a wage and pleasing a spouse and raising a child and caring for a parent and simply trying to go on existing—is different from a football game or a computer course or a criminal case. Life . . . goes on. So too do the stories that mean the most to us. For everyone who was somehow touched by Diane Hawkins and Katrina Harris—their loved ones, most of all, and all of us who came to occupy concentric rings of varying distances from the center—there can be no final act in this play. All these years later, we still find small ways to keep our shared past alive and vibrant in the present, and I suspect that for as long as we live, it will be that way.

A favorite niece in private moments whispers to Diane as if she's just a few feet away. She feels a draft and hears "You go, girl!"

A detective recounts the frenzy of that first night to his colleagues—how it all went right when so easily it could have all gone wrong—so the next time another Norman Harrell flees into the darkness, they'll know what they have to do to catch him.

And every night of his life, a prosecutor joins hands with his wife and children.

They come together in a circle.

They pray for the living and for the dead.

ACKNOWLEDGMENTS

Without the special grace of the family members and friends of Diane Hawkins and Katrina Harris, there would have been no compelling reason for this book to be written—nor, for that matter, could it have ever been. During the investigation and trial that are portrayed here, they gave of themselves in innumerable ways so that justice might be done, and many of the book's insights into the victims and their victimizer were derived from confidences they shared with me then, and that they've since agreed to let me share with the world. In the months following the trial, as I've noted in the epilogue, I returned to several of them to ask for help as I tried to capture the unique vibrancy of Diane and Katrina, and the sustaining spirituality of their survivors. Without exception, everyone I approached offered their cooperation unhesitatingly and generously. Later, when a first draft of the manuscript had been completed, I went back to the well once more, asking several of them—Barbara and Ty Harwood, Carlene Hawkins, Diane's goddaughter Nina Hammond—to read the draft and confirm the accuracy of its particulars; again, all complied. None of this, I'm sure, was easy for them. I know that in this process, I was asking them to dredge up memories that, while precious, were very painful. This book begins with a promise made in a cemetery; more than anything else, I hope that those who best knew Diane and Katrina will read it and be satisfied that the promise was kept, and that their time with me was well spent.

While I'm on the subject of Hawkins contributions to this endeavor, I should note that in delving into the background of the victims and their family, I relied in part on a work entitled *A History of the Black Hawkins Family of Roanoke Rapids, North Carolina,* researched and written for private publication by Terrence Wyche, a resident of that town. This family history was no doubt prepared as a labor of love, and originally intended to be enjoyed by a small group of readers. It gives me great satisfaction to be able to introduce its epic scope to a wider audience.

I thank Eric H. Holder, Jr., the U.S. Attorney for Washington, D.C., during the Harrell prosecution, for his much-needed help and encouragement during the case.

I began working on this book in 1995, and the final product is the result of many drafts, reams of paper, many spent ink cartridges and much frustration. A number of my friends and colleagues read the manuscript in its various incarnations and offered comments that invariably proved helpful. For the hours they devoted to plowing through my unpolished prose, the encouragement they nonetheless extended to me, and the sagacity of the observations they provided me, I thank the following: Thomas Hibarger and his wife, Karla McEvoy, John Gidez, William Blier, Rob Feitel, Pam Norwind, Cliff Keenan, Colleen Bunner (who was also the paralegal on the case and an indispensable part of the prosecution), DeMaurice Smith, Tad DiBiase, Gary Collins, Alyse Graham, Robert Pack, Jeff Londa, Karen Bisset, and Brad Weinsheimer. I'd be remiss if I didn't single out two individuals for special mention: Marty Lobel, a Washington, D.C., lawyer, and Kathy Lesko, an accomplished local writer. Three years ago I was referred to each by mutual contacts, and while I'm now proud to call them my friends, neither knew me well when they took on the task of reviewing this manuscript and giving me feedback. Their detailed, objective, and nurturing critiques greatly assisted me in reshaping this project at a time when it was languishing. I'd also like to thank Jay Acton, a New York–based lawyer and literary agent, for the time, patience, and wise counsel he gave me in the early stages of this endeavor.

Last year, Marty Lobel and Bob Pack referred me to the Gail Ross Literary Agency, and soon thereafter this project took on new life. I thank Gail and her colleague, Howard Yoon, for their fervent advocacy on behalf of this project, not to mention the invaluable insights they gave me as I put the finishing touches on my first "final" draft. They then handed me off to Dan Conaway at Putnam, who has been not just my editor, but my partner and friend. I can think of no higher compliment than to say that in his wisdom, dedication, and integrity, he is the equivalent of the police officers who worked with me on the Harrell case. His assistant, Rachel Holtzman, has also been of great help in bringing this project to fruition.

Finally, I owe no one a greater debt of gratitude than my wife, Patrice, and our two children, Connor and Megan. It's no exaggeration to say that without Patrice's unwavering support and unerringly astute advice, I would never have been able to finish writing this book, let alone shepherd it through to publication. As for our children: When I first embarked on this undertaking eleven years ago, I was thinking that it would be a worthwhile use of my time even if they were the book's only two readers. I wanted them to know the whole story of how members of their family once drew strength from one another and from another wonderful family in a time of great pain. Over the years, I've had the misfortune of having to see them both confront adversity and loss in their own lives, and I'm proud to say that they seem already to know the lessons of this book without ever having read it. They continue to inspire me in ways no one else could.